IMAGES
of America

DENISON

I0806319

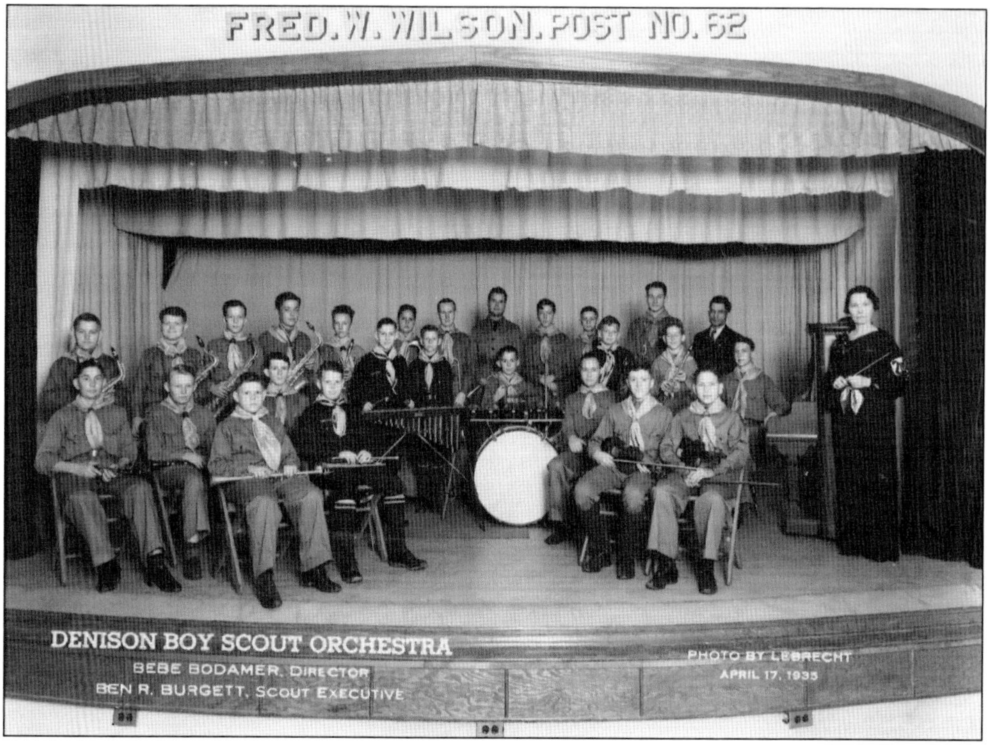

On April 17, 1935, the Denison Boy Scout Orchestra played at the Fred W. Wilson American Legion Post No. 62 at 419 West Crawford Street. Bebe Bodamer (right) was orchestra director; Ben R. Burget (back row, right) was Scout executive. Bodamer gave music lessons in her home until the mid-1950s. Moved from 311 West Woodard Street, the post memorialized Wilson, the first Denison man to fall in World War I. (Walter P. Lebrecht, collection of Mavis Anne Bryant.)

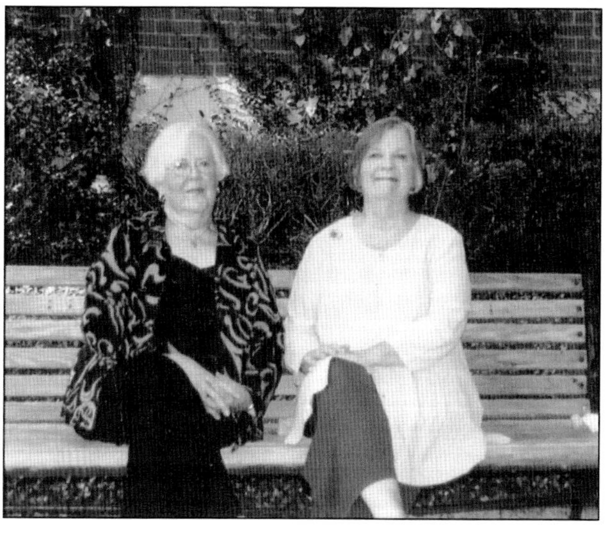

Donna Hord Hunt and Mavis Anne Bryant are lifelong residents of Denison, Texas. Donna Hunt (left), author and retired editor of the *Denison Herald*, writes history columns for the *Herald Democrat*. Mavis Bryant, author and historian, is also a clinical psychologist in private practice in Sherman, Texas. (Kay Casey.)

On the Cover: Dwight David Eisenhower—a five-star general who was born in Denison, Texas, on October 14, 1890—addresses a record crowd, estimated at 10,000, in Forest Park on April 20, 1946. Later, he will become president of the United States. (Donna Hord Hunt.)

IMAGES
of America

DENISON

Donna Hord Hunt and
Mavis Anne Bryant

ARCADIA
PUBLISHING

ISBN 978-0-7385-8474-4

Published by Arcadia Publishing
Charleston, South Carolina

Printed in the United States of America

Library of Congress Control Number: 2010940830

For all general information, please contact Arcadia Publishing:
Telephone 843-853-2070
Fax 843-853-0044
E-mail sales@arcadiapublishing.com
For customer service and orders:
Toll-Free 1-888-313-2665

Visit us on the Internet at www.arcadiapublishing.com

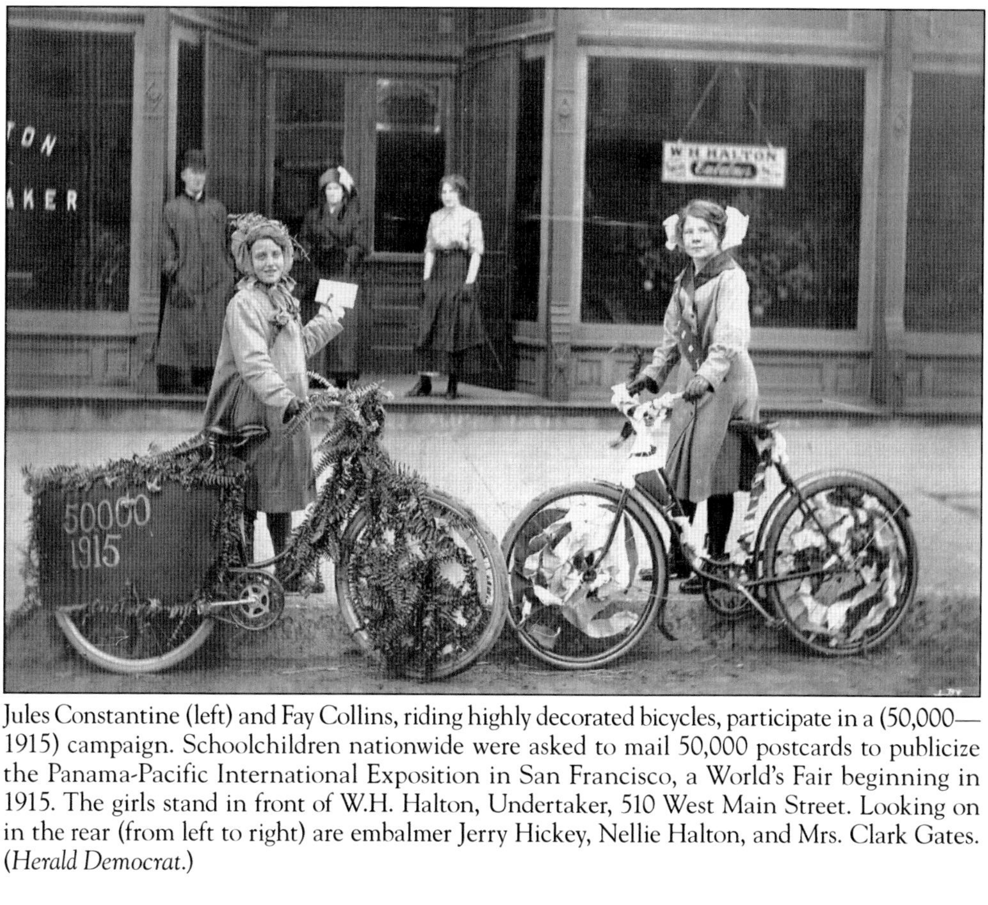

Jules Constantine (left) and Fay Collins, riding highly decorated bicycles, participate in a (50,000—1915) campaign. Schoolchildren nationwide were asked to mail 50,000 postcards to publicize the Panama-Pacific International Exposition in San Francisco, a World's Fair beginning in 1915. The girls stand in front of W.H. Halton, Undertaker, 510 West Main Street. Looking on in the rear (from left to right) are embalmer Jerry Hickey, Nellie Halton, and Mrs. Clark Gates. (*Herald Democrat.*)

Contents

ACKNOWLEDGMENTS

Pictures bring history to life in a way that complements the remembrances and research available in books that are primarily text. The authors have made every effort to shed new light on Denison's history by unearthing images that seldom, if ever, have been seen in print before. Many people have contributed to this effort, and we are grateful to all of them.

Images in this photographic history book come from many different sources. Because people started documenting the history of Denison almost 150 years ago, in 1872, most of the craftsmen who created our pictures are no longer with us. The current custodians of these images, however, have been very generous in loaning them.

Belinda Burget McKee shared her rare copy of *Art Work of Grayson County* (1895), perhaps the oldest collection of high-quality photographs of the Denison area. It formed part of the estate of her aunt Dean Burget Harris. John Wright, publisher of the *Herald Democrat*, generously gave permission to use many of the historical pictures that were in the files of the *Denison Herald* when it merged with the *Sherman Democrat* a number of years ago.

Among those who shared photographs or other material used in this book are Bobby Blankenship, Betty Jane Hickey Brodie, Kay Casey, Michelle Castle, John Crawford, Anne Clymer Goddard, Grayson County College, Billy Holcomb, Lyndon and Paulette Hyatt, Betty Lou Ferguson Johnson, Mary Karam, Lavada Crook Linder, Don Mace, Mia Marsico Munson, Richard Munson, Perrin Air Force Base Museum, Becky Fisher Oubre Rains, C.J. Ransom, Red River Railroad Museum, Jim Sears, Dr. Don and Kay Skelton, and Bredette C. Thomas Jr. We thank you, one and all.

The book's authors, Donna Hord Hunt and Mavis Anne Bryant, are historians who have been collecting Denison photographs and postcards for many years—long before having any thought of putting this book together. A majority of the remaining photographs and postcards are from their collections. Several come from Mavis Anne Bryant's archive of negatives and prints by Denison photographer Walter P. Lebrecht. A number of rare images included here once belonged to Helen Murray (Mrs. Alfred A.) Thomas, daughter of newspaperman Bredette C. Murray, and came to the authors by surprisingly varied routes.

Throughout the book, sources of photographs are indicated with the following abbreviations (for full book citations, see Suggested Reading). AWGC = *Art Work of Grayson County*; courtesy of the Benjamin Burget family. BCT = Bredette C. Thomas Jr., Foster City, California; used by permission. DHH = Collection of Donna Hord Hunt. HD = *Herald Democrat*, Sherman and Denison, Texas (includes items formerly in files of the *Denison Herald*); used by permission. IndDen = *Industrial Denison*. MAB = Collection of Mavis Anne Bryant. WPL = Photograph by Walter P. Lebrecht, Denison, Texas.

Introduction

From its very beginning, Denison was destined to be a railroad town. O.B. Gunn, chief engineer for the Missouri–Kansas–Texas (MKT) Railroad, was responsible for the town being named Denison. He made a personal inspection of North Texas and selected the location of the new city to become the Katy railhead in Texas. A tent city had sprung up near the banks of the Red River, where a lawless community existed, but the frontier village called Red River City was so temporary that, five years later, nothing was left but one log cabin. The location that Gunn selected for Denison was kept secret until the lots went up for sale on September 23, 1872, and Denison was born.

December 24, 1872, was a biting cold day, but a heavily loaded construction train came chugging into Denison. It was piled high with rails and ties to test the strength of the newly built bridge over the Red River. The first official train came in on Christmas day.

Denison was one of the first planned communities in Texas, and one of the first to use zoning as a guide to growth. The Denison Town Company laid the town out on a grid pattern with wide streets, and it specified the uses that could be made of particular areas. Blocks were reserved for schools, a major park, and churches.

Denison's population grew to 3,000 during the town's first 100 days. Tents and wooden buildings popped up like magic, and every third building was a saloon. But the businessmen of Denison were a stern, self-reliant group determined to tame both the wild terrain and the wild behavior of early inhabitants. On March 7, 1872, Denison was incorporated by an act of the Texas Legislature. L.S. Owings, former governor of the Arizona Territory, was the town's first mayor.

Denison has the distinction of being the first city in Texas to have a free, graded public school. Formal opening of the Denison Educational Institute, also called Washington School, took place on October 12, 1874, with Nat Sommerville as the first superintendent.

Few cities of its size had more churches or better schools than Denison. Nearly all the evangelical denominations have had good buildings through the years. St. Luke's Episcopal Church has the oldest church building, completed just four years after the town's first lots were sold. A portion of that building is still being used today. The First Presbyterian Church, however, formed the first church on December 23, 1872, with Rev. Josiah Milligan as pastor.

The Leeper/Security Building was the tallest structure in North Texas in the late 1800s. The top floor was removed later because of fear that the building would fall. Denison also was the first town in Texas to provide free delivery of rural mail, beginning in 1901.

William Benjamin Munson Sr. is remembered as the man who put Denison on the map. Trained as a surveyor, he helped select and develop the original townsite. His brother Thomas Volney Munson was recognized as one of the world's foremost horticulturalists. In 1876, he established nurseries here and rose to the pinnacle of fame when the grape industry of France was threatened with a root disease. He used grafts from his vineyard to save the vines of France. A grateful French nation awarded him the coveted Legion of Honor medal.

In 1896, Denison's XXI Club constructed the first women's clubhouse in Texas. The impressive two-story brick building, which housed Denison's first public library, was made possible by an endowment from a third Munson brother, Theodore.

From the point of view of many Denisonians, one of the greatest civil wars in US history happened July 23–26, 1931, between Texas and Oklahoma—the Red River Bridge War. German leader Adolph Hitler even used pictures of Texas Rangers in Denison as propaganda to prove that there was physical strife in the United States. The Rangers also had been in Denison earlier, camping out in Forest Park in 1922, when a strike by railroad workers split the town in two.

When the Denison Dam across Red River and Lake Texoma was constructed and the lake filled over a five-year period, the dam carried a modest price tag of $54 million. The project was formally dedicated on July 1, 1944.

The native Denisonian who gained greatest international fame was born in a small, unassuming house at 208 East Day Street on October 14, 1890. Dwight David Eisenhower, whose father was a Katy engine wiper, became a five-star general. In 1953, he was inaugurated as the 34th president of the United States.

Perrin Air Force Base came to town to train Air Force pilots, but it closed in 1971. In 1987, the MKT Railroad merged with the much larger Union Pacific Railroad. Both events were setbacks for the town, but the city has since developed new industries and become a center for the delivery of health-care services for a large region in North Texas and Southern Oklahoma. Lake Texoma and historical areas reflecting the importance of railroading in the town's past make Denison attractive for young families, visitors, and retirees alike.

Suggested Reading

Art Work of Grayson County. Published in Twelve Parts. 12 vols. N.p.: W.H. Parish Publishing Co., 1895.

Bryant, Mavis Anne. *Donald Mayes of Denison, Texas: An Architectural Legacy.* Denison, TX: Denison Heritage, Inc., 2001.

Bryant, Mavis Anne, and Donna Hord Hunt. *Two Schools on Main Street: The Pride of Denison, Texas, 1873–2007.* Denison, TX: Gate City Publishing, 2009.

Holcomb, Billy. *Theater Row: Movie Palaces of Denison, Texas.* Edited by Mavis Anne Bryant. Denison, TX: Denison Heritage, Inc., 1999.

Images: A Pictorial History of Denison, Texas. Denison, TX: Denison Herald, 1994.

Maguire, Jack. *Katy's Baby: The Story of Denison, Texas.* Austin, TX: Nortex Press, 1991.

McLeRoy, Sherrie S. *Black Land, Red River: A Pictorial History of Grayson County, Texas.* Virginia Beach, VA: The Donning Company, 1993.

McLeRoy, Sherrie S., and Roy E. Renfro. *Grape Man of Texas: Thomas Volney Munson and the Origins of American Viticulture.* Rev. ed. San Francisco, CA: Wine Appreciation Guild, 2008.

Reflections: Sharing Sherman and Grayson County's Past. Vol. 1. Sherman, TX: Sherman Democrat, 1994.

Reflections: Sharing Sherman and Grayson County's Past. Vol. 2. Sherman, TX: Herald Democrat, 1996.

Robinson, Frank M., comp. *Industrial Denison.* N.p.: Means-Moore Co., c. 1909.

One

Gateway to Texas

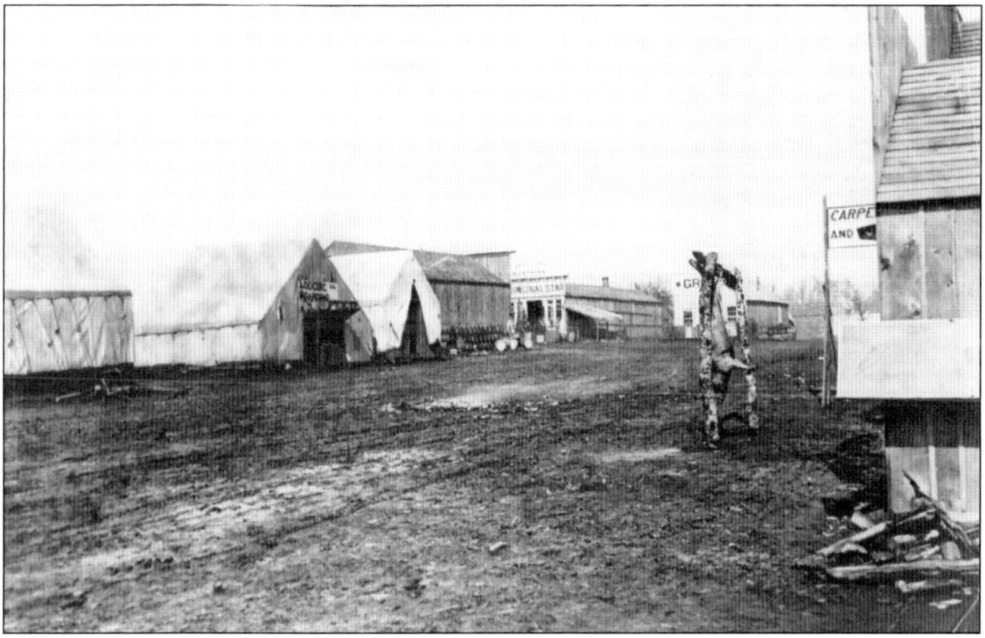

Taken in 1872, this is the earliest known photograph of Denison's downtown. A clothing store and grocery already have been established. One tent, bearing the "Original Star" logo, offers "Lodging, Boarding, Feed." Here Samuel Star and Charles Waterman will build a prosperous company. On the right is a carpentry shop. Note the side of beef hanging next to the street. The town drew 3,000 inhabitants during its first 100 days. (HD.)

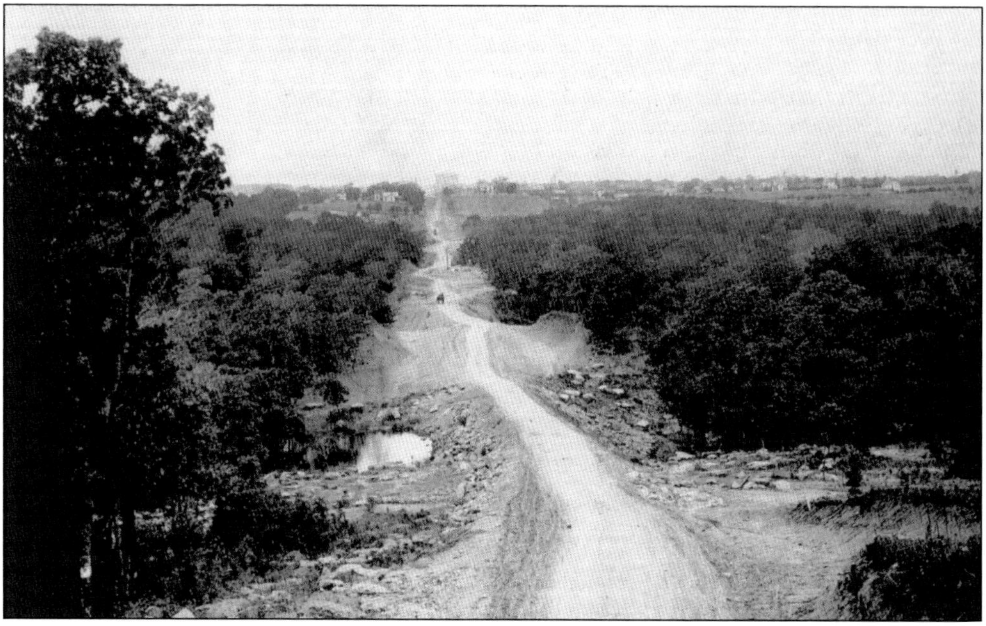

In 1872, the Missouri–Kansas–Texas Railroad built its tracks southward across the Red River into Texas. To house its first depot in Texas, the company carved the town of Denison out of prairie, grasslands, and woodlands in the Cross Timbers ecological region. This photograph, published around 1895, shows an unpaved road—dusty when dry and muddy when wet—taken by travelers coming from the east toward the railhead at Denison. (AWGC.)

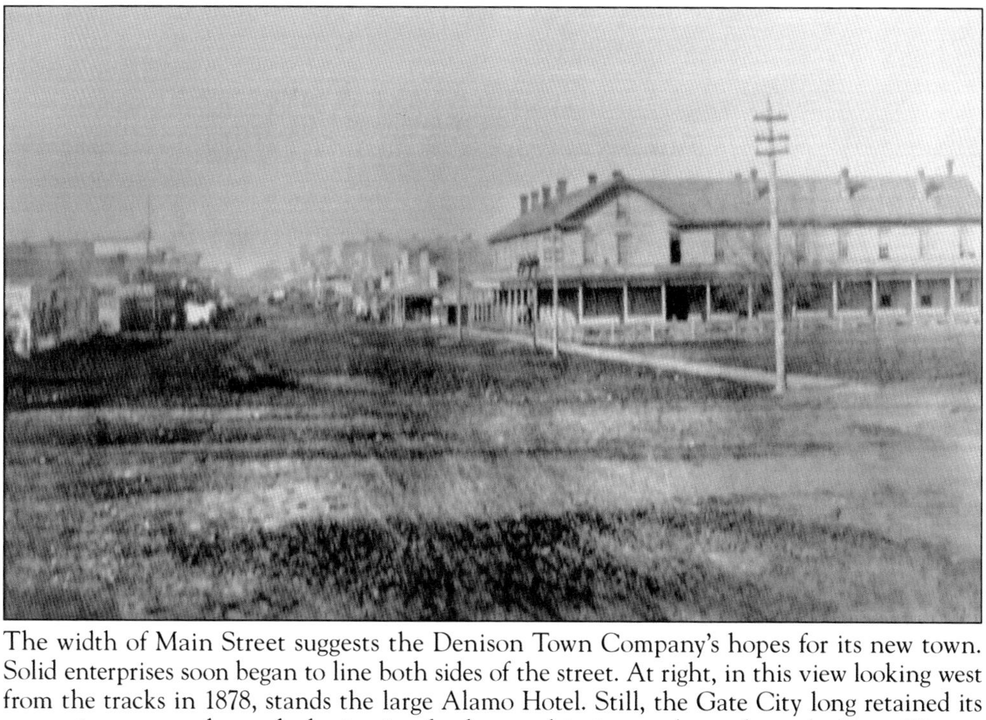

The width of Main Street suggests the Denison Town Company's hopes for its new town. Solid enterprises soon began to line both sides of the street. At right, in this view looking west from the tracks in 1878, stands the large Alamo Hotel. Still, the Gate City long retained its reputation as a rough, rowdy destination for drovers shipping cattle north on the Katy. (George Perkins, in HD.)

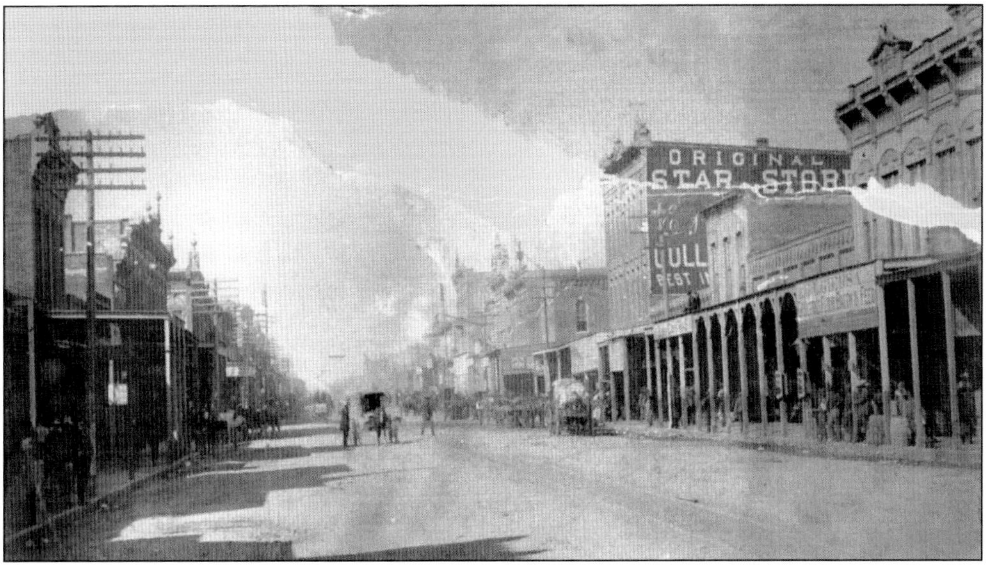

Prominent in local commerce was the Original Star Store erected at 125–131 West Main Street in 1881 by three of Denison's earliest clothing purveyors: Samuel Star (1843–1899), his brother-in-law Charles Waterman, and Max Grundstein (1849–1916). Star arrived in Denison in 1872 and ran the store until 1900. The building is still in use in 2010 after housing, most notably, a bowling alley, skating rink, and pawnshops. (DHH.)

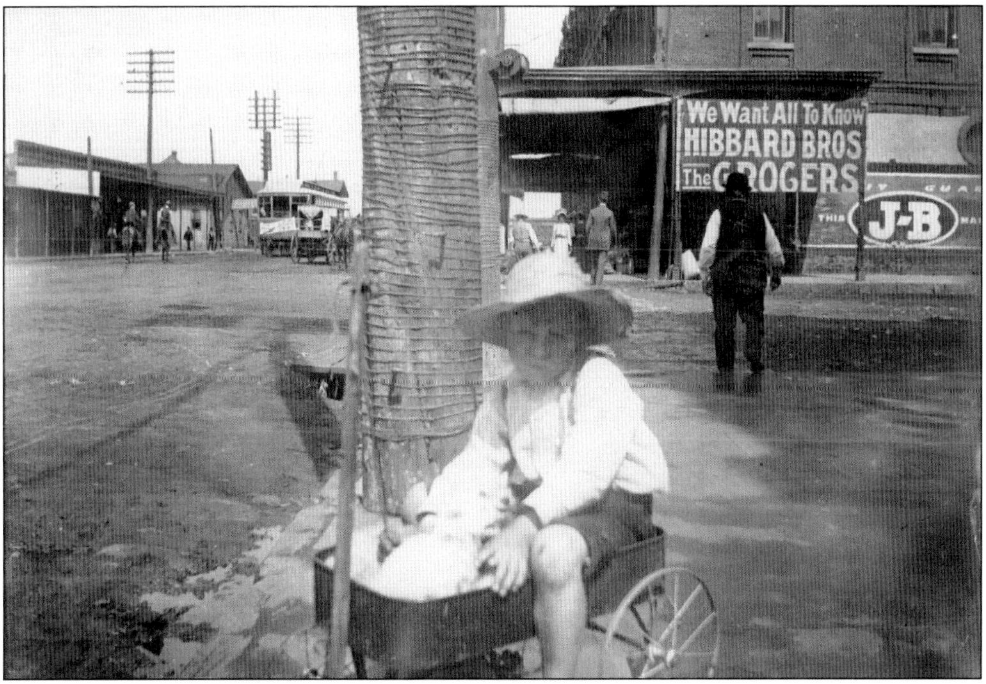

The Hibbard brothers (Walter, Fred, Charles, and H.A.) came to Denison in 1876 from Troy, Wisconsin, to begin one of the city's earliest successful grocery companies. From 1897 through 1902, the firm occupied 100 East Main Street, shown here, looking east. Across the street, just west of the MKT freight office, are saloons, cafés, and a loan office. Note the electrical poles and trolley car. (Lyndon and Paulette Hyatt, in MAB.)

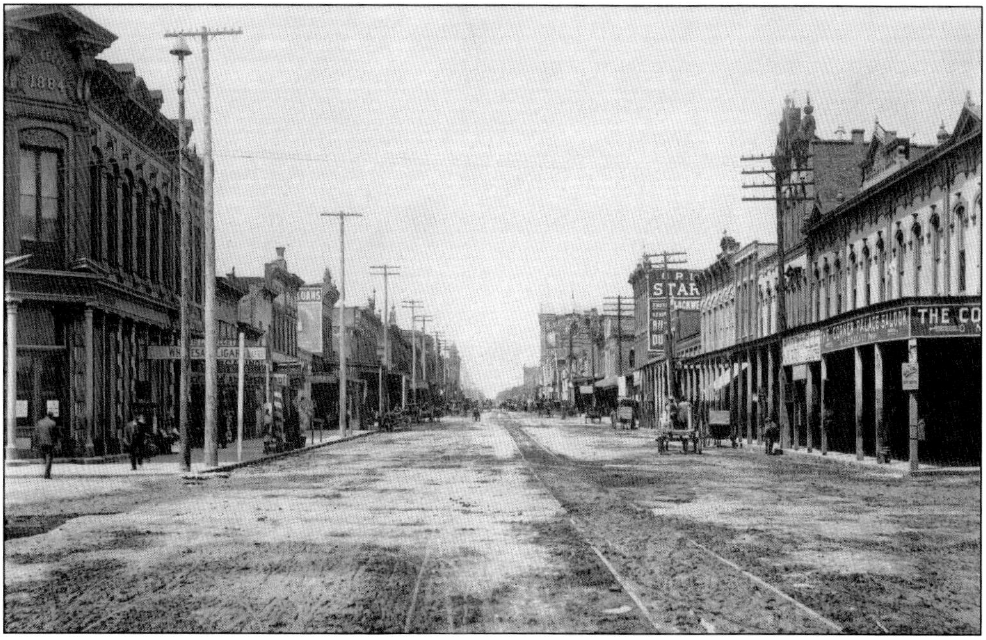

By 1895, Denison's Main Street was full of fine buildings accessed by mule-drawn trolleys (see tracks, center). Poles carried electricity, rapidly replacing gas for lighting. Liquor and cigars were still big moneymakers, indicated by Sweeney's Corner Palace Saloon at the northwest corner of Houston Avenue and Main Street. Across Main Street, German-born Louis Lebrecht, who later became mayor, had built an elegant store for his wholesale tobacco business in 1884. This view looks west. (AWGC.)

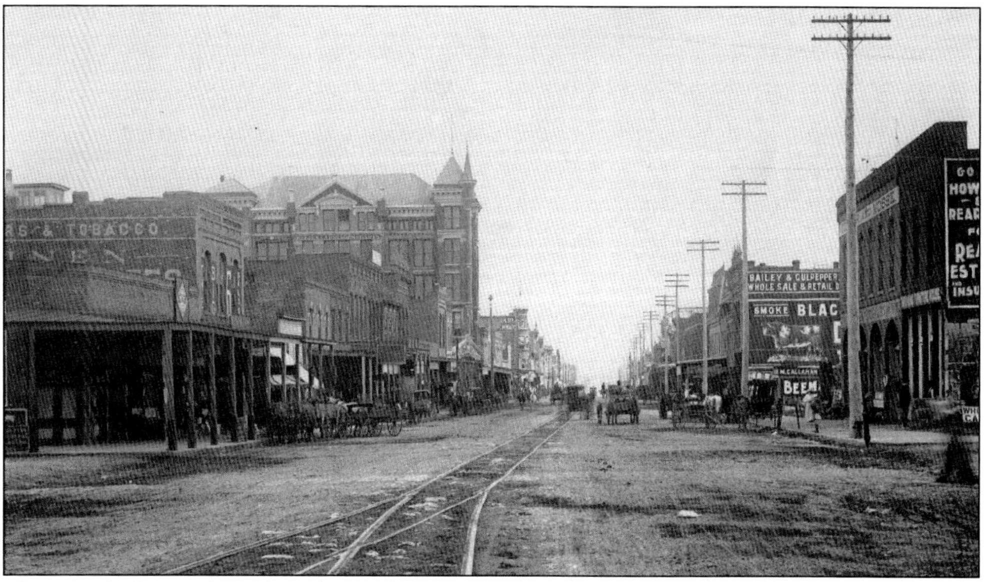

This view looks east from the other end of Main Street in 1895. The large structure, once the tallest building in North Texas, is the five-story Leeper/Security Building, 331 West Main Street. Like the Big 6 Saloon (left), stores built awnings to shelter customers arriving in wagons. According to a newspaper advertisement, Tignor and Mosse (right), later the site of the Rialto Theater, dealt in "carriages, buggies, harness . . . wagons, harvesting machinery, etc." (AWGC.)

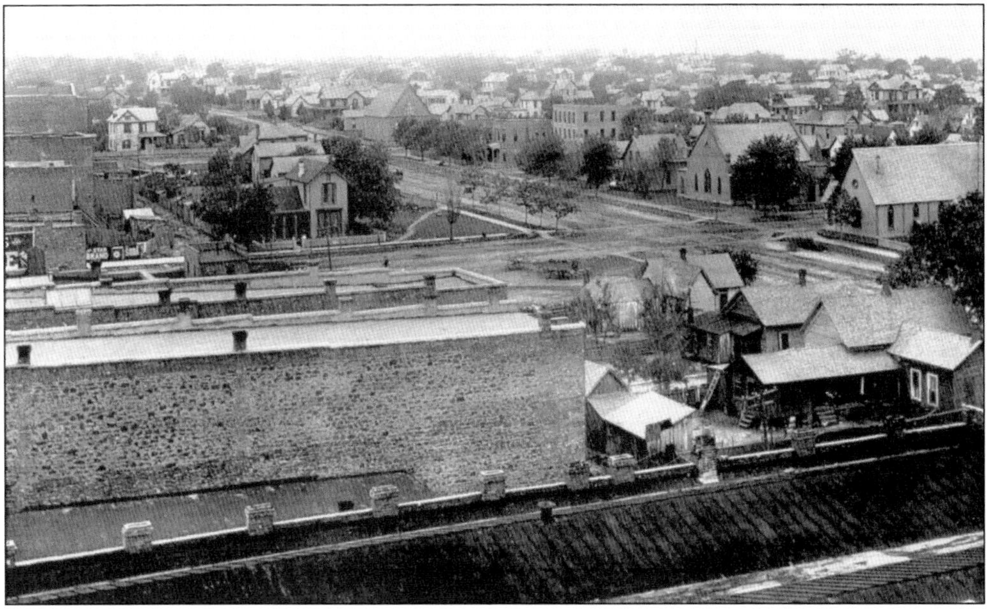

Here are two 1895 views of Denison taken from the town's highest point, the Leeper/Security Building. The photograph above is a view to the northwest, centered on the intersection of Woodard Street and Fannin Avenue. An impressive residential district stretches beyond St. Luke's Episcopal Church (upper right) and the First Methodist Episcopal Church across the avenue. A block west on Woodard Street is the First Baptist Church. Intimate views are afforded of backyards (lower right) and an alley (upper left). The photograph below provides a view to the southeast. Charles M. Davis's big livery stable and wagon yard are seen where Chestnut (Skiddy) Street crosses Rusk Avenue. The large brick house across Rusk Avenue will, in a year or two, be listed as a private boardinghouse belonging to Mrs. H.C. Bray. In the distance, barely visible, is Denison's first (wooden) viaduct. (Both, AWGC.)

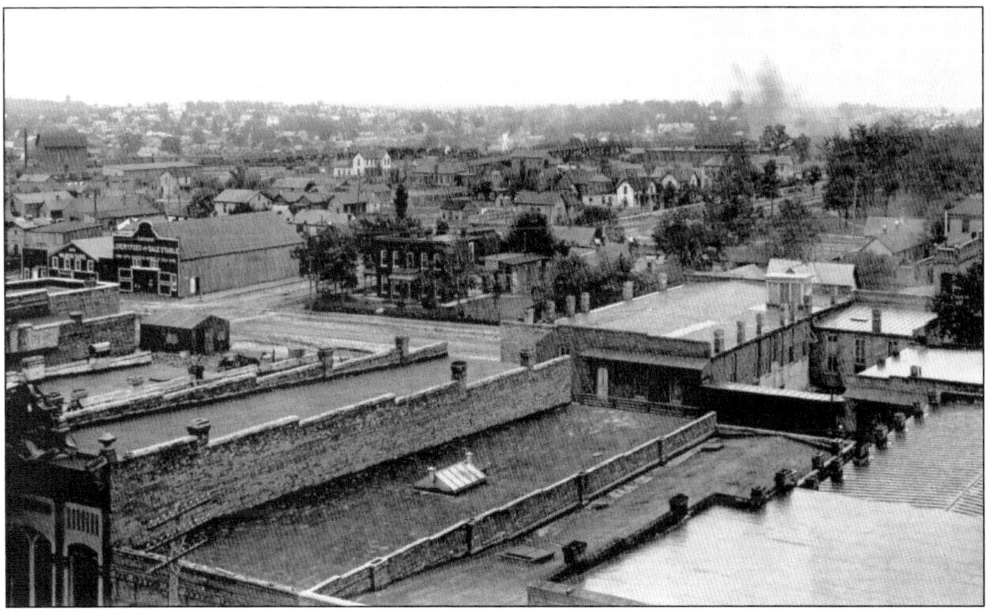

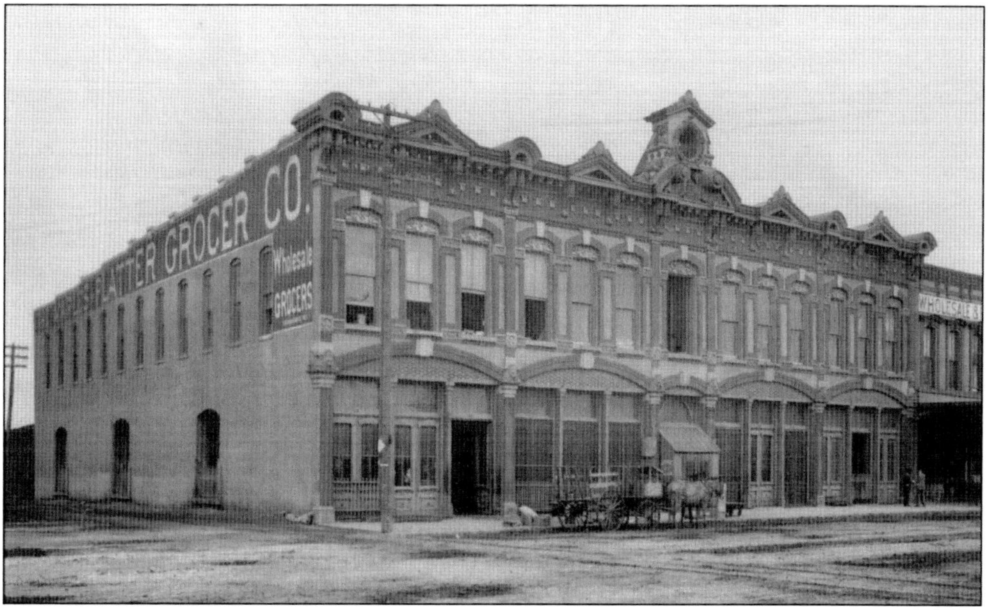

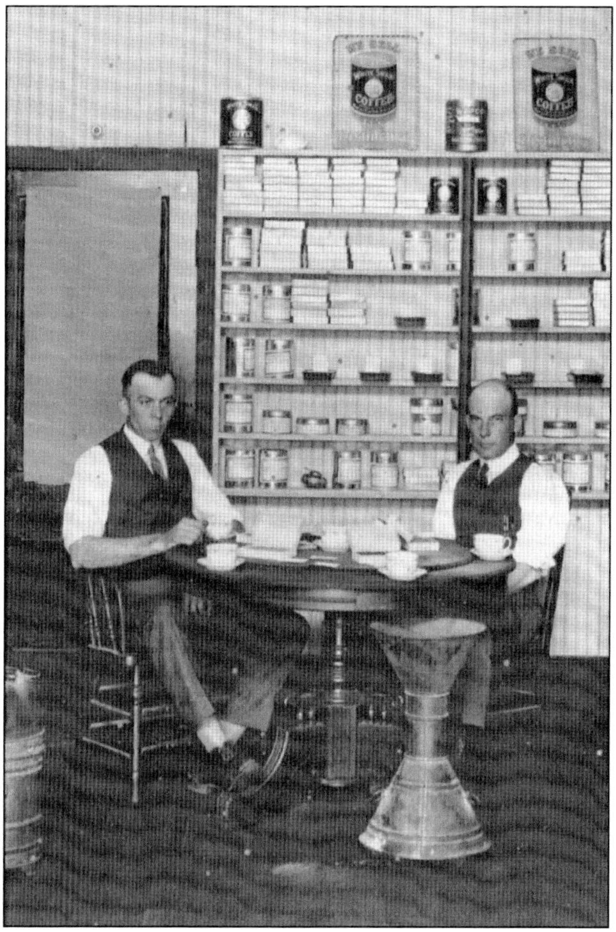

Located next to the railroad tracks at 104 East Main Street, this large, elegant warehouse was built in 1885 for the Waples-Platter Grocer Company (above). That year, Andrew Fox Platter had formed a partnership with Edward B. Waples and his two sons, Paul and John. Founded in Denison, the company became one of the largest wholesale grocery firms in the Southwest, with its salesmen covering five states. As the Wapco and White Swan brands became widely known, coffee importing, roasting, packaging, and sales became major elements of Waples-Platter's business. W.J. Cockrell Sr. (1889–1947) managed the coffee-roasting operation, which produced 20,000 pounds of coffee daily. Shown at left in the coffee-testing room around 1920 are Cockrell and Lingo Platter (1890–1929), a nephew of Andrew Fox Platter. (Above, AWGC; left, HD.)

The McDougall Opera House at 221–223 West Main Street provided some of the young Gate City's earliest entertainment. Col. John B. McDougall, a colorful pioneer, operated numerous successful businesses. His opera house occupied the top two floors of the imposing structure in this stereoview from construction in 1881 until 1907. Seen here in a rare 1883 view, the building was demolished in 1959. (Hardesty and Dean, in MAB.)

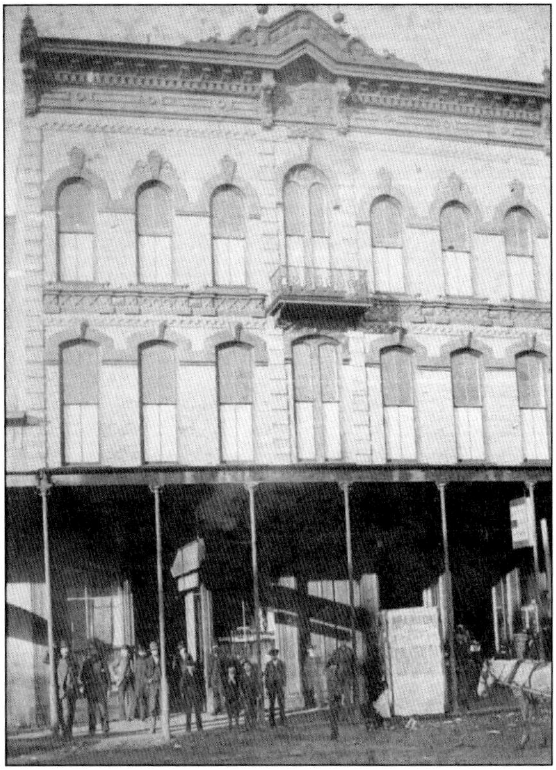

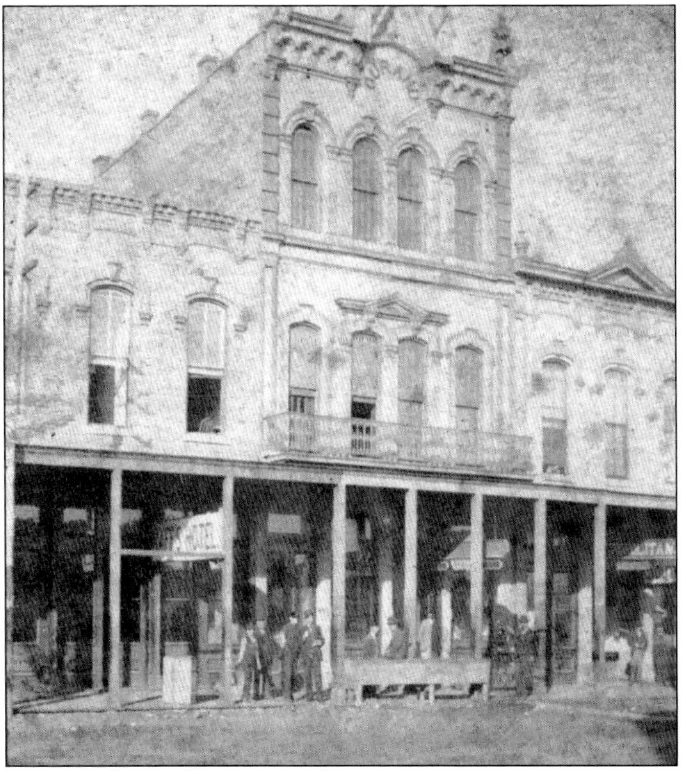

John D. Ourand (1834–1913) arrived with the Katy in 1872, opened a saloon, and built his Ourand Hotel at 109 West Main Street in 1881. Upon Ourand's death, Robert W. Rentz, a former MKT engineer, took charge, advertising meals for 30¢, "clean beds a specialty," and telephones. Seen in this 1883 stereoview, the hotel's motto was "Stop here and feel at home." (Hardesty and Dean, in MAB.)

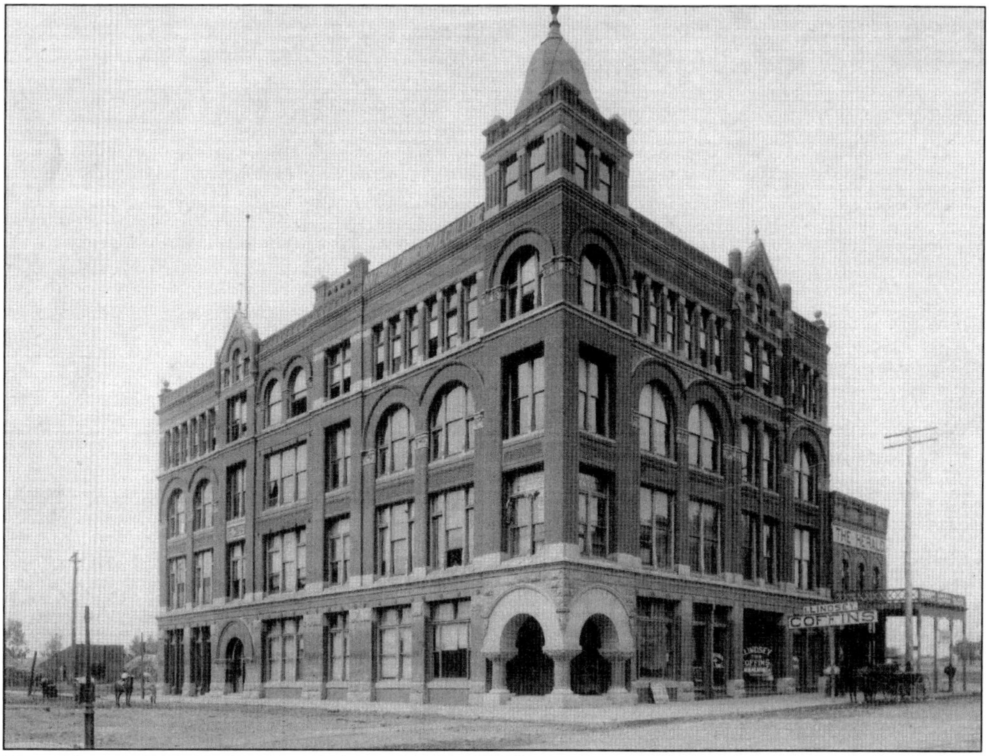

Erected around 1890, the National Commercial College at 500 West Main Street was an ambitious undertaking for a small city. Calling itself "the largest business college in America," it expected to handle 1,500 students a year. After a decade, however, the structure was converted into the first Denison Hotel, boasting numerous amenities. It continued in operation until January 1920, when it was destroyed in one of Denison's greatest fires. (AWGC.)

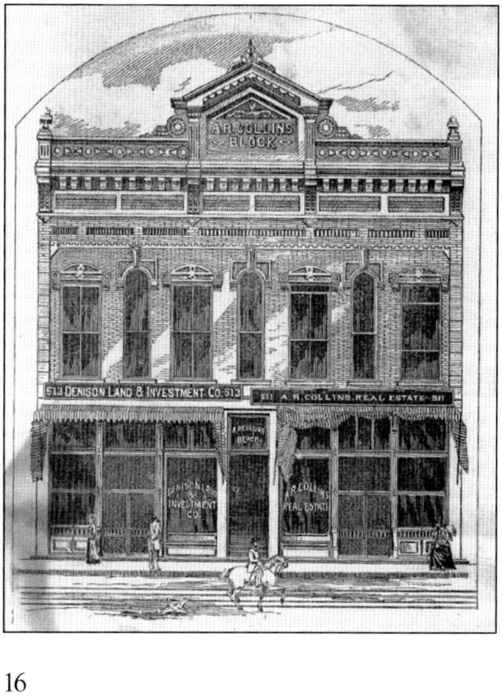

In 1889, Alpheus Remember Collins built the Collins Block at 511–513 West Main Street. It housed his real estate office, which was founded in 1872. Businesses leased space, and the Firemen's Hall upstairs hosted fraternal and labor union meetings. A son, self-taught architect Walter D. Collins (1877–1952), later operated his Collins Safe and Bank Fixture Company here for 38 years. This is one of Denison's finest Italianate commercial buildings. (DHH.)

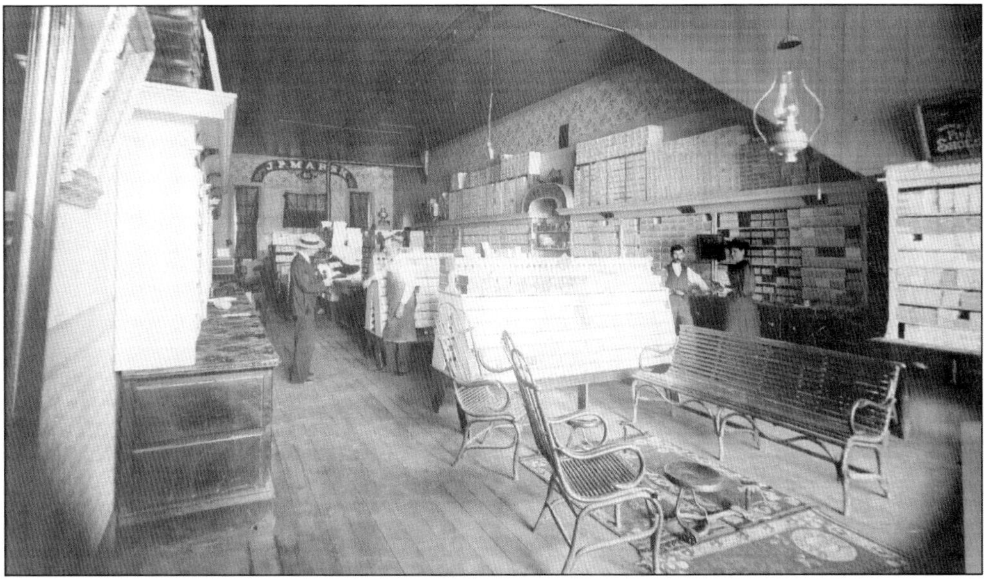

Born in New York in 1833, Julian P. Marsh came to Denison around 1885 after prospecting for gold in California. He manufactured and sold boots and shoes on Main Street from his arrival in town until his unexpected death in 1898. Starting in 1891, son Walter worked with his father in the business, as seen here. Daughter Minnie Marsh was a noted teacher, principal, lecturer, and clubwoman in Denison during the 1890s. (MAB.)

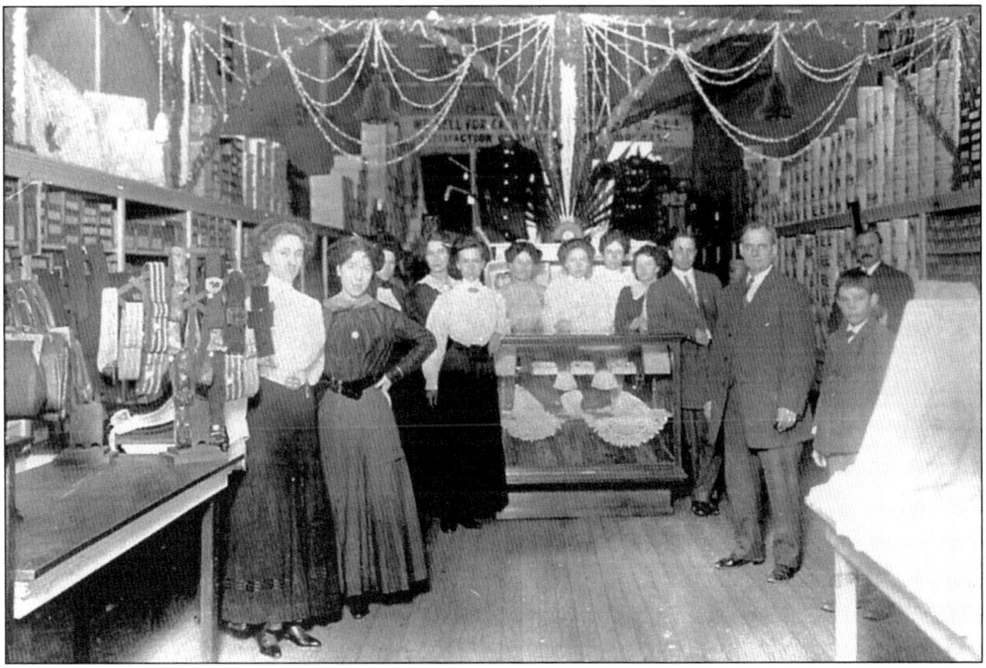

Most early stores occupied standard 25-foot-wide rectangular spaces, so displays were crucial in establishing a unique character. This one, probably William A. Baity Dry Goods at 306–308 West Main Street, rose to the challenge. Nettie Anderson Hickey (1892–1971) worked here sewing as a young girl. Among the employees shown here around 1907 are the family of Preston Tapp, Hickey, Rose (Mrs. George W.) Bodkin, Della Criswell, Carrie Martin, and Florence Perry. (MAB.)

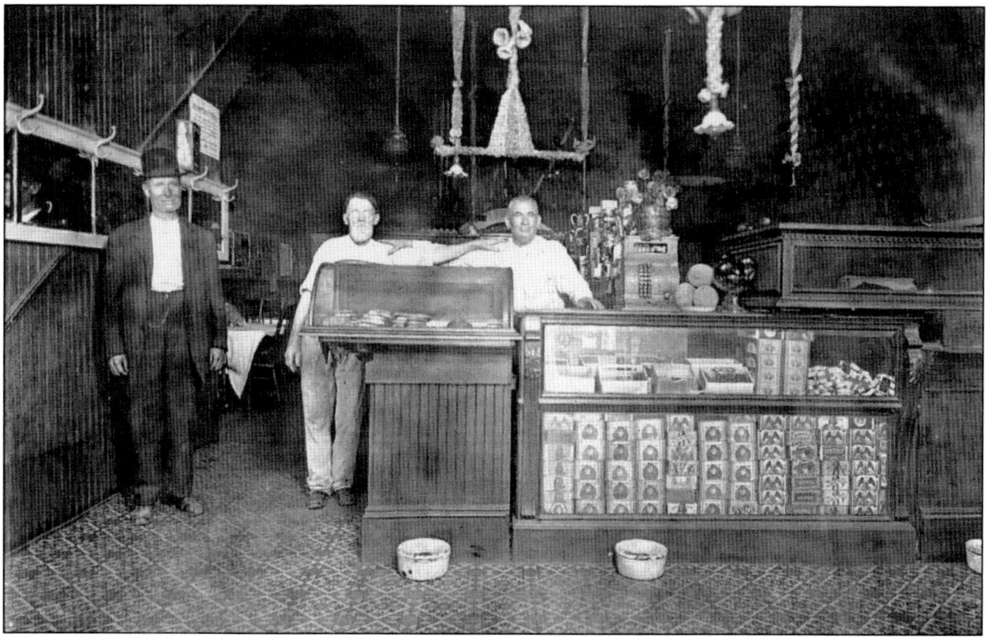

Fancy cases house cigars, chewing tobacco, little bags of tobacco for rolling cigarettes, and souvenir advertisements in this early tobacco store located on Main Street in Denison. Spittoons are placed on the carpet for ease of use as customers test the products. A pyramid of melons in front of the cash register strikes an amusing note. It sits beneath decorative electric light fixtures and a ceiling fan. (MAB.)

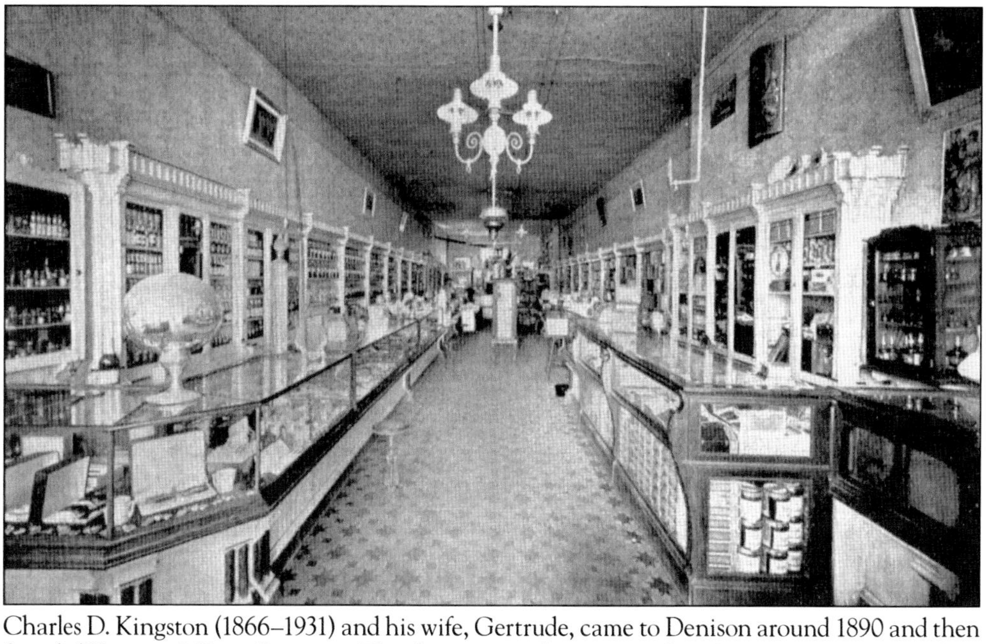

Charles D. Kingston (1866–1931) and his wife, Gertrude, came to Denison around 1890 and then founded Kingston's Drug Company. This firm operated continuously at 322 West Main Street from its founding in 1892 until it merged with another drugstore in 1985. Its recording thermometer on the front of the building once was the town's official temperature gauge. The company began with five employees and had grown to 22 by 1955. (IndDen.)

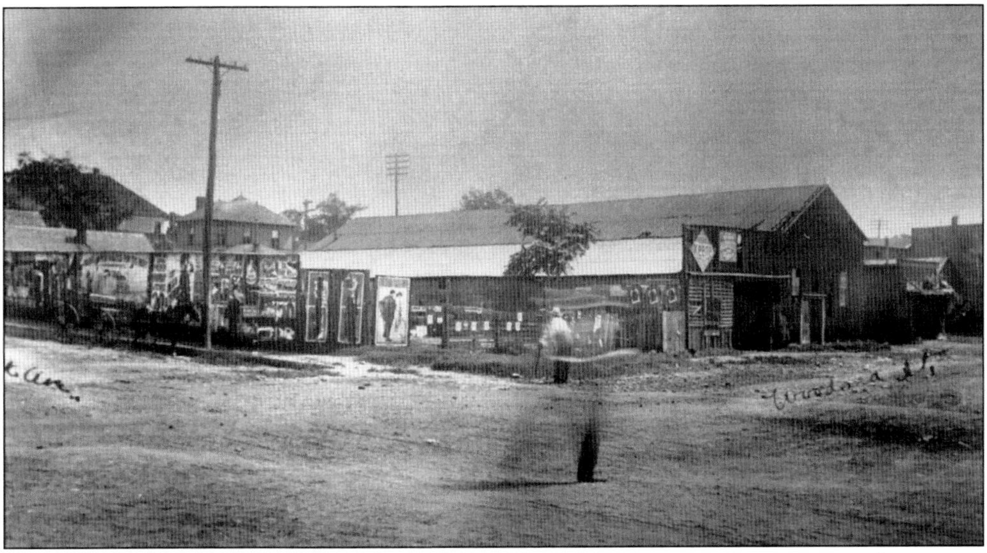

As early as 1896, D. Osborne Fisher of Tishomingo, Indian Territory, was operating his wagon yard at 231 West Woodard Street and Rusk Avenue. He also sold wood and coal. Heavy traffic at this intersection made it a prime place to advertise products and coming events. The photograph also captures an early photographer with his tripod. The Denison Post Office was constructed on this site in 1910–1912. (HD.)

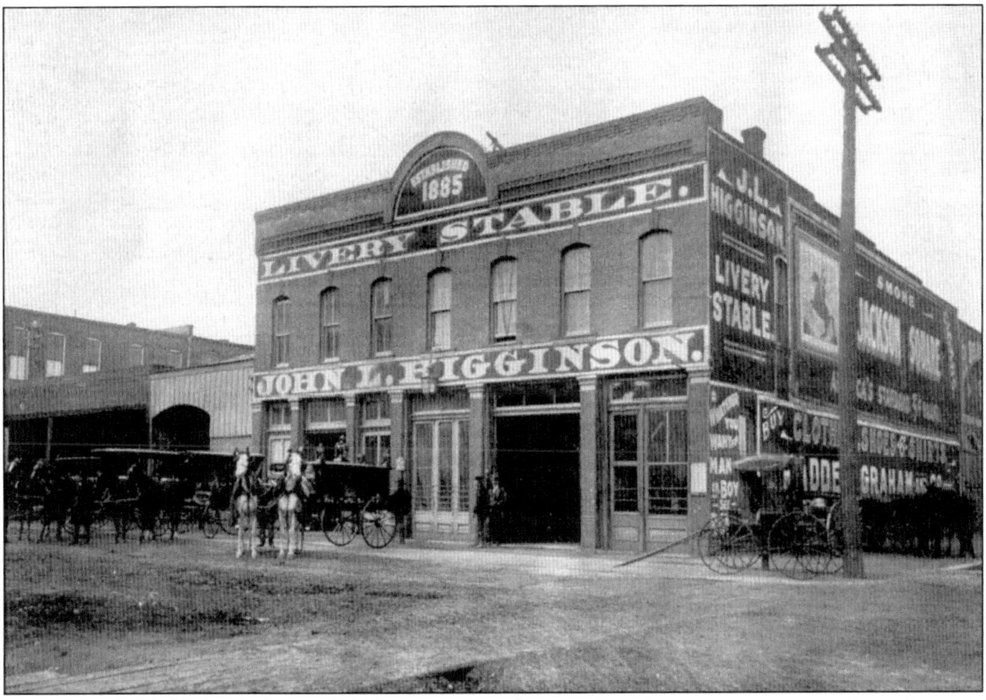

Before automobiles became popular, horses and mules were key for transporting people and goods. Stables and horse lots were important businesses. John L. Higginson (1868–1936) operated one of Denison's best stables, the White Elephant at 115–122 Rusk Avenue at Woodard Street. Before 1900, the business belonged to Jerry Nolan and, later, to M.T. Mathes. The corner location, seen here around 1908, was ideal for eye-catching wall advertisements. (IndDen.)

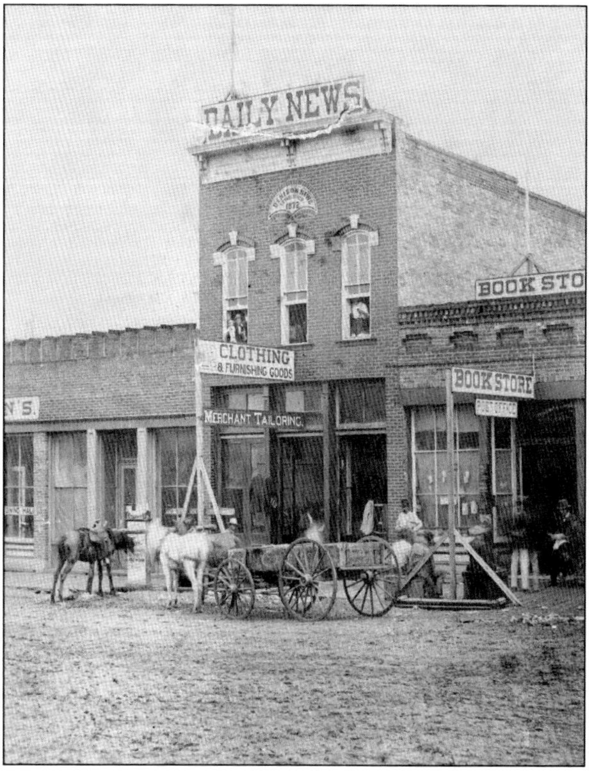

Bredette Coryden Murray (1837–1924) was a key figure in Denison's early history. A pioneer newsman active in politics, Murray was friend and personal secretary to L.S. Owings, who was governor of the Arizona Territory and, later, Denison's first mayor. Murray founded the *Denison Weekly News* in December 1872 and became a city alderman in March 1873. In a year, the *Weekly News* grew into the *Denison Daily News*. (DHH.)

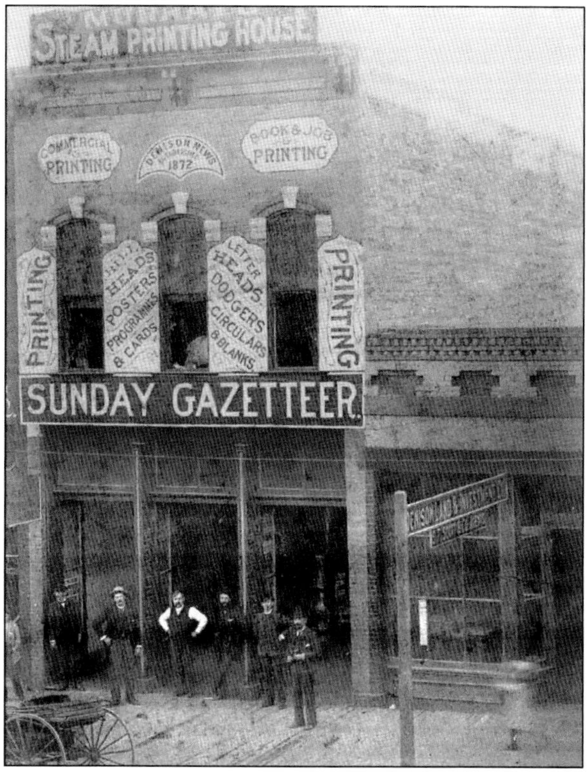

Murray sold the *Denison Daily News* in 1881 and later founded another weekly, the *Sunday Gazetteer* (he called it "Your Sunday Glass of Beer"). Running it until 1913, Murray also operated Murray's Steam Printing House, perhaps "the largest and best-equipped shop in the Southwest," as noted in the *Denison City Directory*. Seen here at 112 West Main Street, Murray (center) remained influential in Denison until his death in 1924. (BCT.)

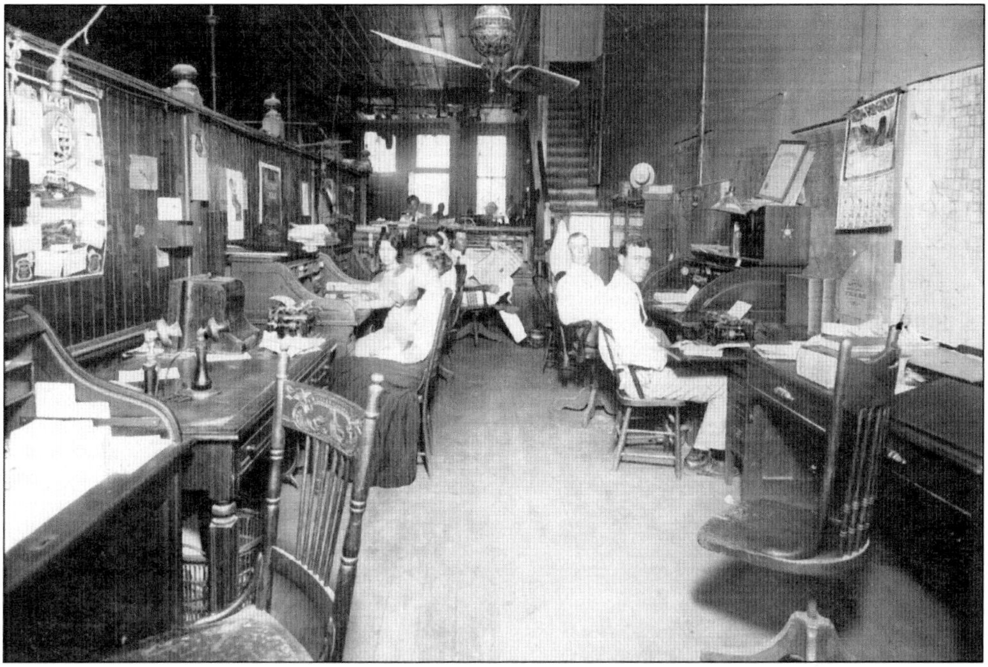

Before the Internet, television, or radio, newspapers were the primary means of disseminating information. Newspapermen like M.M. Scholl (the "Snake Editor" of the *Denison Dispatch*) and B.C. Murray were local celebrities who entertained readers and tirelessly promoted local growth. This *Gazetteer* newspaper office, seen around 1912, sports tall telephones, curious typewriters, ornate ceiling fans, improvised wiring, maps, and female and male employees in almost equal numbers. (DHH.)

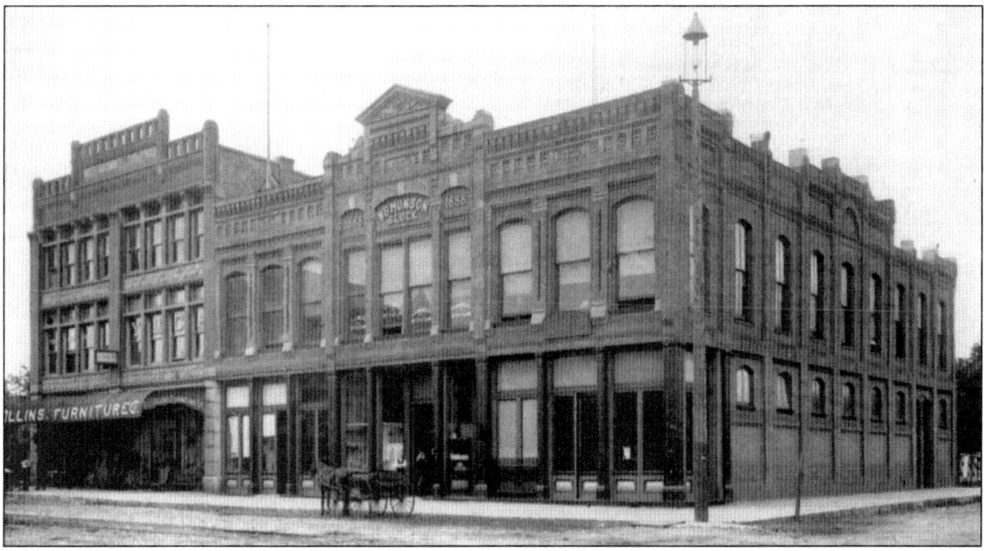

The first William Benjamin Munson, an early Denison real estate developer from Illinois, built the Munson Block at 301 West Woodard Street in 1888. He was one of three brothers (the others were Thomas Volney and Theodore) who had a lasting impact on Denison's history. Many important enterprises started out leasing space here. One, shown on the left around 1895, was Collins Furniture. The YMCA occupied the upper floors. (AWGC.)

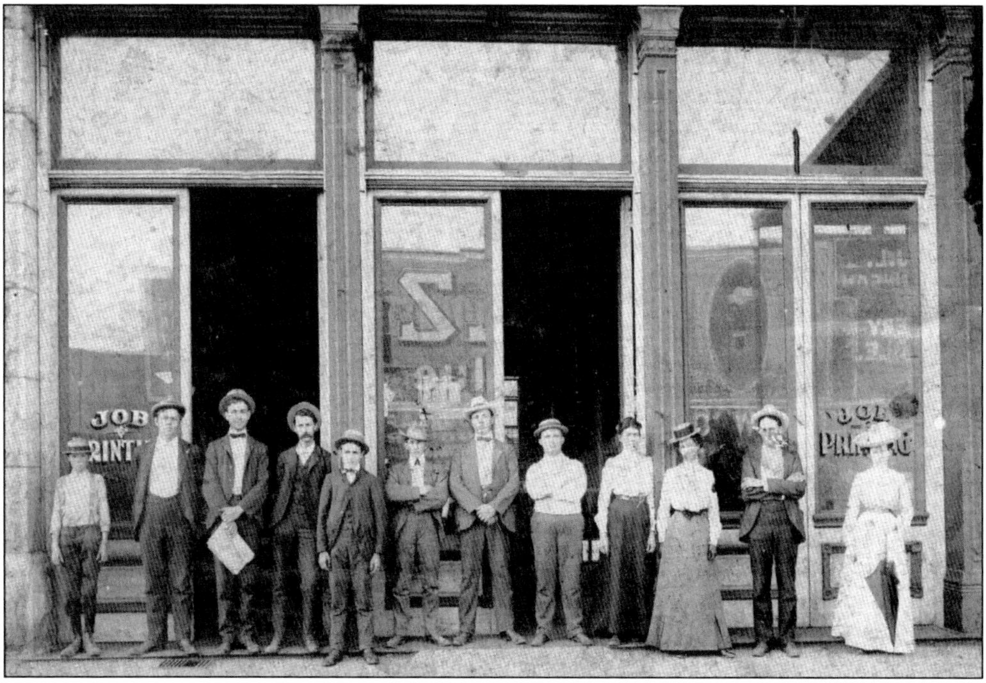

In 1902, the *Denison Herald* was located in the Munson Block at 305 West Woodard Street. In addition to publishing the news, the firm used its presses for commercial job printing. The staff included a publisher, reporters, editors, an advertising solicitor, advertisement compositor, linotype operator, pressmen, circulation collector, bookkeepers, stenographers, and others. A number of those seen here later went on to success at newspapers in Dallas and Fort Worth. (HD.)

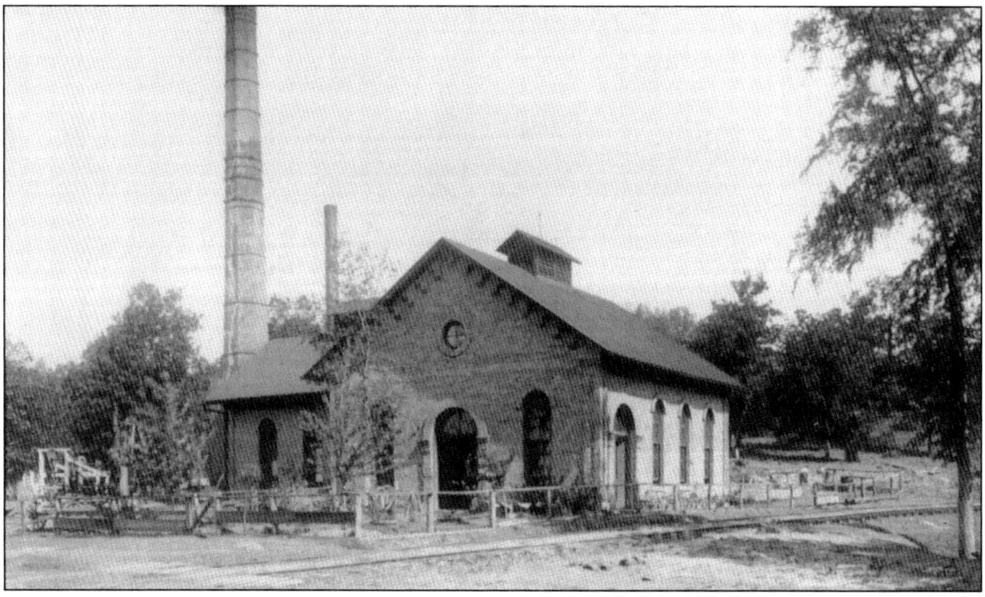

As early as 1895, Denison was the only city in North Texas with an inexhaustible supply of clear water from two lakes. The waterworks system furnished fire protection and water beginning in 1884. By 1914, Denison owned 42 miles of water mains and 30 miles of sewers, together costing $540,000. The lake water was filtered at the Denison City Waterworks pumping station. (AWGC.)

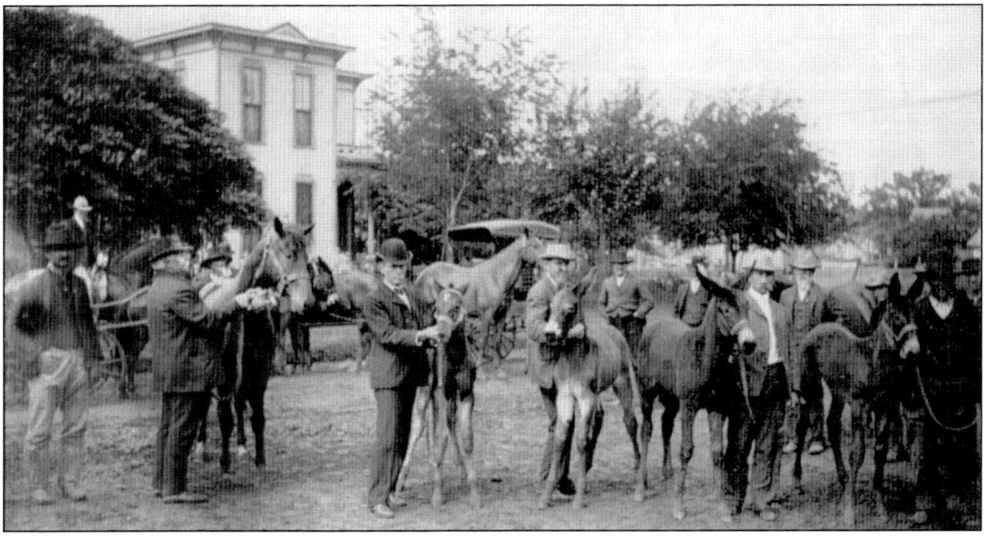

A feature of June Sales Day in 1902 was a colt show, said to be at the home of T.V. Munson in Denison. Several nice prizes were offered, and some fine horses were shown. Men had much to gain by becoming expert judges of horses, and they enjoyed the fun of bargaining and trading horses and mules. (Hendricks, in HD.)

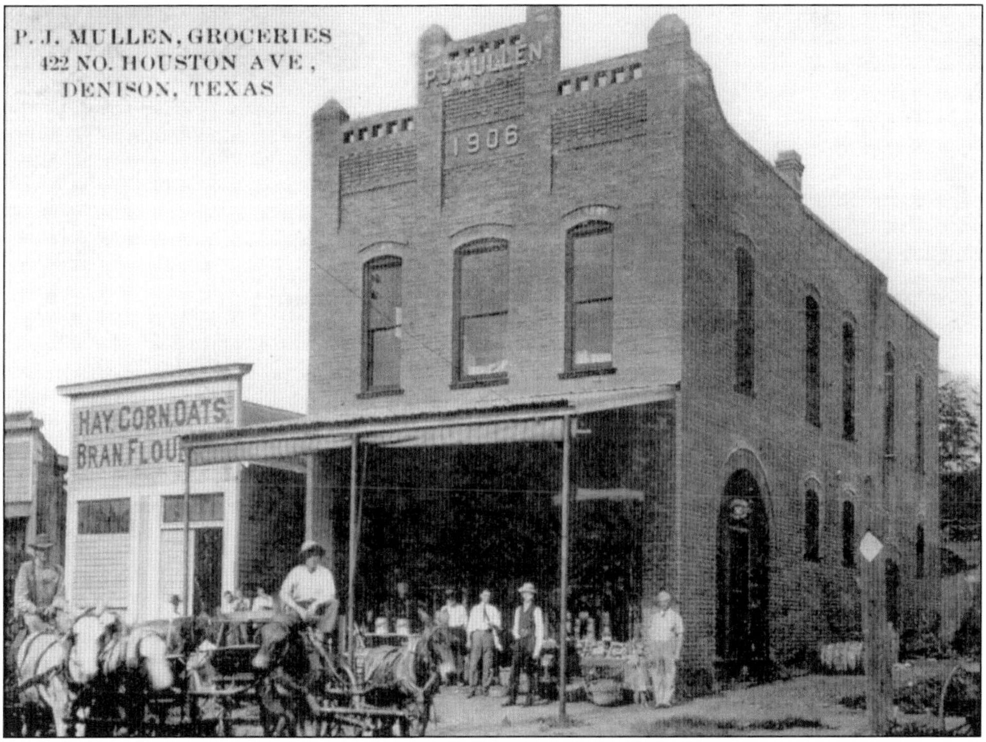

Patrick J. Mullen built this fine brick grocery store in 1906 at 421 North Houston Avenue, the southwest corner of Morton Street. Mullen, a single man, lived in a boardinghouse near the grocery in 1910 but, by 1917, had moved to 411 West Sears Street. William J. Stanford took over the store later. Many types of business have used it since. Recently it has been a motorcycle shop. (MAB.)

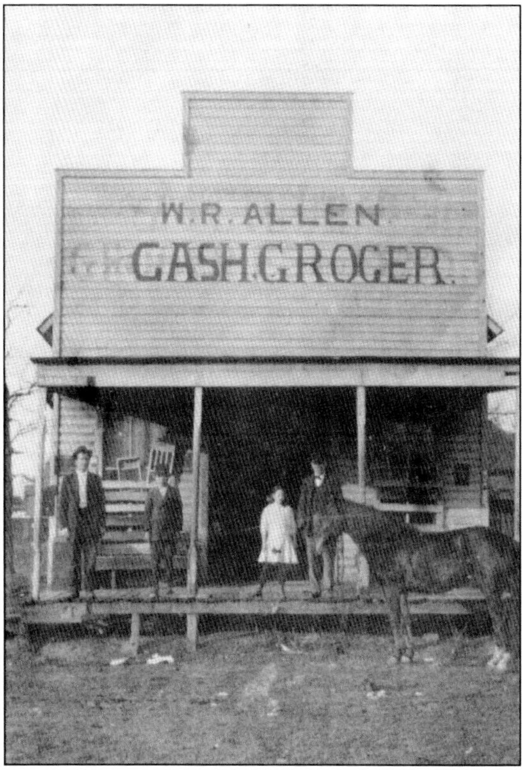

William R. Allen (1843–1921) and family operated the W.R. Allen Cash Grocery at 1031 West Crawford Street, beginning around 1897. The building shown here (about 1909) burned and was replaced by a neighborhood grocery. Pictured here, from left to right, are William R. Allen, a delivery boy named Daniels, eight-year-old Libby J. Bogar Allen (later mayor), and Tom Cox. Cox was killed in 1910 in a train wreck in Greenville, Texas. (DHH.)

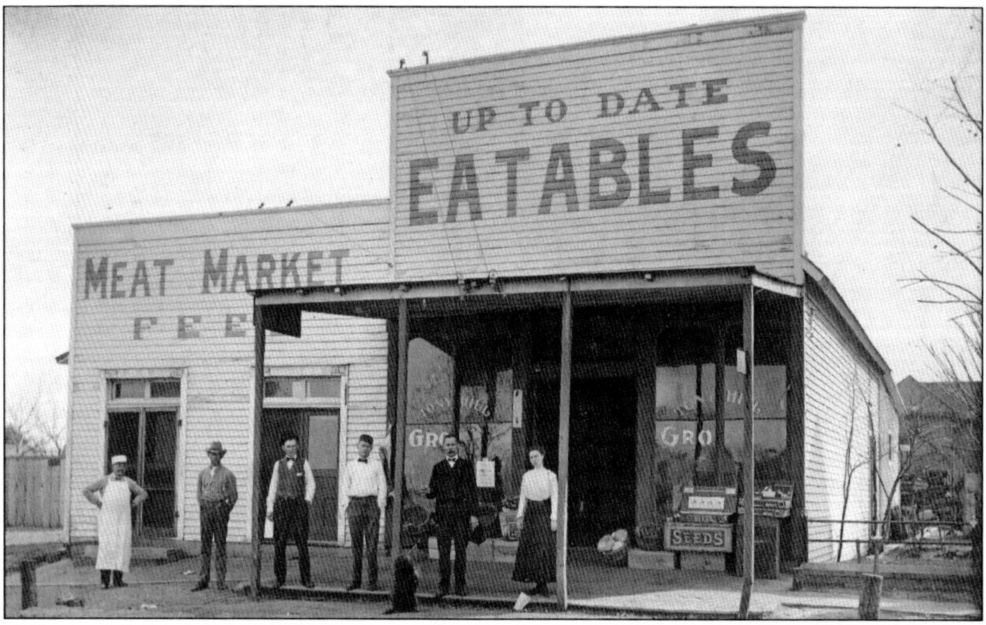

Offering "Up To Date Eatables," Tony Hill Grocery was located at 1220 West Gandy Street in 1889. It was named for its placement in the tony, or better, part of Denison. By 1899, Allen L. Jones owned the store, but Jesse Whitehurst acquired it before 1907. Pictured around that time are Mr. Fredrick, two unidentified people, Coley Hubbard, Whitehurst, and Mae Murphy. Note Whitehurst's dog sitting up and begging. (HD.)

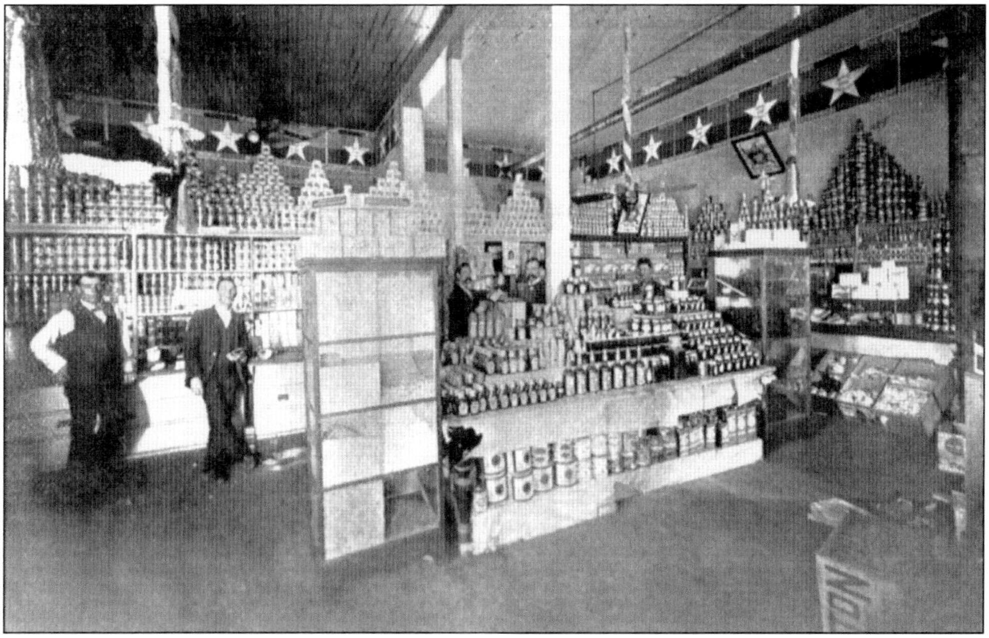

Dan Tracy (born about 1866) opened his High Grade Grocery around 1900 at 118–120 North Rusk Avenue. Mamie Tracy was bookkeeper and cashier, and Frank R. Tracy was clerk. Bulk containers of beans, flour, corn, and other foods stand near the front, while bins of potatoes and onions can be seen on the right. Canned foods stacked decoratively made the store high-grade. Well-dressed employees stand waiting to serve customers. (IndDen.)

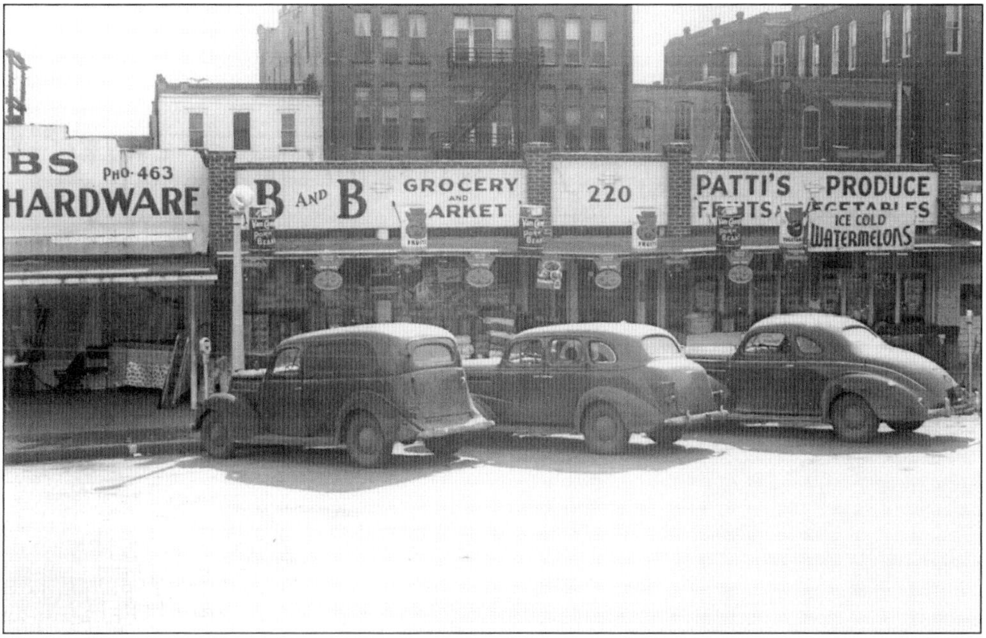

If one wanted vegetables fresh from the garden, ice-cold watermelon, canned goods, fresh meat, or maybe furniture or hardware, the 200 block of West Woodard Street was the place to go in the 1940s. Patti's grew most of its produce on the family farm. B and B Grocery had a meat market, and Combs Furniture and Hardware had almost anything else a family might need. (DHH.)

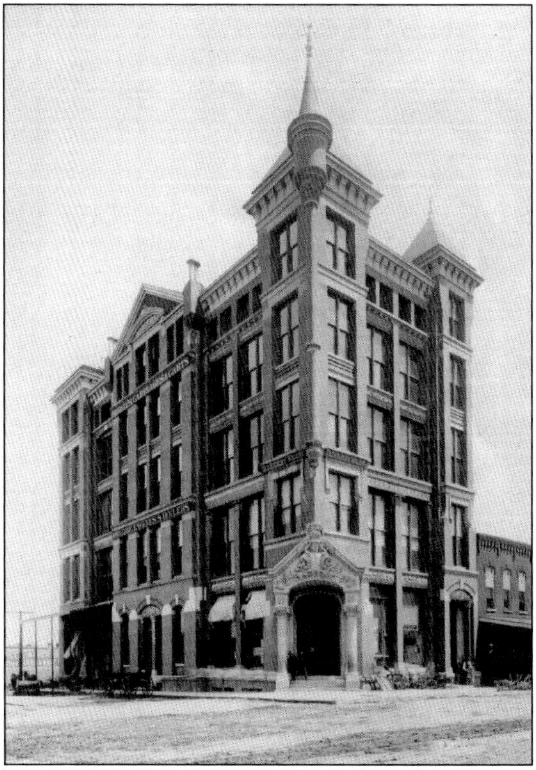

Edward Leeper and Thomas Boldrick, ambitious young owners of a hardware business, wanted their building at 331 West Main Street to be the talk of Texas. In that, architect Pierre Lelardoux succeeded. Completed in 1891, the elegant skyscraper (shown at left around 1895) drew gawkers from as far away as Dallas. Initially named for Edward Leeper, the structure later was called the Security Building after a short-lived tenant, Security State Bank. Before 1905, the turret and top floor were "dangerously too high" and later removed, leaving Old Stoneface above the main entrance as the building's chief ornament (shown below in 1954). While banks occupied the prominent ground floor corner space, professionals had offices on the upper floors. Carrie Cole operated the small elevator for many years. In 1954, the building was demolished. Its granite foundation was reused for the Lilley-Linn Department Store. (Left, AWGC; below, MAB.)

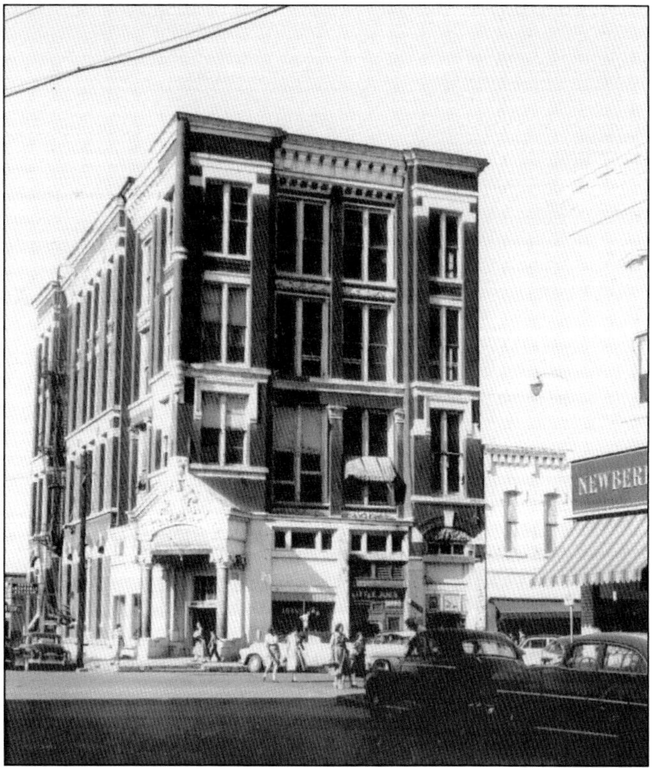

The State National Bank opened at 300 West Main Street in 1883, replacing a residence hotel, the Nelson House. Initially only 25 feet wide, the three-story bank expanded by stages around its ornate Beaux-Arts–style core. Bank leaders have included Edward Perry, S.G. Bayne, G.L. Blackford, Andrew Fox Platter, W.L. Peterson, Ralph Porter, and Jack Berry. In 1957, a drive-through facility was added on the south side of the bank (below). Later, to enlarge the parking lot, the drive-through was moved and a larger version installed a block away. In 1970 and 1971, nationwide, large banks were acquiring small community banks. At this time, Interfirst Bank purchased the State National Bank and demolished the historical Main Street building. A boxy new two-story structure made of white marble replaced it on the same site. (Right, AWGC; below, MAB.)

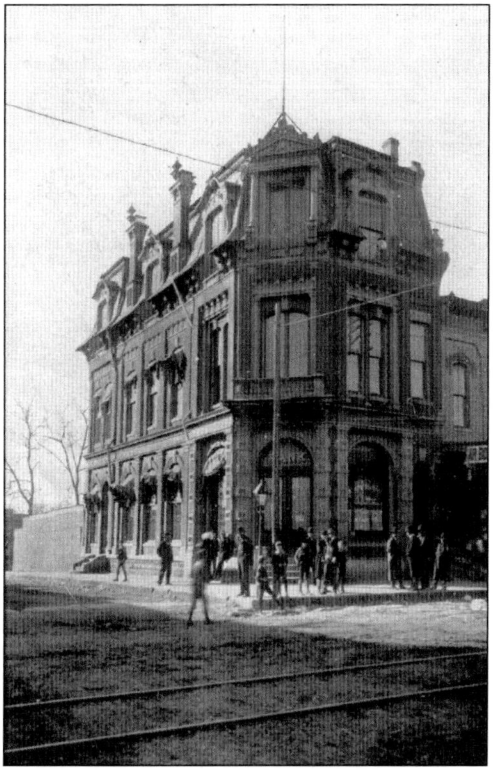

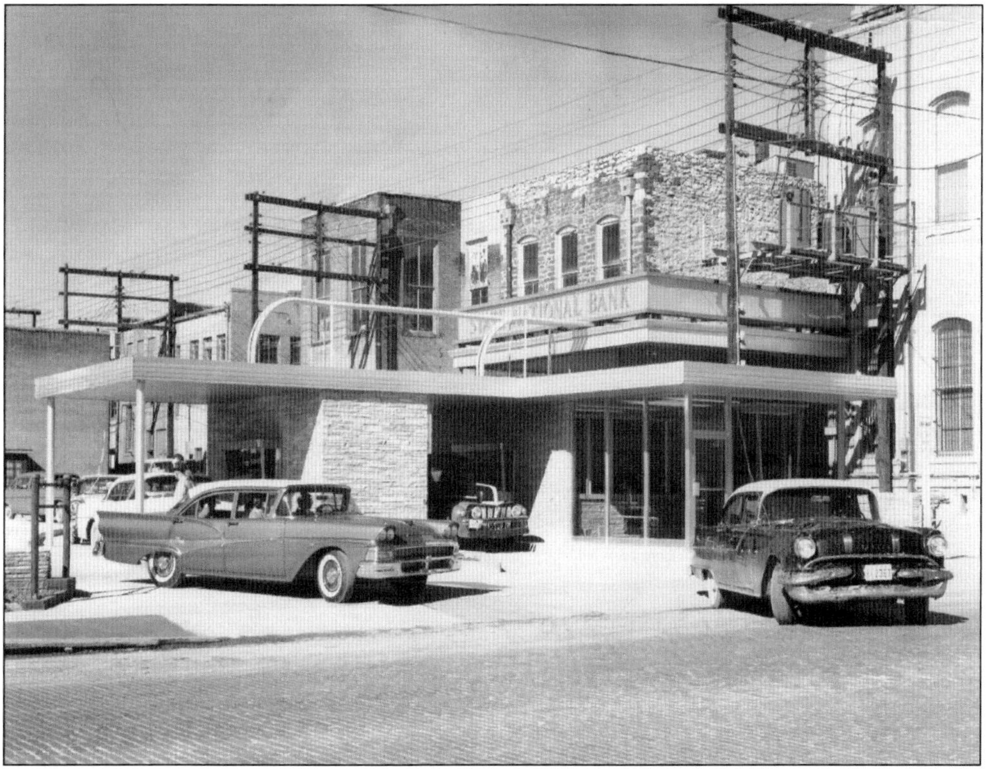

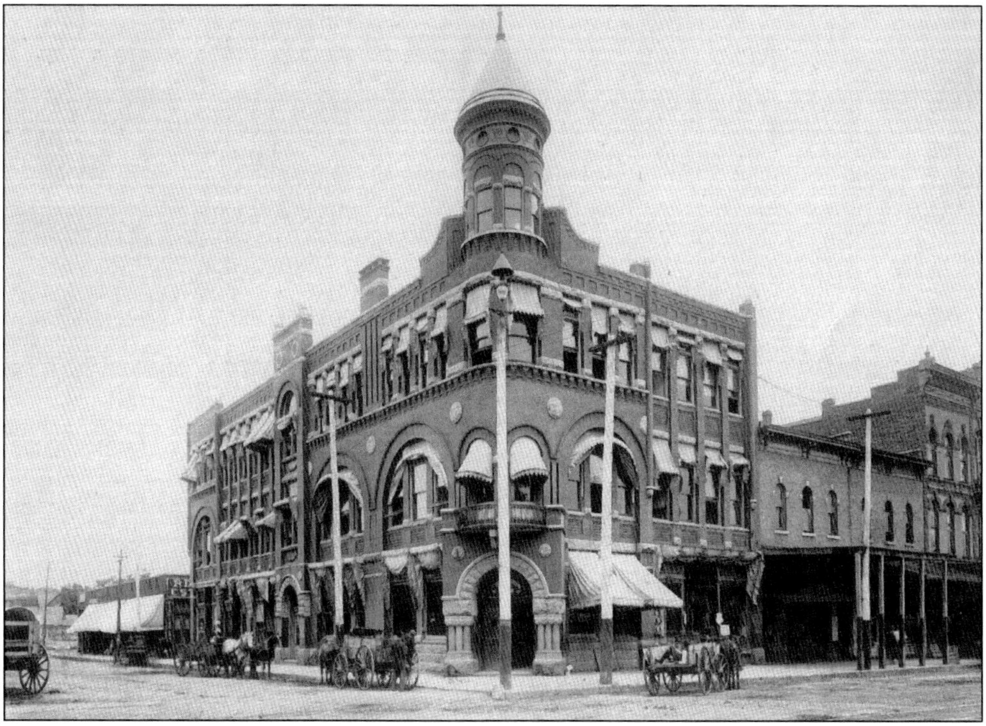

The northeast corner of Main Street and Rusk Avenue has been a bank location since Denison was founded. The First National Bank (shown above around 1895) was established at 231 West Main Street in 1873, with a new building erected there in 1881. The structure was called the Ford Building, after J.M. Ford, then bank head. Around 1921, when the Citizens National Bank was founded, the tower was removed. Early leaders included W.B. Munson Jr., R.W. Stoddard, D.E. Blackburn, Clarence Scott, Henry Etter, and M.A. Regensburger. Building tenants included insurance companies, other banks, and the offices of the US Army Engineers in charge of building the Denison Dam. In 1959, after clearing most of a city block, the bank replaced the Ford Building with a sleek, new stucco facility designed by architect Donald Mayes. (Above, AWGC; below, MAB.)

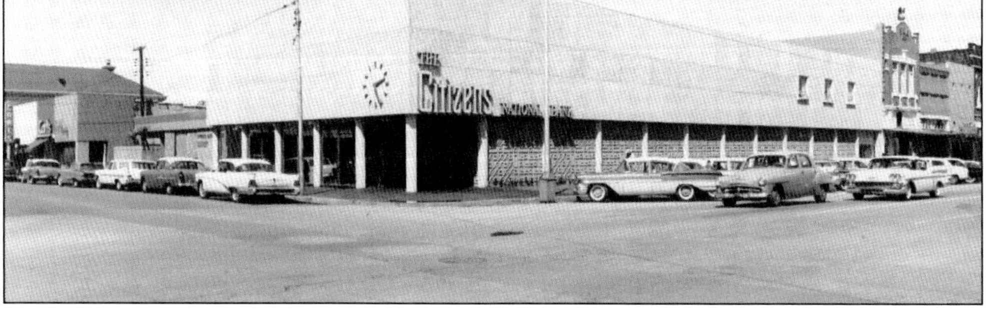

Two

THE RAILROAD STEAMS INTO TOWN

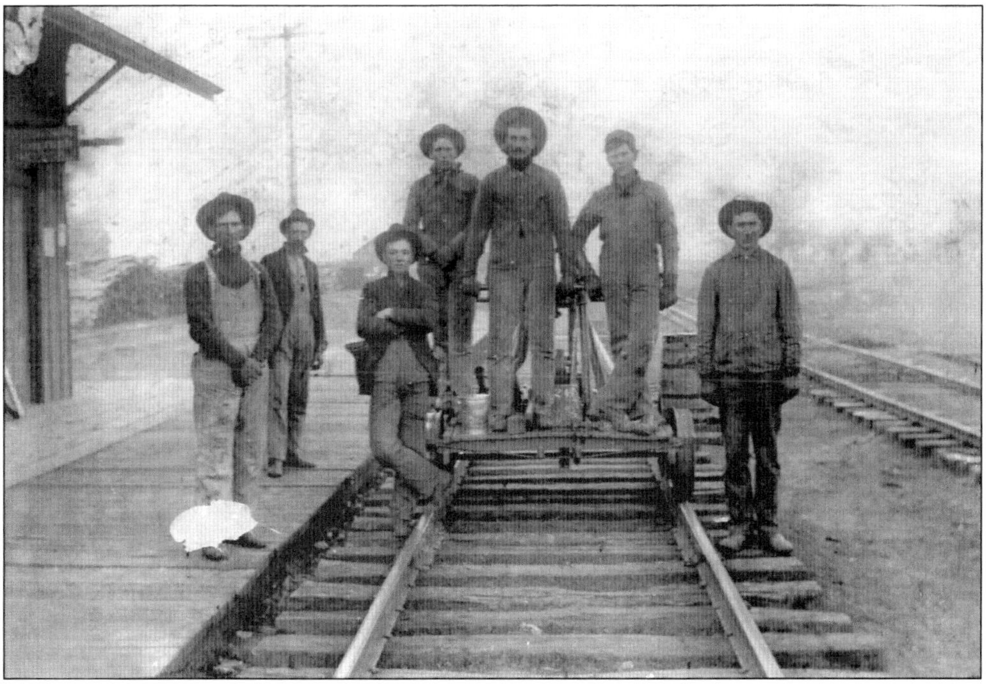

Pumper cars like this one were used to transport crews charged with maintaining rails and other equipment needed to keep trains running smoothly. This crew pauses beside an early railroad telegraph office. In the center is William M. Cordell. (Betty Ferguson Johnson.)

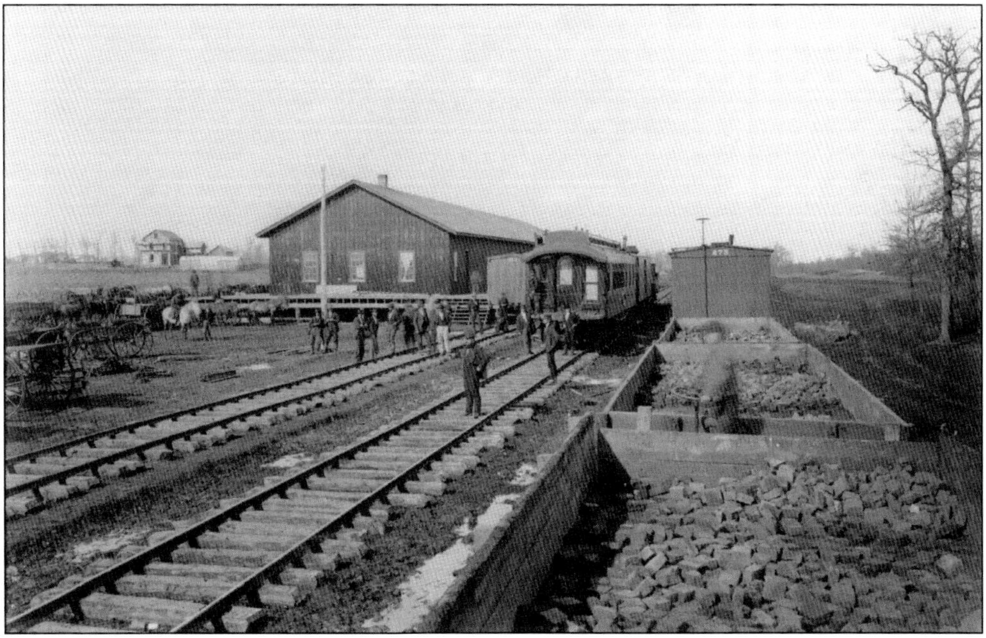

Soon after the MKT tracks reached Denison in December 1872, the railroad hired a St. Louis photographer Robert Benecke to document the operation at Denison. The first Katy Depot was the frame building shown here. Only three months later, it would go up in flames. This photograph shows carloads of bricks being unloaded as onlookers, possibly on a rest stop while traveling through Denison, observe. (HD.)

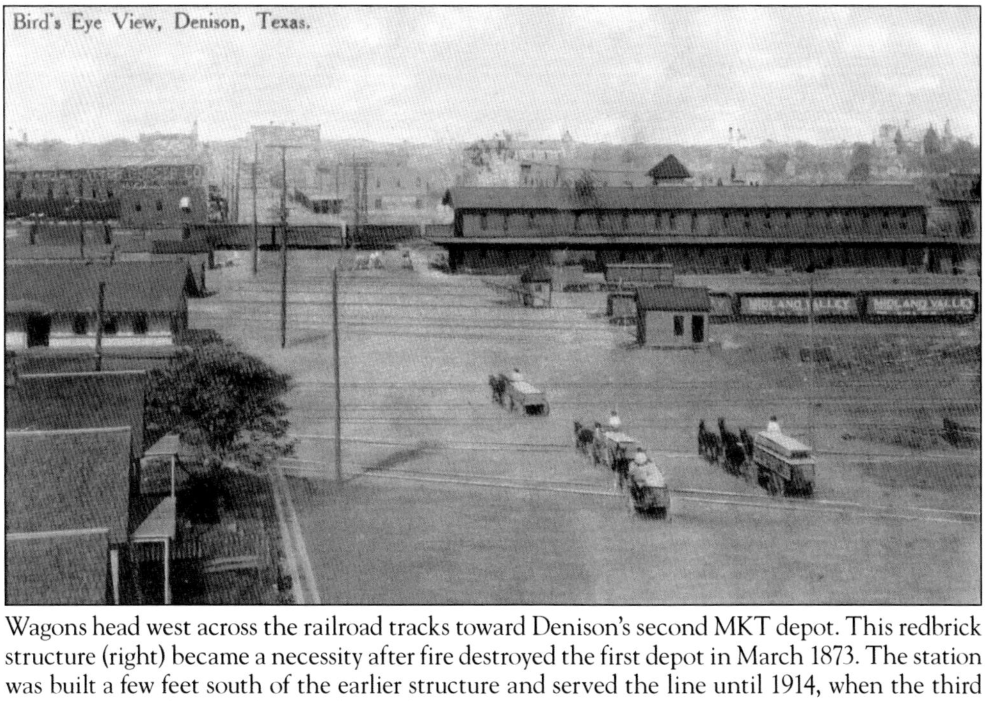

Wagons head west across the railroad tracks toward Denison's second MKT depot. This redbrick structure (right) became a necessity after fire destroyed the first depot in March 1873. The station was built a few feet south of the earlier structure and served the line until 1914, when the third depot was completed. Also visible (top left) is the redbrick Waples-Platter Grocer Company, an important firm founded in Denison. (DHH.)

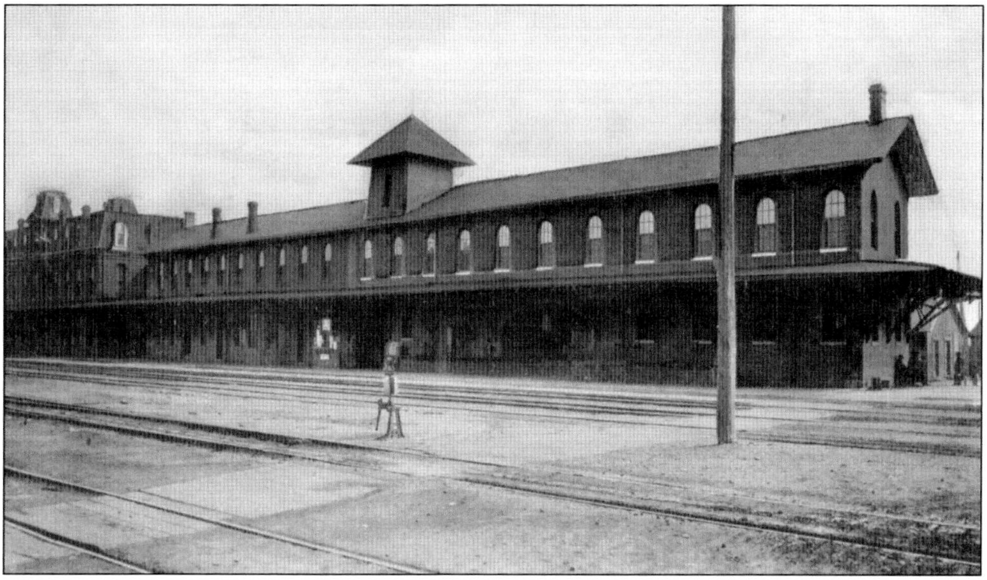

The second train depot, called Union Station, is seen looking east from Houston Avenue around 1905. The McDougall Hotel, constructed before 1886, stands at the north (left) end. The Katy's growth soon forced the depot to expand. In addition to passenger and freight stations, the building housed offices of the Houston and Texas Central (HTC) Railroad on the second floor until the McDougall Hotel extended into the space. (MAB.)

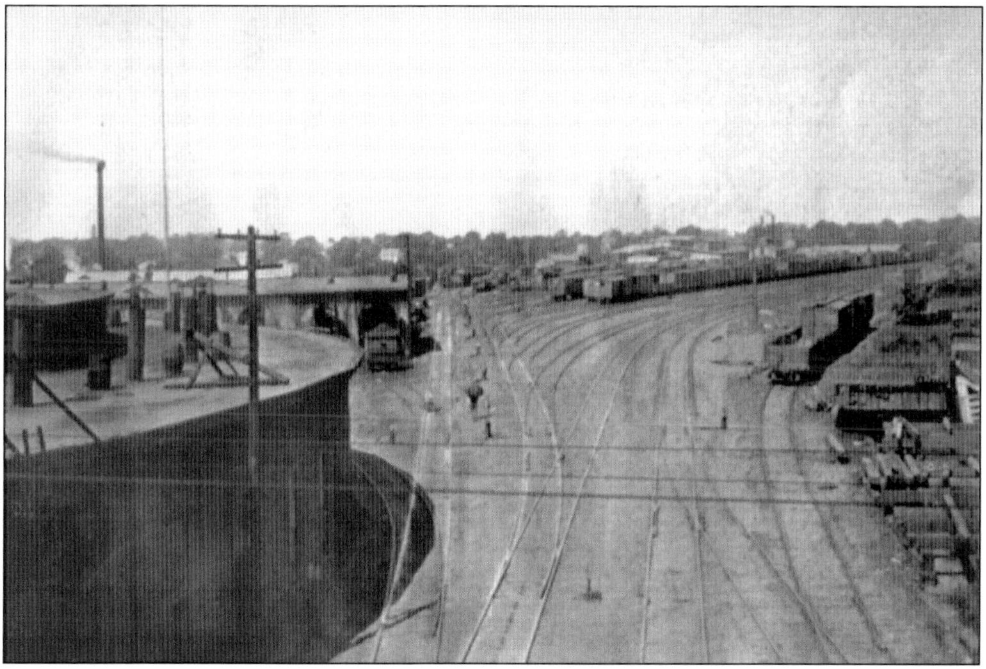

In 1895, this scene would have been visible at the MKT shops. On the left is the roundhouse. Today, the Austin Avenue viaduct covers the location of the former shops. It was here that engines, passenger cars, and boxcars were repaired and put back on the tracks. Every year, countless cars passed through the shops, which employed hundreds of Denison workers. Strong labor unions represented the various trades. (AWGC.)

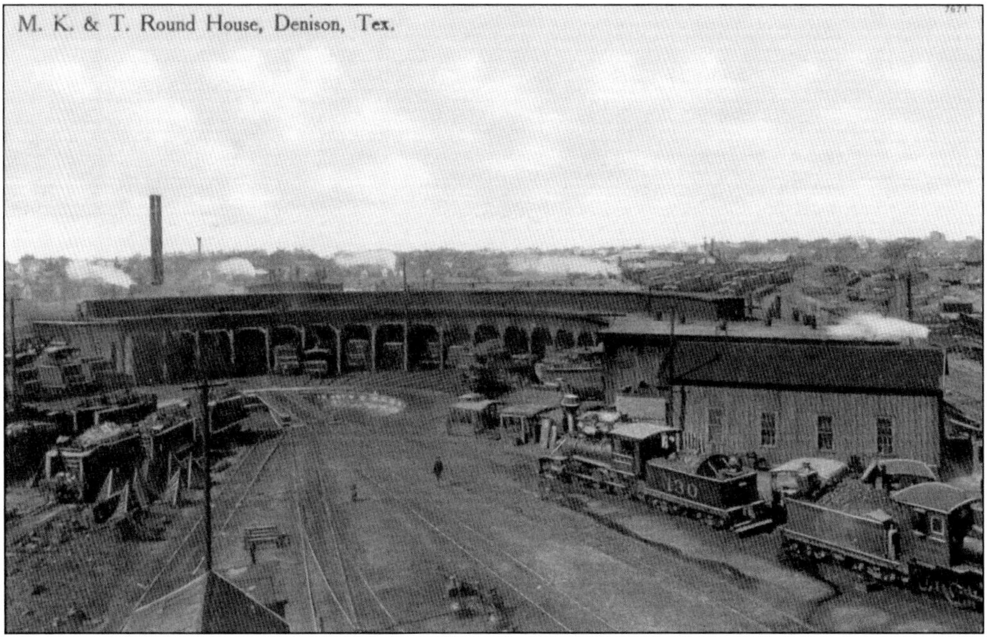

Railroad shops were located near a roundhouse because its turntable allowed steam locomotives to be turned around for repair or storage. The Katy's Denison roundhouse can be seen here in the late 1800s. A "teapot" locomotive is sitting out front. A portion of the shops can be seen to the rear and right of the structure. This roundhouse ceased to be used after the Ray Yards were built. (DHH.)

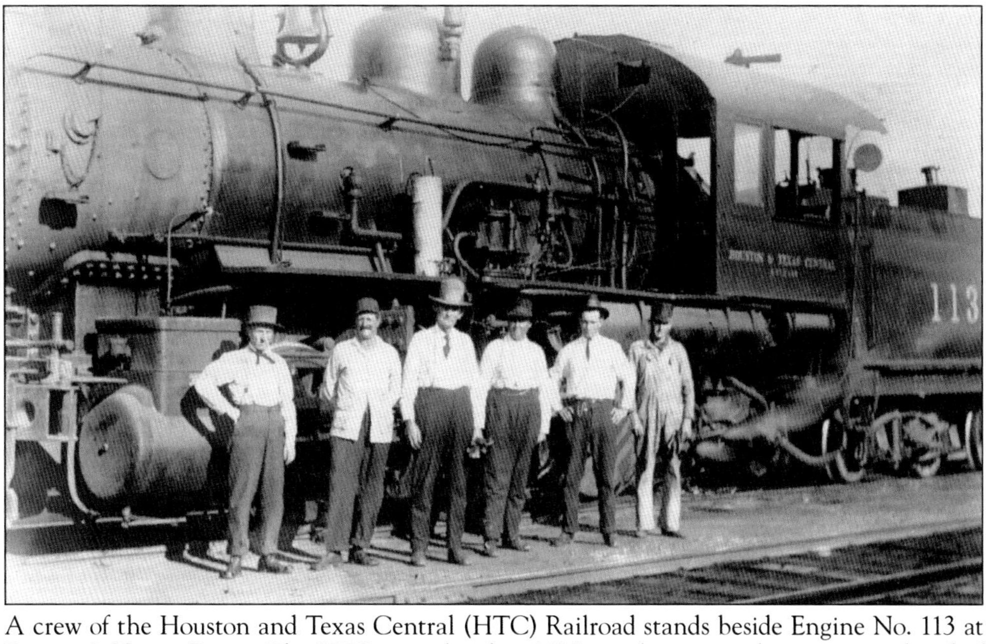

A crew of the Houston and Texas Central (HTC) Railroad stands beside Engine No. 113 at Denison's Union Depot. The HTC, completed in 1876, was known as the pioneer railroad of Texas. It traveled from the Gulf through Sherman and Denison to Hearne. In Denison, its office was in the Union station building. As of 2010, controlling interest in HTC was in the hands of the Southern Pacific Railroad. (DHH.)

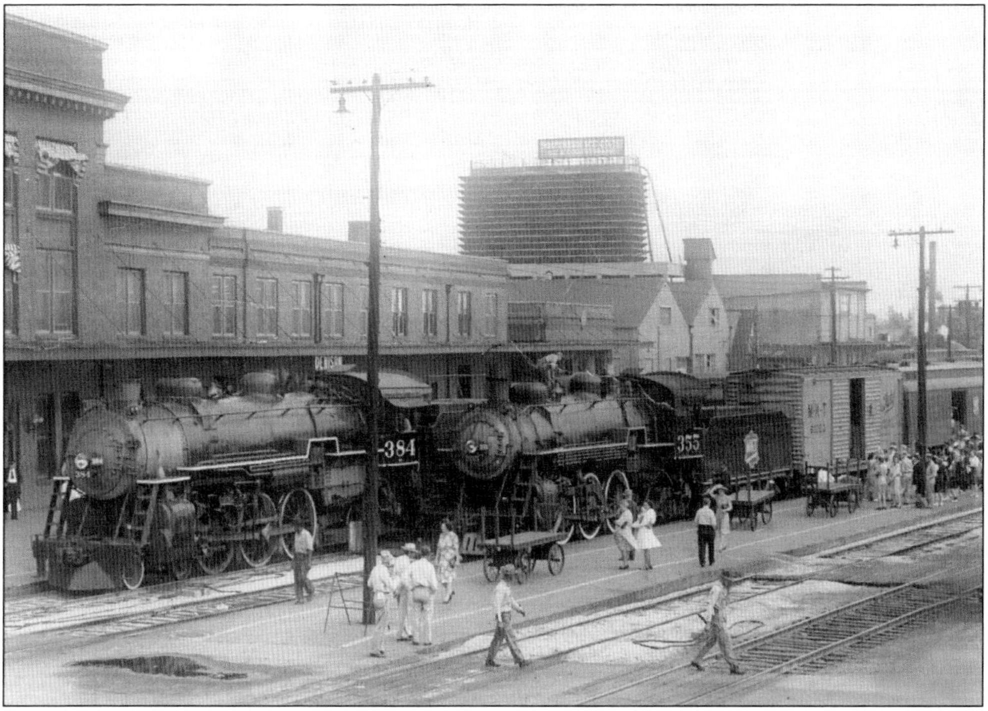

Two MKT trains piloted by familiar steam engines make stops at the depot in downtown Denison in 1965. Passengers await the appointed time for their train to depart. Katy trains ceased to exist on August 12, 1988, when the railroad merged with the much larger Union Pacific Railroad. The water tower of the Southern Ice Company can be seen in the background. (HD.)

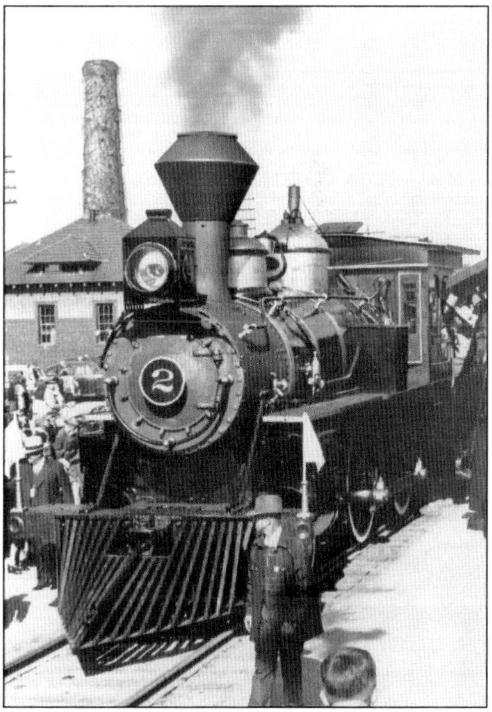

This steam engine is the kind used by the MKT Railroad in Denison's early days. It also resembles those on which David Eisenhower, father of US president Dwight David Eisenhower, worked as an engine wiper in the Katy car shops during the three years the family lived in Denison. This picture formed part of an official exhibit during the Katy Railroad centennial in 1970. (Claud Easterly, in HD.)

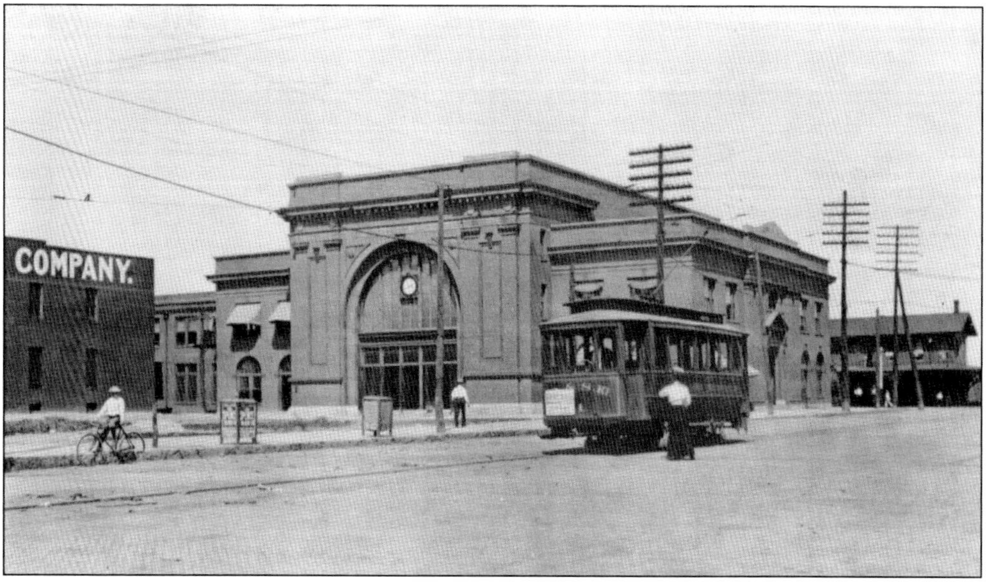

In 1901, the Denison and Sherman Railway (DSR), the first electric interurban railway in Texas, began taking passengers on the 10.5-mile route between the two cities. A precursor to the Texas Traction and Texas Electric Railway companies, the DSR operated for only one year. Its terminal was near the Katy Depot, and its turnaround was on the south side of the Katy Depot, seen here. (DHH.)

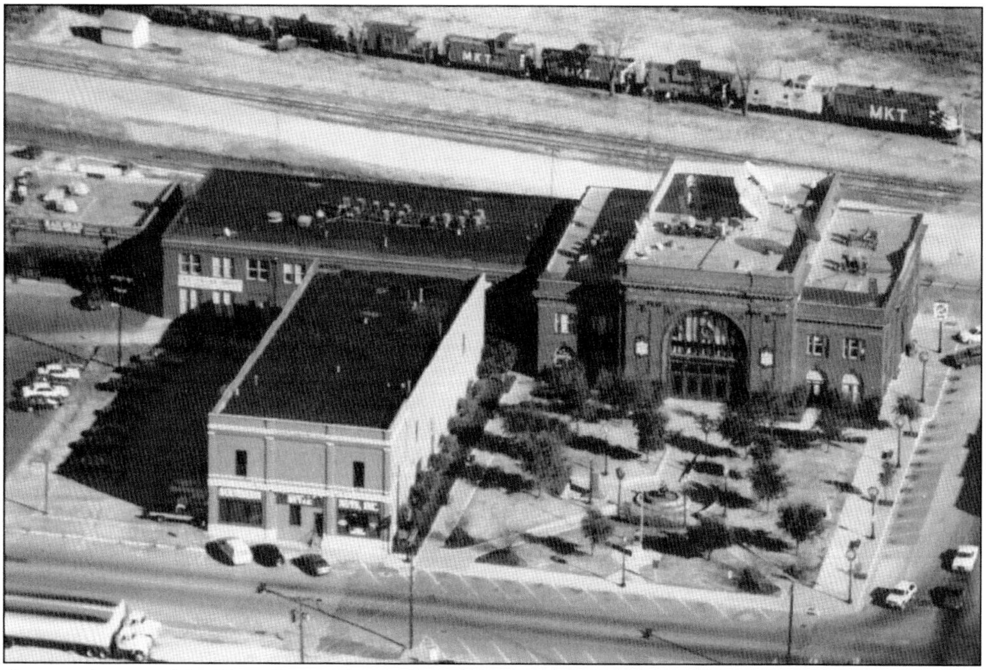

An aerial view of the Katy Depot shows the rolling stock of the Red River Railroad Museum today. The park in front of the depot was reestablished after C.J. McManus purchased the property in 1983. Southern Style Nuts occupied the original Denison Grocer Company building on Houston Avenue, and in this photograph, the Railhead Restaurant stands at the north end of the depot. (Red River Railroad Museum, Denison, Texas.)

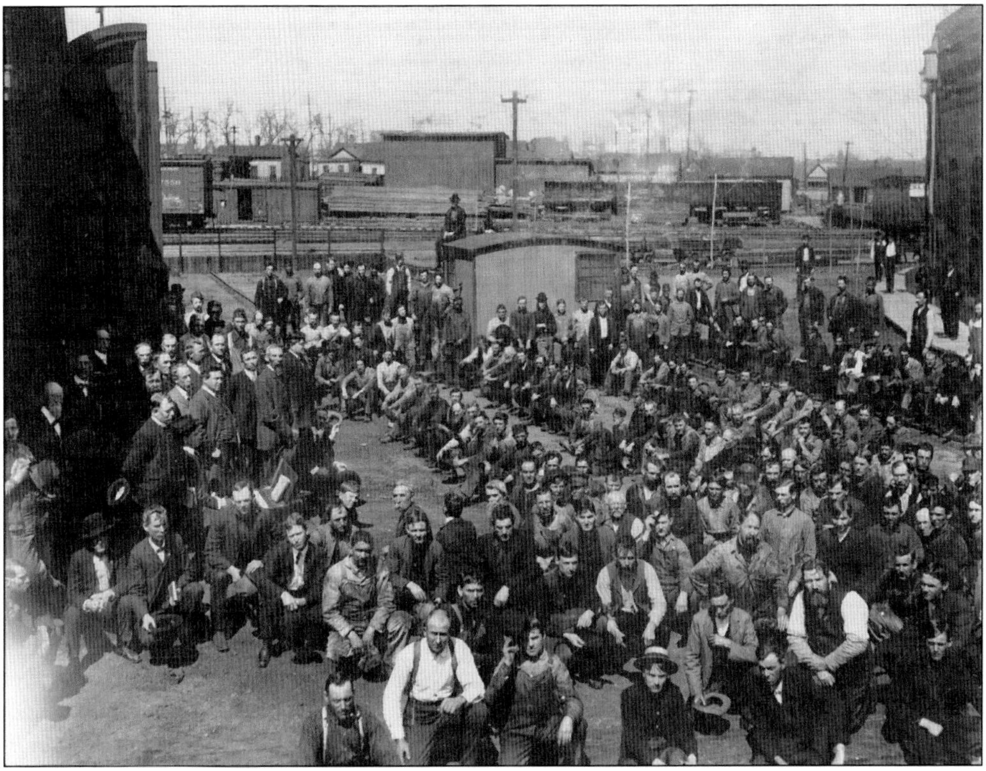

Men who repaired the engines and cars in the MKT shops on South Mirick Avenue and underneath the Austin Avenue viaduct got together with office employees and Katy dignitaries for a photograph in the early 1900s. The photographer who made this picture, Hendricks, also photographed the Katy Car Shops after a 1909 fire; that photograph is in the collection of Grayson County Frontier Village. (HD.)

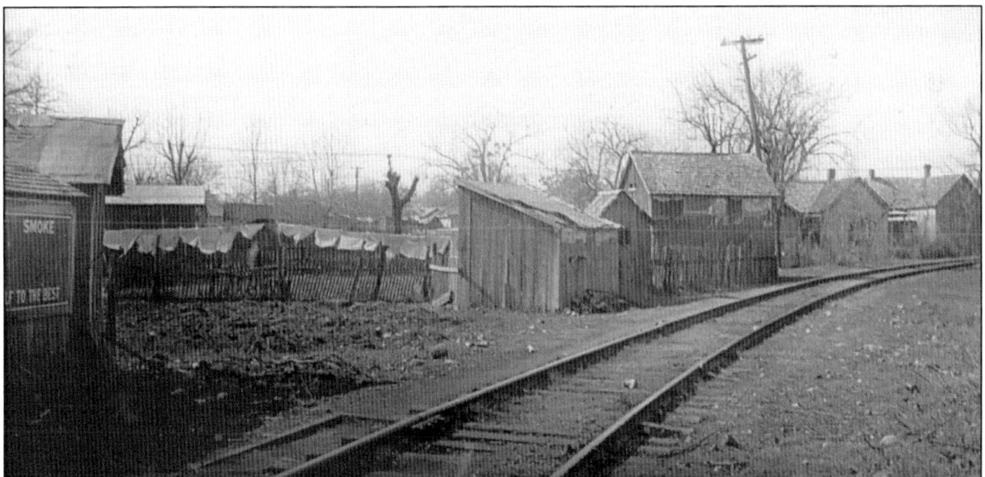

Called "A Beautiful Spot," this photograph is near a railroad track leading into Denison. A frame house on the left of the picture has an outdoor privy, and other sheds hold up a clothesline on which underwear, and possibly diapers or dish towels, are hanging. The picture is reminiscent of the 1920s. A portion of a cigarette sign is plastered on a wall on the left. (DHH.)

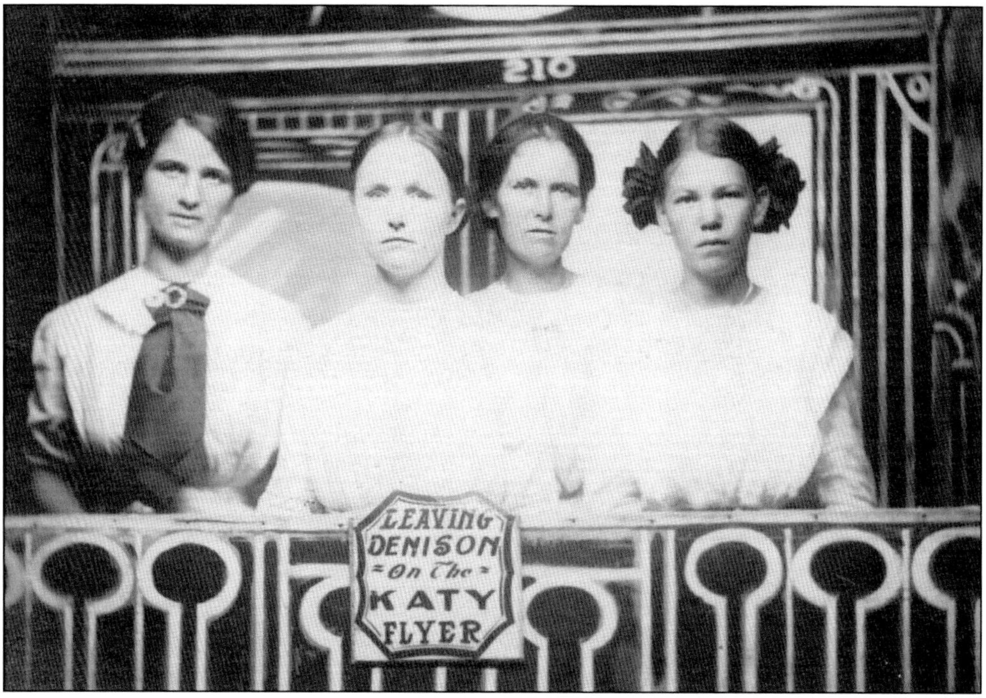

Four unsmiling young women pose for a picture taken on a photographer's prop, Caboose No. 210. A sign indicates that the train is "Leaving Denison on the Katy Flyer." Photographers all along the Katy routes (and other railroads as well) used similar backdrops to create real-photo postcards. This enabled travelers to send amusing portraits back home to family and friends. This postcard belonged to Julie Mathis. (DHH.)

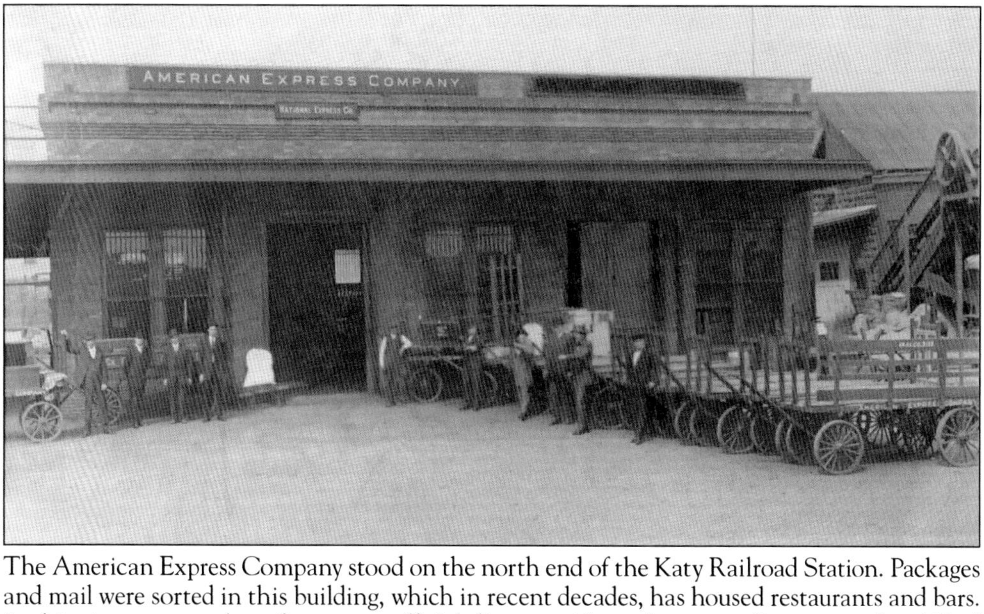

The American Express Company stood on the north end of the Katy Railroad Station. Packages and mail were sorted in this building, which in recent decades, has housed restaurants and bars. In this picture, a number of company officials line up with mail wagons. One pictured is Alfred Thomas, who married Helen Murray Thomas, daughter of Bredette C. Murray, publisher of Denison newspapers. (BCT.)

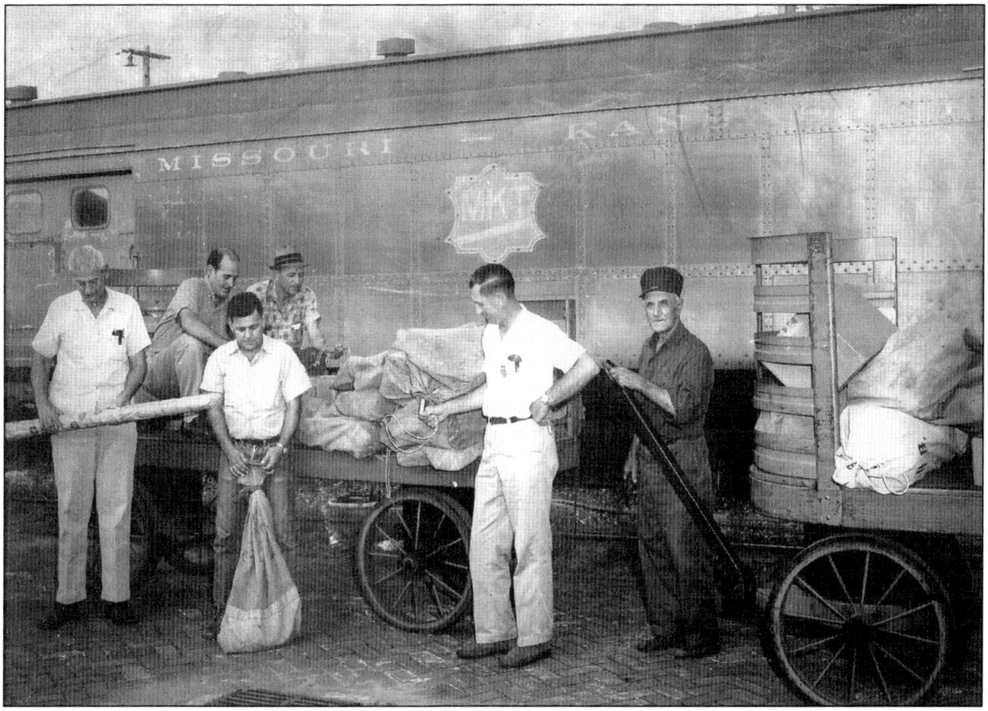

Railway postal clerks assemble the mail for a southbound MKT train headed to San Antonio at the close of passenger service in 1965. The workers include, from left to right, (front) Hillary Womack, Connie Brown (with mailbag in hand), Roland Krueger, and Homer Hayes; (back) T.E. Stokes and John Zepeda. The Railway Mail office was on the north end of MKT depot. (HD.)

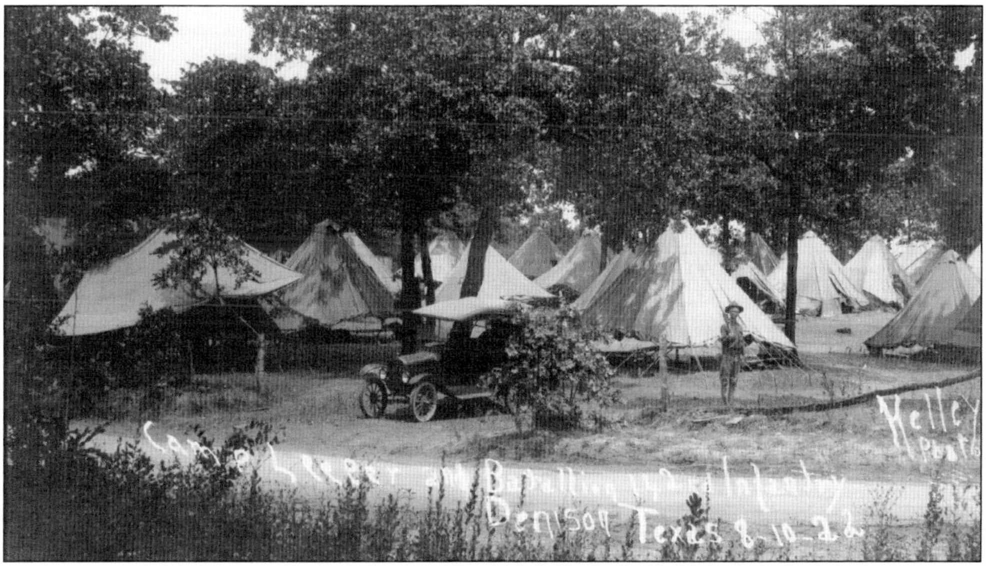

Violence flared in 1922 when Gov. Pat Neff sent the Texas National Guard to Denison to keep order during a three-month strike by more than 1,400 Katy Railroad workers. Third Battalion, 142nd Infantry set up Camp Leeper in Forest Park on August 10, 1922. The guard made almost 300 civilian arrests during the occupation. Troops were sent home by the governor on October 21, 1922. (DHH.)

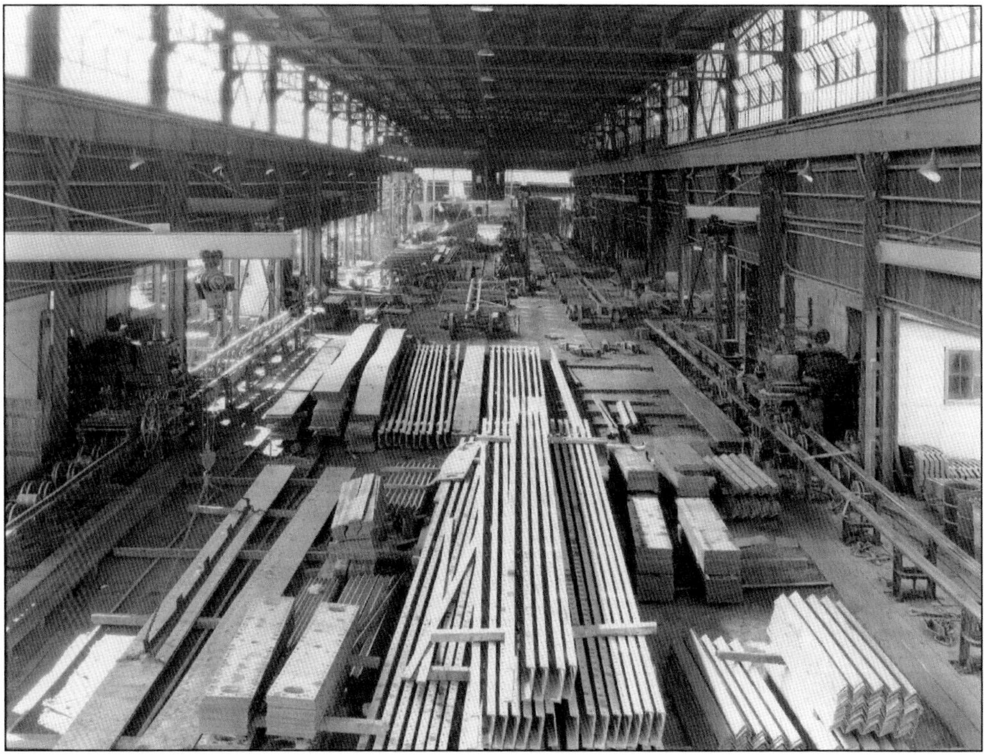

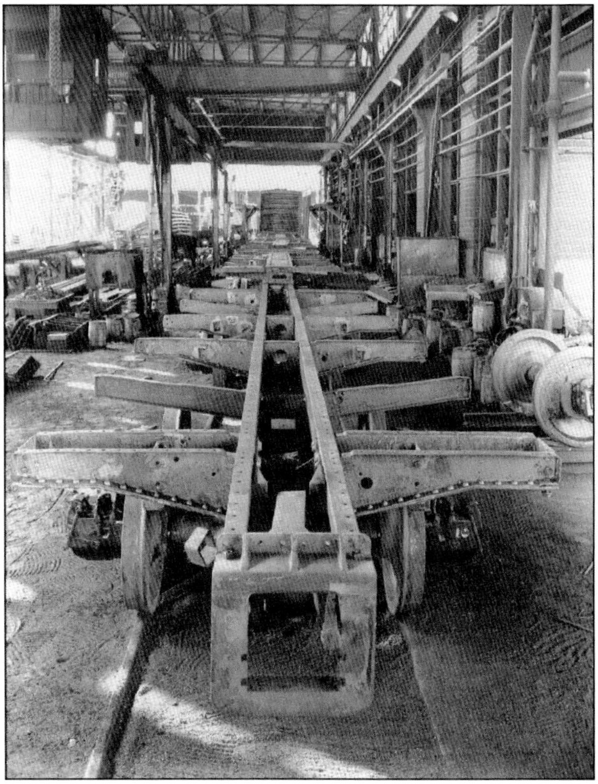

These two photographs, made by Walter P. Lebrecht in the late 1920s or early 1930s, are interior views of the Katy Car Shops on South Mirick Avenue in Denison. Railroad cars and engines were taken here for repairs. Materials were stockpiled so that almost any type of repair could be made. Windows high on each sidewall provided light and ventilation in the days before air-conditioning made it easier to endure working in the hot Texas summers. At the ends of the long buildings were sets of railroad tracks upon which the cars could be rolled so that the railroad workers could perform their duties. Lebrecht, grandson of a German rabbi and son of a Denison mayor, was a commercial photographer in Denison during the 1920s and 1930s. Then he became city tax assessor and collector. (Above, MAB; left, DHH.)

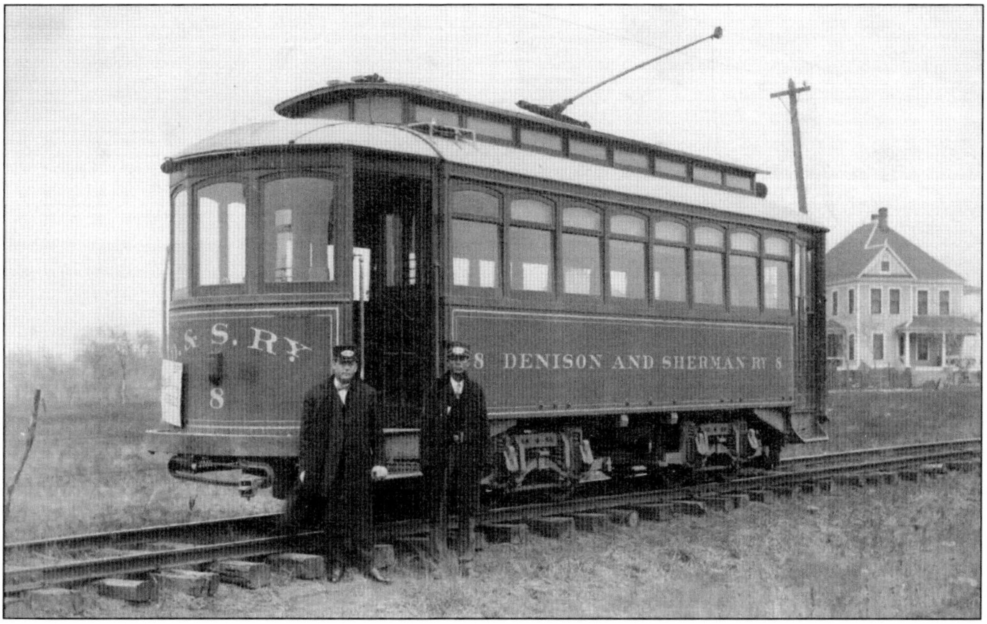

Electric railways, or trolleys, provided convenient and quick travel between many Texas cities for more than 40 years. The first interurban, the Denison and Sherman Railway, began running over its 10.5-mile route in 1901. The trip took 30 minutes and cost 25¢. The company built Woodlake Park between the two towns to promote travel, recreation, and amusement, with special excursions. Coaches were powered by overhead cables. (DHH.)

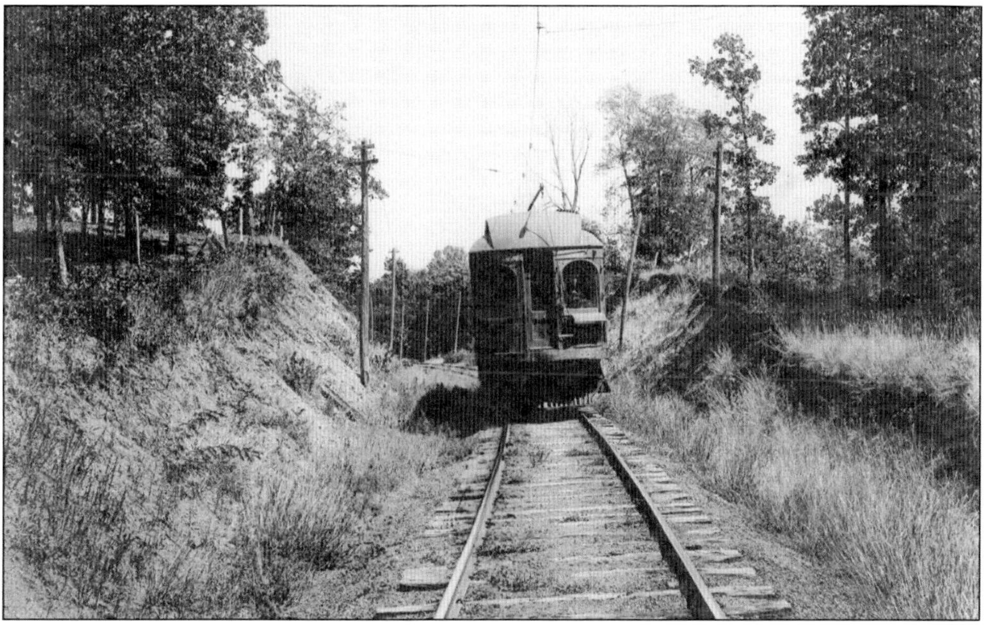

A Dallas-bound Texas Electric Railway interurban leaves Denison on September 2, 1909, headed to Dallas via Woodlake and Sherman. The interurban line to Dallas and later to Waco opened that year. Electricity was generated in power stations along the line. Each car had from two to four motors of 30 to 75 horsepower. By 1920, near four million passengers had been carried, yet runs halted on December 31, 1948. (DHH.)

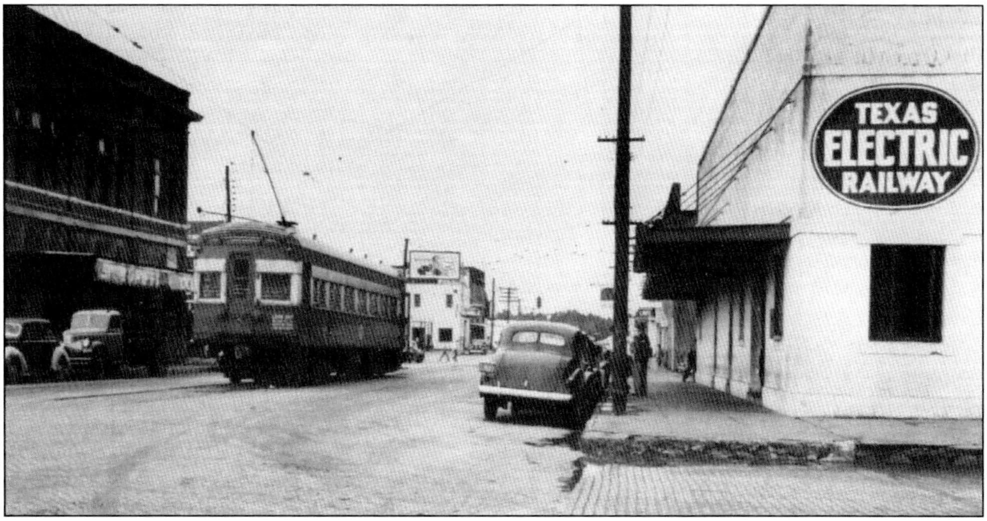

The Texas Electric Railway (interurban) office in Denison was located at the southwest corner of West Woodard Street and Houston Avenue. The interurban would leave the station across the avenue from the Katy Depot, head south to Main Street and turn right, then proceed west up the middle of Main Street on its way to Sherman and beyond. A turnaround was located on Main Street, just south of the depot. (DHH.)

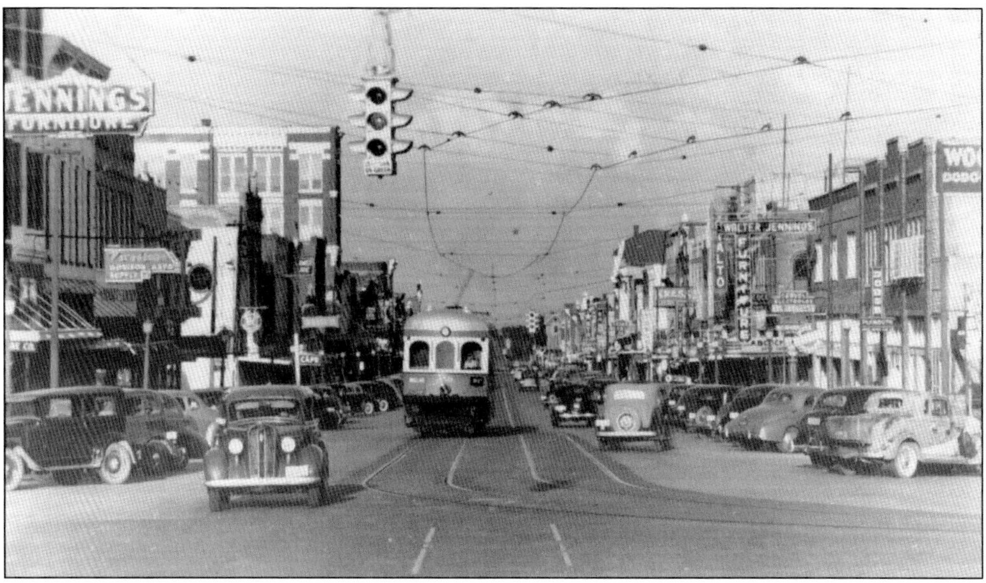

Traffic speeded up on Denison's Main Street with the construction of the Denison Dam. Hordes came to work, and the Great Depression wound down. This view looks east from the 500 block of Main Street on October 22, 1940. Traffic lights keep automobiles in line near the Woods Dodge-Plymouth dealership and Babcock Auto Supply. Two Jennings Furniture stores face each other across the street. (MAB.)

Three

The Finer Things in Life

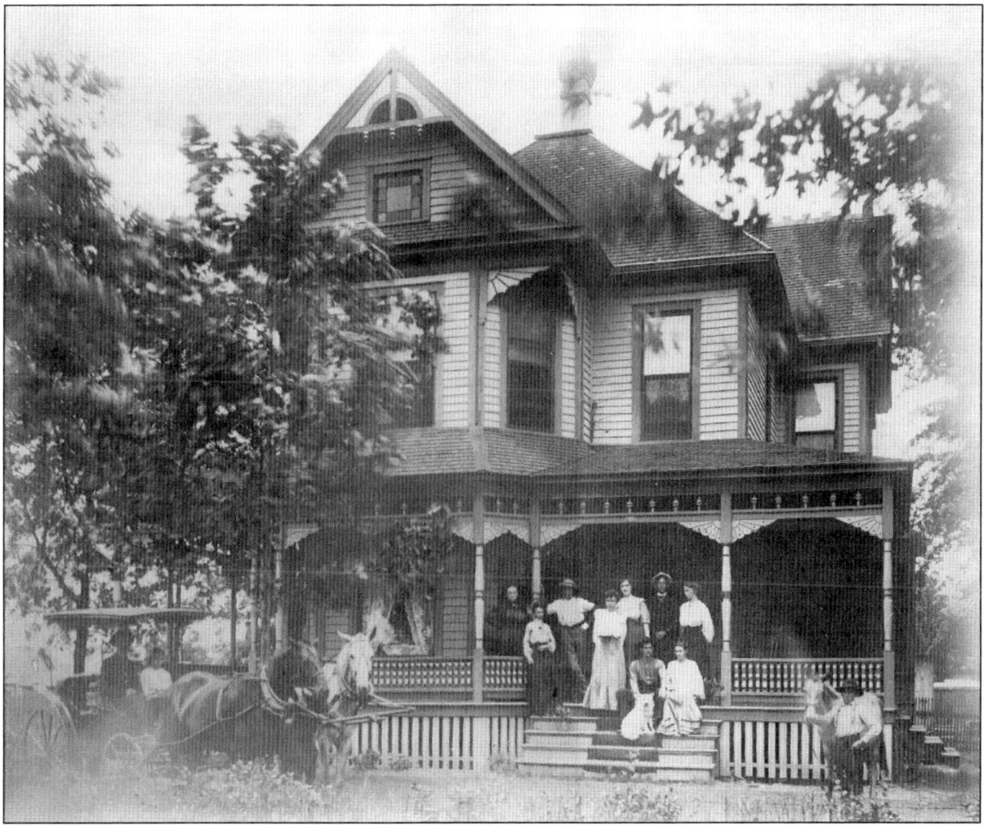

It could have been a movie: the big Victorian house full of adults and children at the corner of South Austin Avenue and Texas Street. William R. Young, a locomotive engineer, brought wife Mary south from Illinois around 1885. Son William W. became a Katy fireman and machinist, daughter Annie taught at Peabody Elementary School, and son Frederick kept books at the State National Bank and captained the Denison Rifles. (HD.)

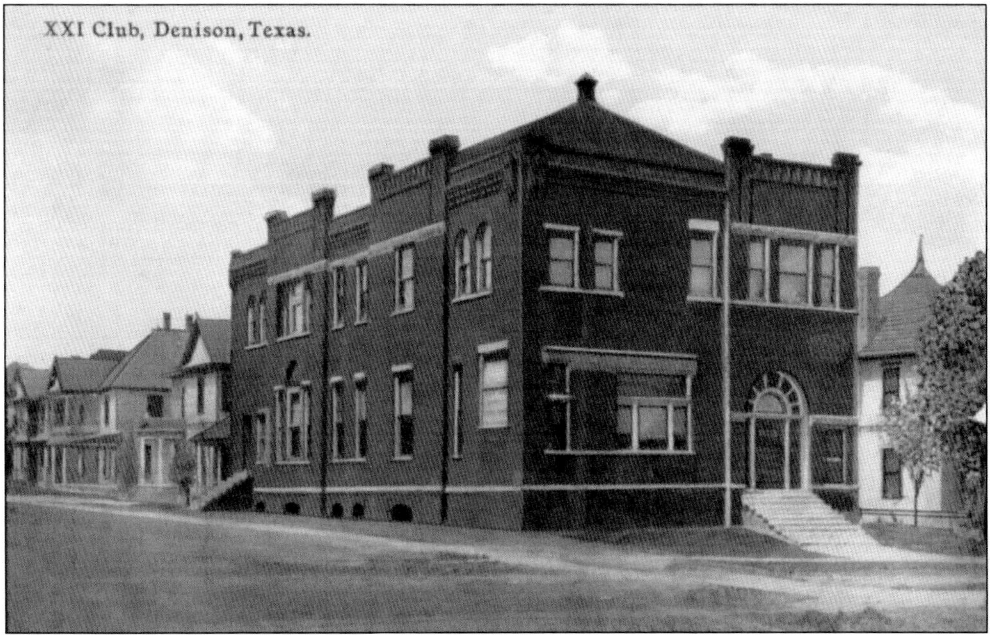

The first headquarters for a woman's club in Texas was erected in 1896 at 901 West Gandy Street. Denison's XXI Club had facilities for music, drama, and art, as well as a large auditorium and the town's first public library. Bachelor J.T. Munson donated land and $4,000, and Andrew Carnegie contributed $1,700 toward construction. In 1925, the city council ordered the building demolished after engineers identified unsafe "subsoil conditions." (MAB.)

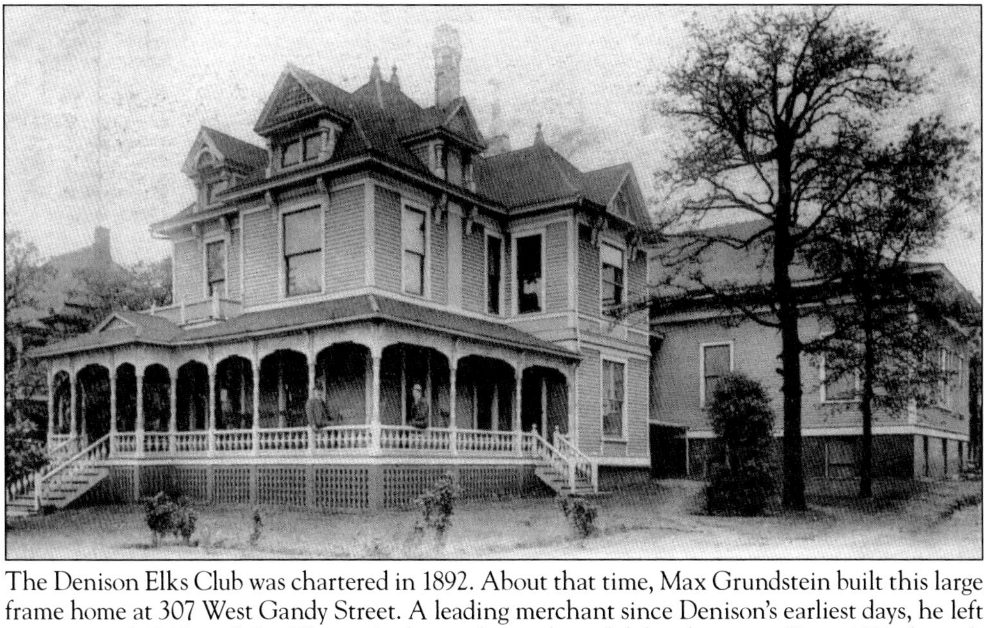

The Denison Elks Club was chartered in 1892. About that time, Max Grundstein built this large frame home at 307 West Gandy Street. A leading merchant since Denison's earliest days, he left town around 1900, and the Elks made the residence their club headquarters. From 1910 through the 1920s, they organized elaborate entertainment starring local talent. The house burned in 1916, and the current brick structure replaced it. (MAB.)

Denison was one of the first planned communities in Texas, and one of the first to employ zoning. The Town Company laid out streets and lots, specifying what uses could be made of them. By 1883, many blocks were covered with neat homes and yards, as seen in this stereoview. Less glamorous aspects of daily life—cooking, washing, animals—were relegated to backyards. (Hardesty and Dean, in MAB.)

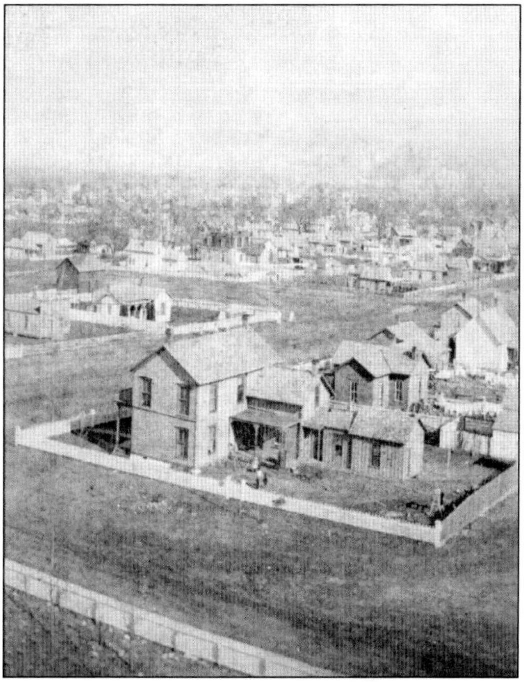

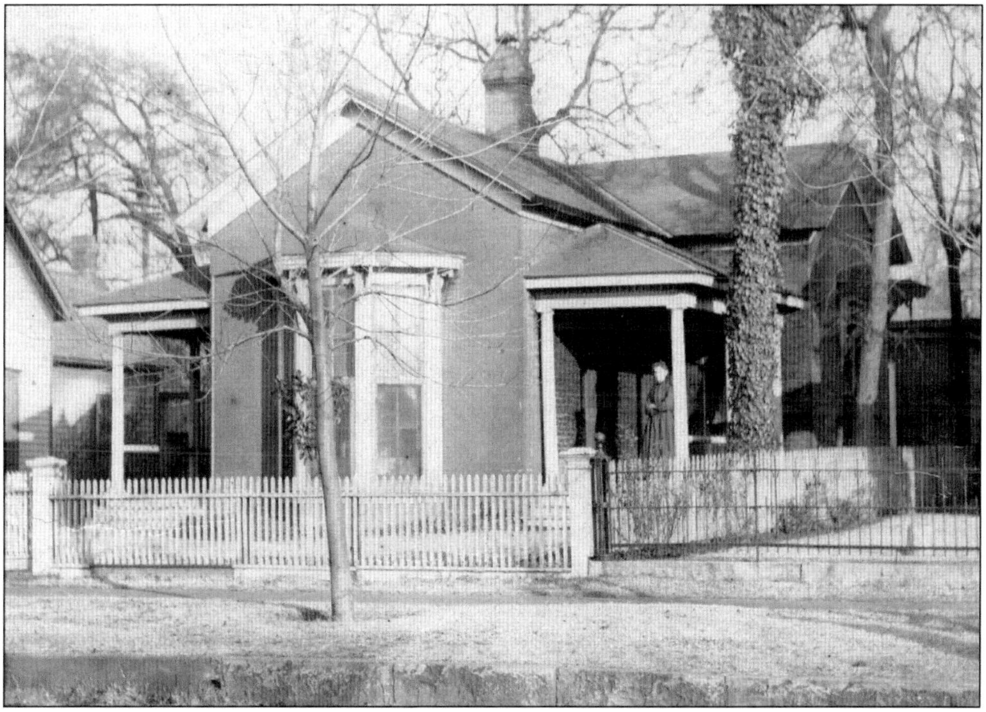

Joseph Koehler was the original contractor charged with building Denison's first high school, the Educational Institute. In 1873 and 1874, he built the Italianate brick residence seen here around 1900 with its charming bay window and twin porches at 321 West Gandy Street. He brought his bride, Lizzie Hopkins, here after their marriage on December 23, 1874. Four months later, burdened with debts, Koehler sold the property. (MAB.)

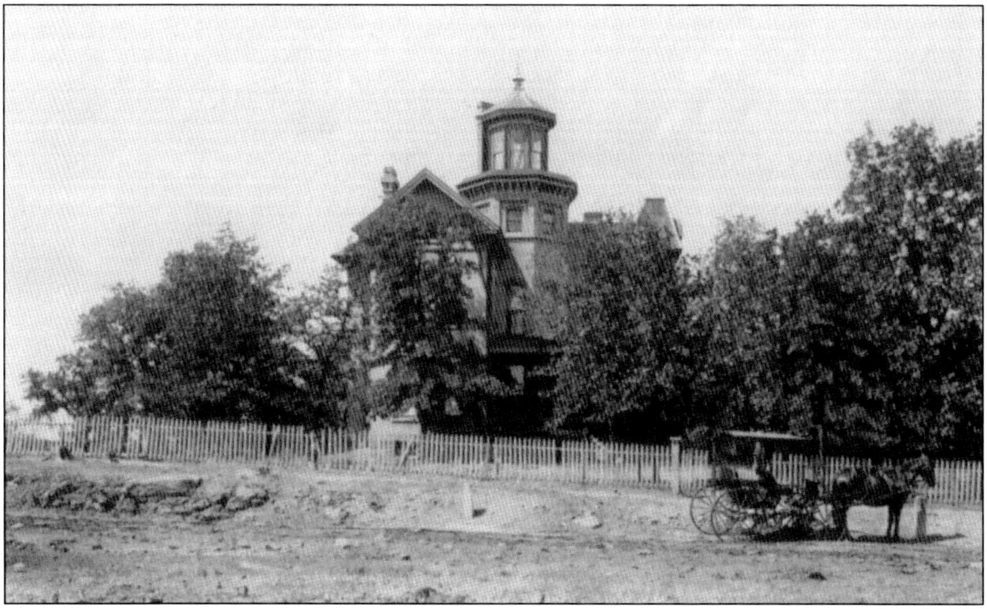

Before 1885, Dr. Alexander W. "Sandy" Acheson (1842–1934) and his wife, Sarah "Sadie" Cooke Acheson (1844–1899), built this elegant Italianate home on an elevated block at 1419 West Woodard Street. Sarah Acheson was a leader in Texas temperance and women's suffrage movements. Her husband, a Civil War Union veteran, was an influential doctor and politician. In this photograph, his horse and buggy stand ready for emergency house calls. (AWGC.)

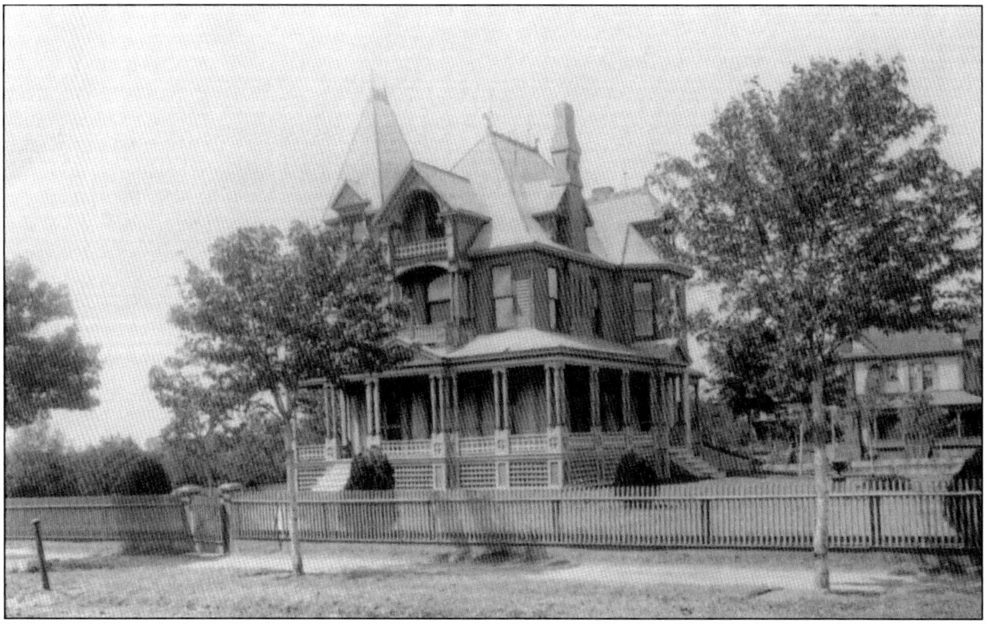

Andrew Fox Platter (1850–1932) arrived in Denison at its founding from Chillicothe, Missouri, and helped found Waples-Platter Grocer Company. He married Frances "Fannie" Waples and built this home at 1201 West Sears Street between 1891 and 1895. The Platter, Waples, and Lingo families intermarried, living in close proximity. The Platters' only child, Berenice, married Adm. Adolphus Andrews, commander of the US Navy's Third Naval District during World War II. (AWGC.)

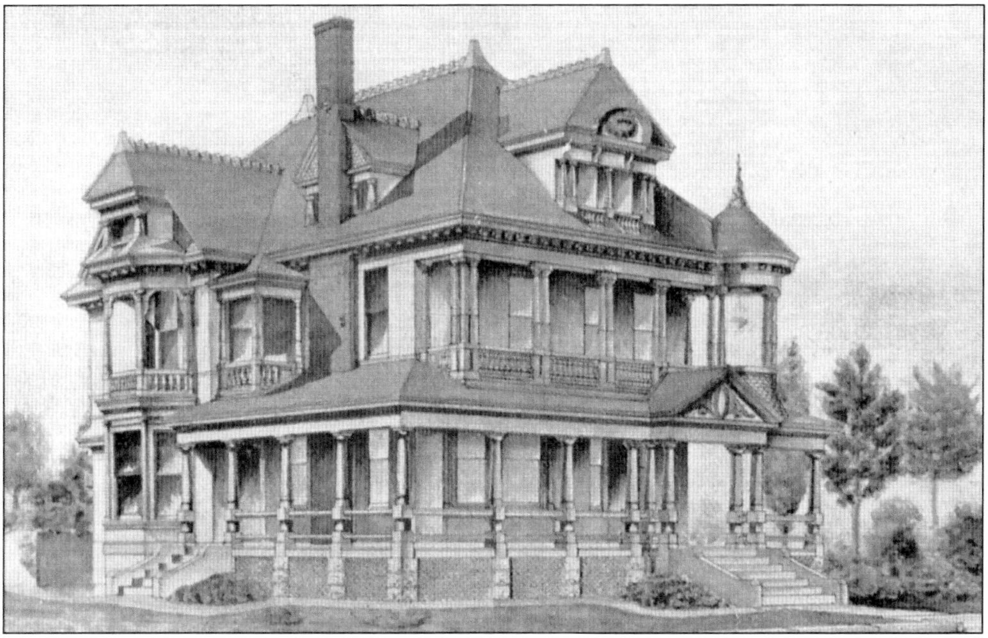

John B. McDougall opened a saloon upon his arrival in Denison in 1872. After his bartender died, McDougall married his Irish-born widow, Margaret Moulton, and helped raise her three children. The couple operated a large hotel at the train station; John also founded an opera house, an electric company, banks, an insurance company, and a laundry. The McDougalls built this imposing residence at 412 West Morton Street in 1897. (IndDen.)

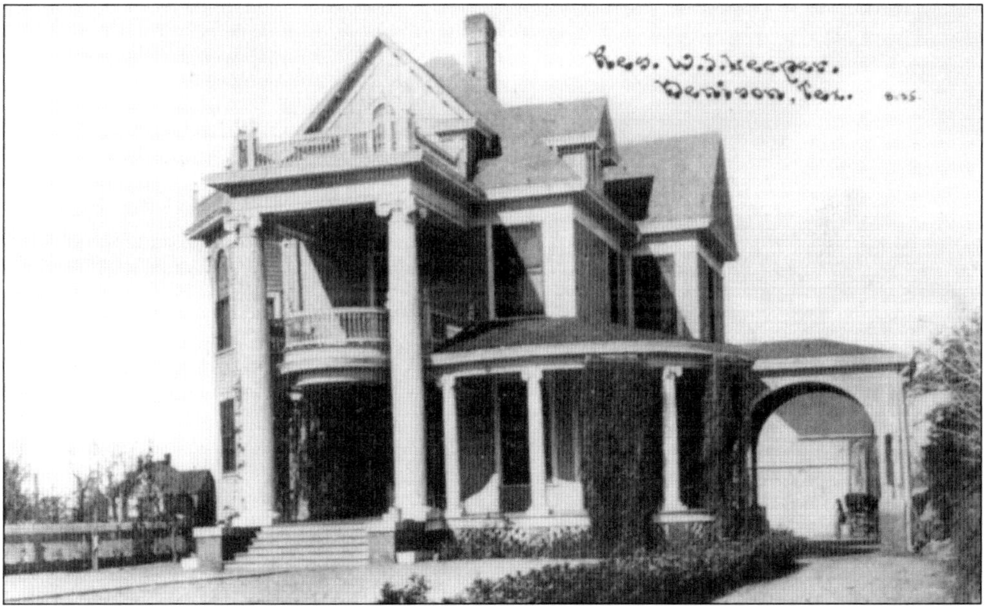

With its two-story columned portico and porte cochere entry, this house at 1123 West Sears Street combined neoclassical revival and Victorian architectural styles. It was constructed in 1902 for Walton James Leeper (1863–1939) and his wife, Clara. He was vice president of Lingo-Leeper Lumber Company, then one of Denison's leading businesses. Leeper descendants owned the house until 1952. Dr. Donald H. and Helen Brandt subsequently raised their children there. (MAB.)

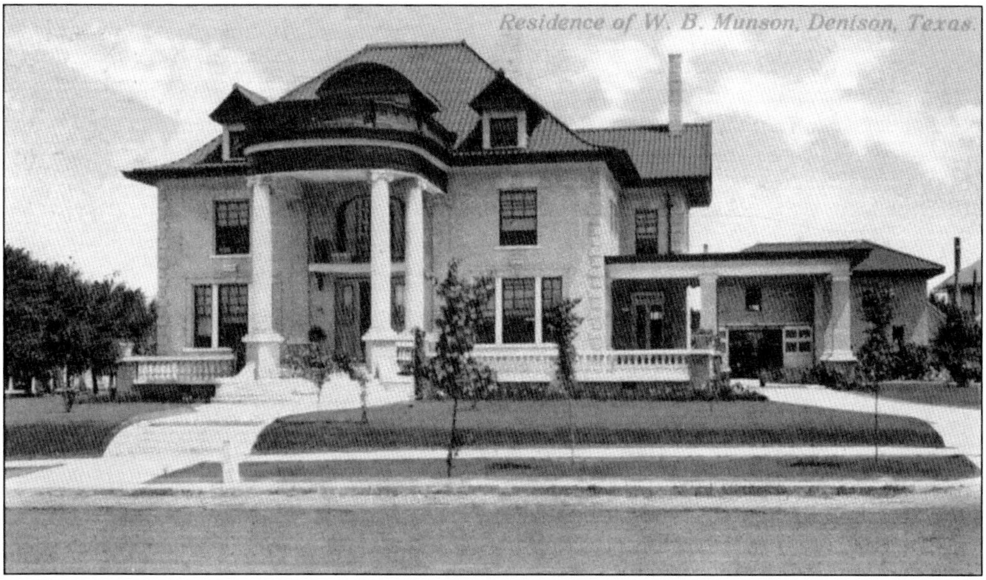

William Benjamin Munson (1846–1930) was one of three brothers who came from Illinois to Grayson County before Denison was founded and helped to define the town's character. An investor and real estate developer, Munson and wife Mary Ella built this striking neoclassical revival–style residence in 1912, at 1127 West Morton Street. In time, magnolia trees overshadowed the home still occupied by Munson descendants in 2010. (MAB.)

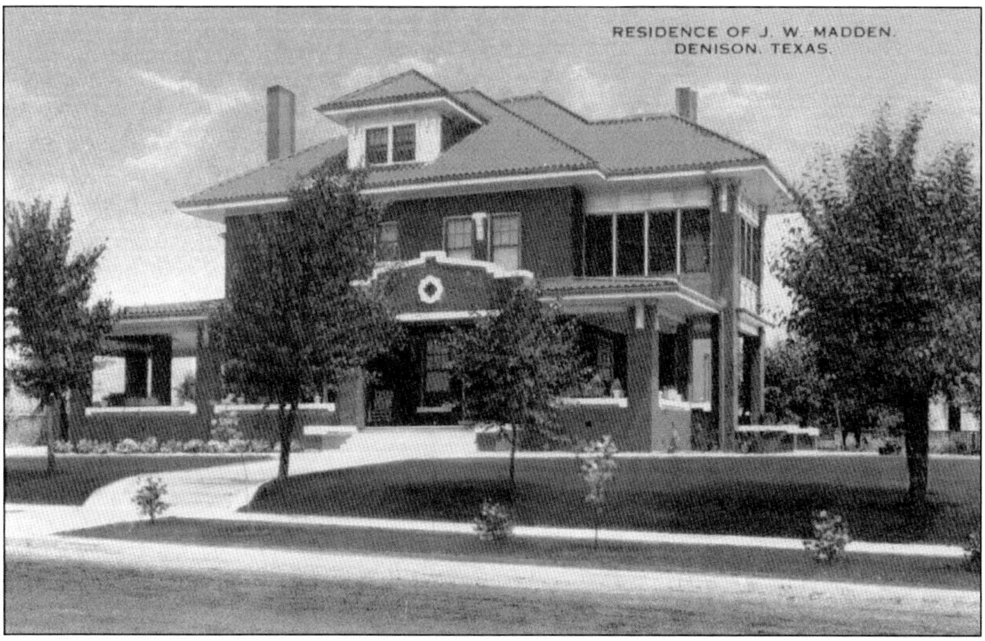

Architect John Tulloch designed this Spanish Colonial Revival and prairie-style home for John William and Lilla (Graham) Madden. He came from Tennessee to Denton as a boy and entered the dry goods business with his wife's brothers, expanding to Denison around 1898. By 1912, when this impressive residence was built at 1103 West Morton Street, he owned Madden's Department Store and headed the North Texas Loan and Trust Company. (MAB.)

Built around 1896 by Dr. Julian C. Feild (1841–1906), this Queen Anne residence stands at 1004 West Bond Street. After serving as Denison's first official city physician, Feild practiced less and became a successful entrepreneur. Around 1918, Nicholas Marsico bought the house as an anniversary gift for his wife. The Marsico family, owners of the Denison Mattress Company, lived there until 1989. Ken Daniel recently renovated the property. (IndDen.)

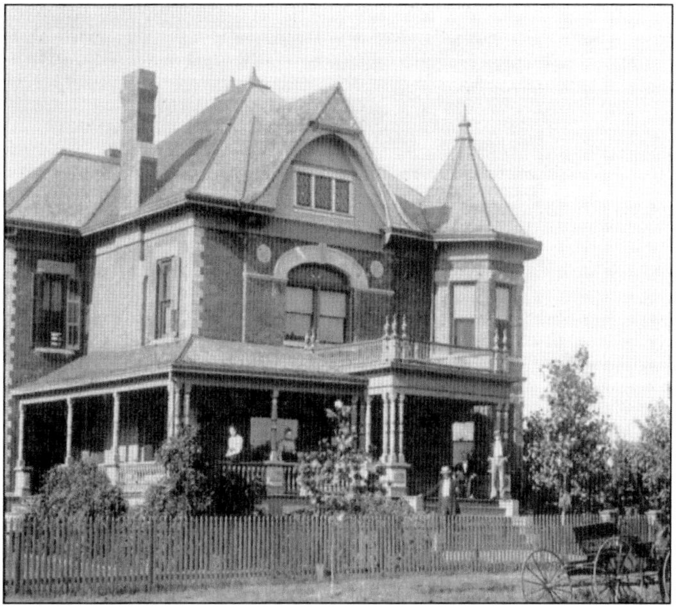

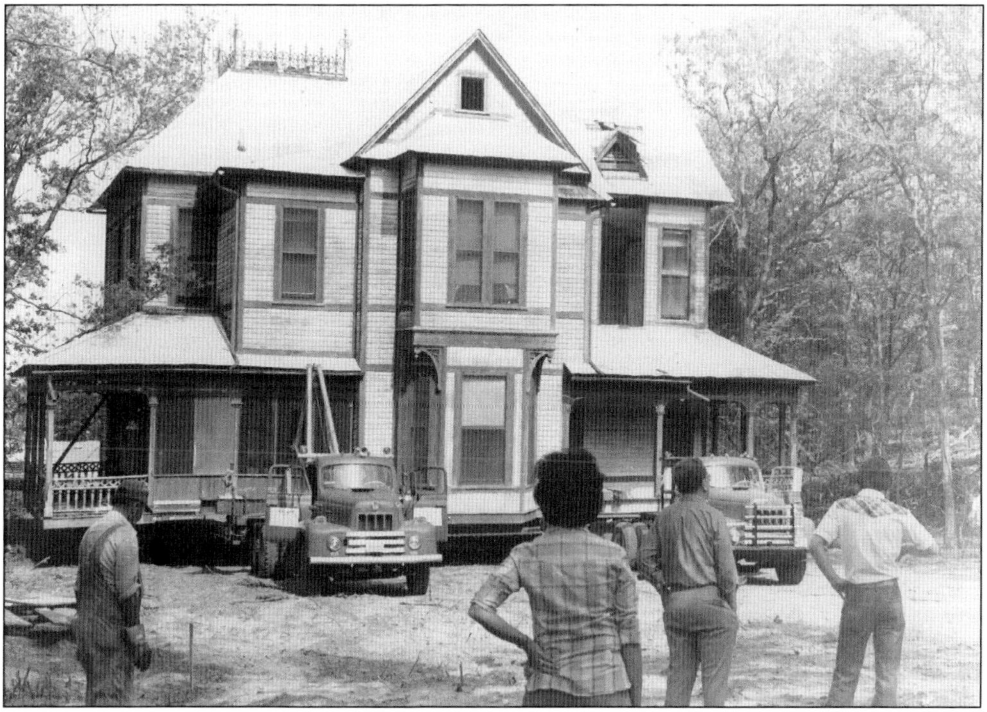

John Joseph Fairbanks (1840–1923) previously had lived in New Jersey, Indiana, and Kansas when he arrived in Denison before 1880. He honed his skills as a farmer and bookkeeper and then succeeded in real estate. By the mid-1880s, this imposing residence stood on South Austin Avenue, where Fairbanks reportedly hosted gambling activities. In 1979, the home was dramatically moved to make way for an automobile dealership. In 2010, it was a bed-and-breakfast inn. (DHH.)

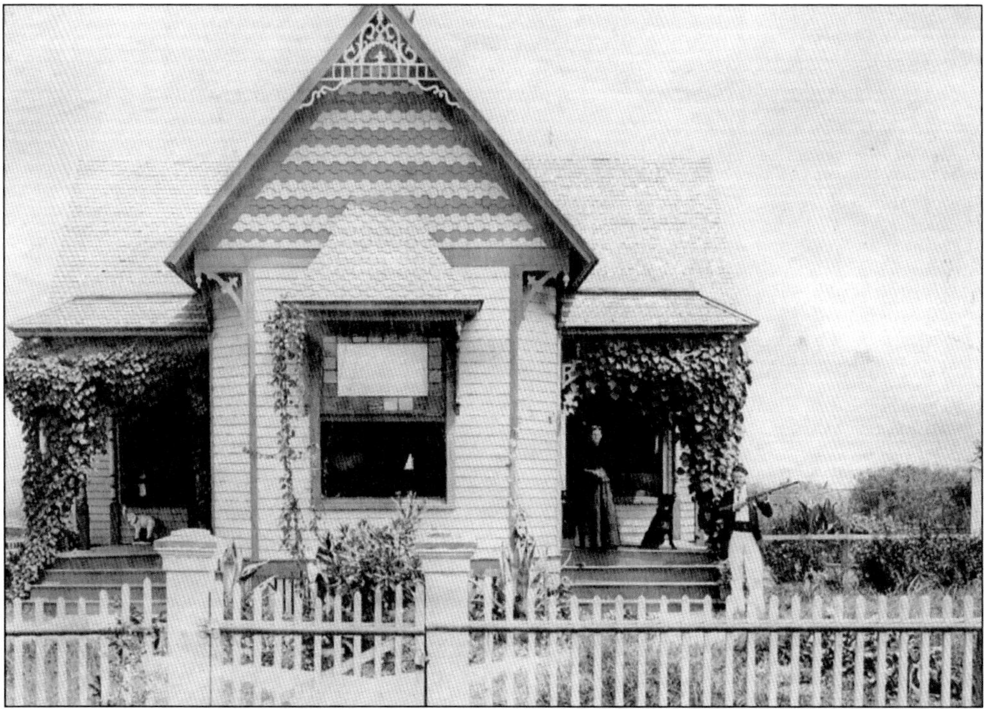

Mortimer M. Scholl (1864–1952) left Missouri for Denison and, with brother Charles, founded the *Denison Dispatch* on July 4, 1888. Later, he was a *Denison Herald* columnist and a local justice of the peace. Popularly known as the "Snake Editor," Mort had a provocative pen, flowing white sideburns, and a penchant for dueling. He wore a rose in his lapel, carried a cane, and was noted for his hats—stovepipe, derby, or Panama. With wife Euphrates, he owned this Victorian cottage at 1230 West Walker Street, seen above around 1900. Both elegant and charming, Euphrates matched her husband for adventurous spirit. Below, the couple is about to embark on a ride in one of those newfangled horseless carriages. Note the well-polished lanterns on either side of the car. (Both, Don Mace, in DHH.)

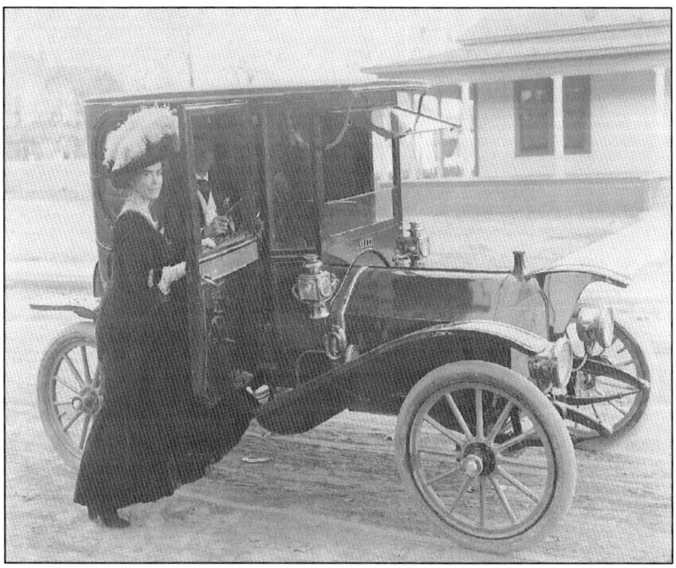

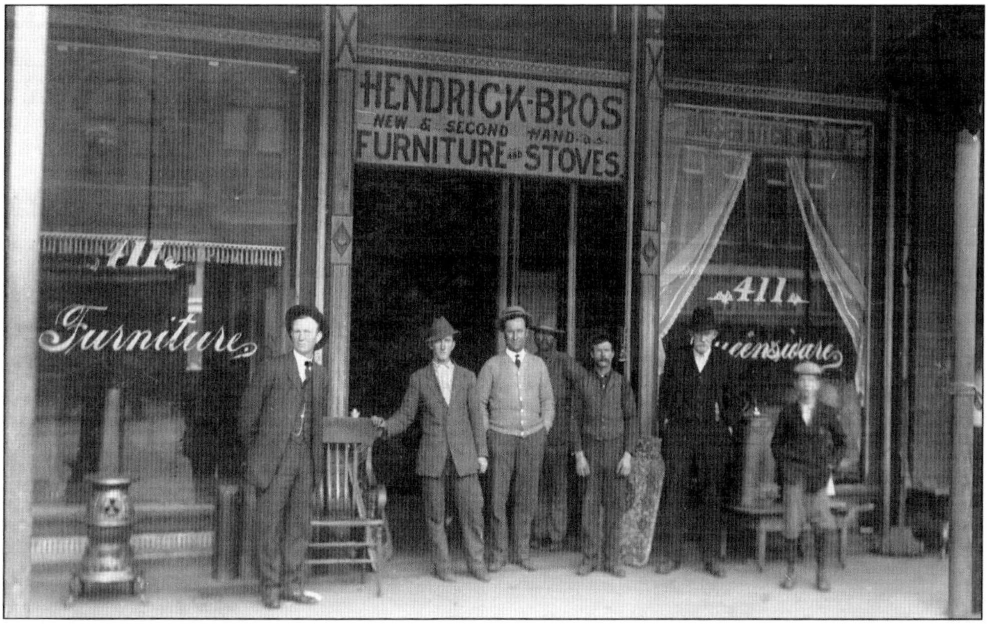

As Denison blossomed, its newly prosperous residents enjoyed furnishing their homes in the latest styles. Laborsaving devices, telephones, and other inventions became must-haves for the elite. Eager merchants catered to these desires with advertising and advice. O.L. Bailey, Hendrick Brothers, Charles H. Jones, and Scott and Jennings were among Denison's early purveyors of furniture, carpets, stoves, sewing machines, china, cookware, and related items. The Hendrick clan began migrating westward from Virginia after the Civil War, first to Tennessee and then, by 1880, to Fannin County, Texas. Several were experienced carpenters, dry goods salesmen, and preachers. After 1902, they came together to open Hendrick Brothers (exterior above and interior below), succeeding Bailey at 411 West Main Street. By 1907, James W. Hendrick was sole owner, taking Jones's posh spot at 517–519 Main Street. By 1917, Hendricks had sold out and retired. (Both, MAB.)

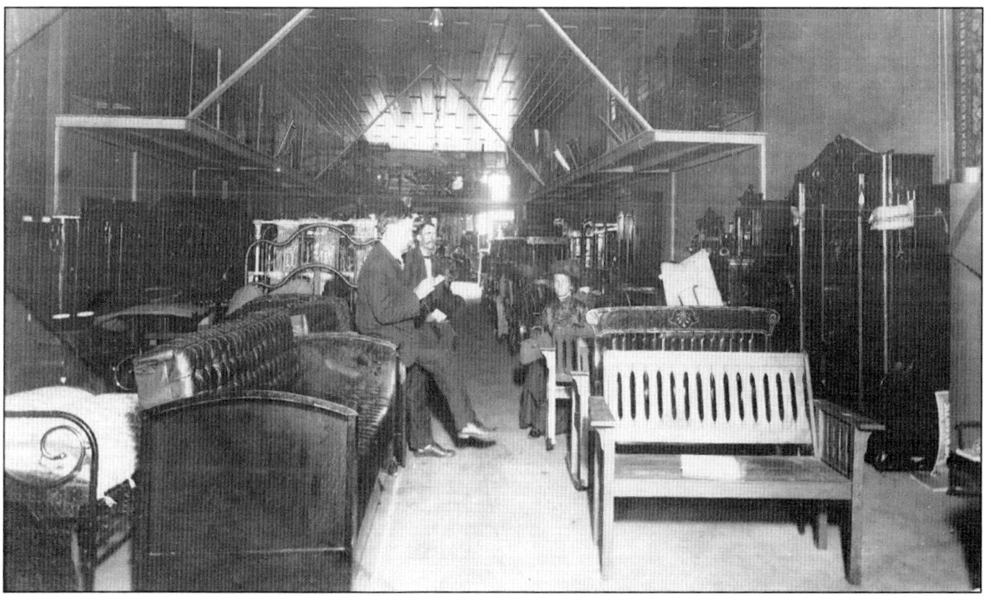

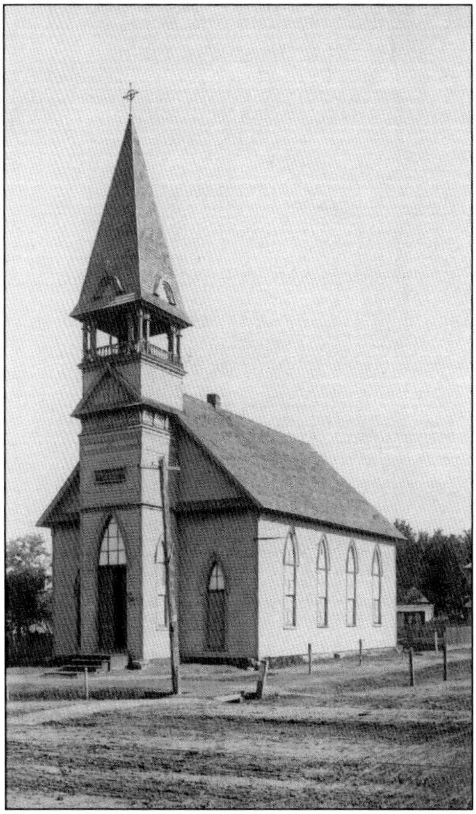

In 1873, the North Texas Conference of the Methodist Episcopal Church South established a mission in the raucous new frontier town of Denison. Two years later, the growing congregation erected a frame church at 430 West Skiddy (now Chestnut) Street, in the heart of the red-light district. That one-room structure with bell tower (seen at left in about 1894) was formally chartered as a church in the Methodist Episcopal Conference in 1881. It served the congregation until a wealthy church member, Edward B. Waples (1814–1898), spearheaded efforts to construct a new edifice at 830 West Main Street. Completed in 1899, the church was heralded as the finest in North Texas. European artisans crafted the remarkable stained-glass windows. Sadly, Waples did not live to see the new church completed, but Waples Memorial Methodist Church, South, seen below around 1930, was named in his honor. (Both, AWGC.)

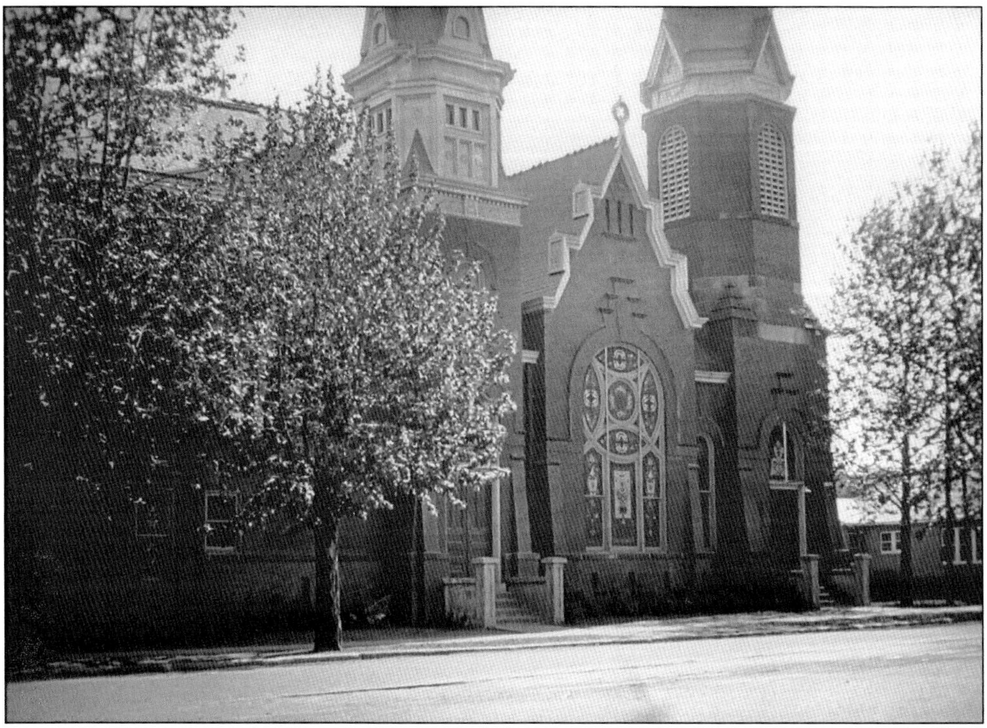

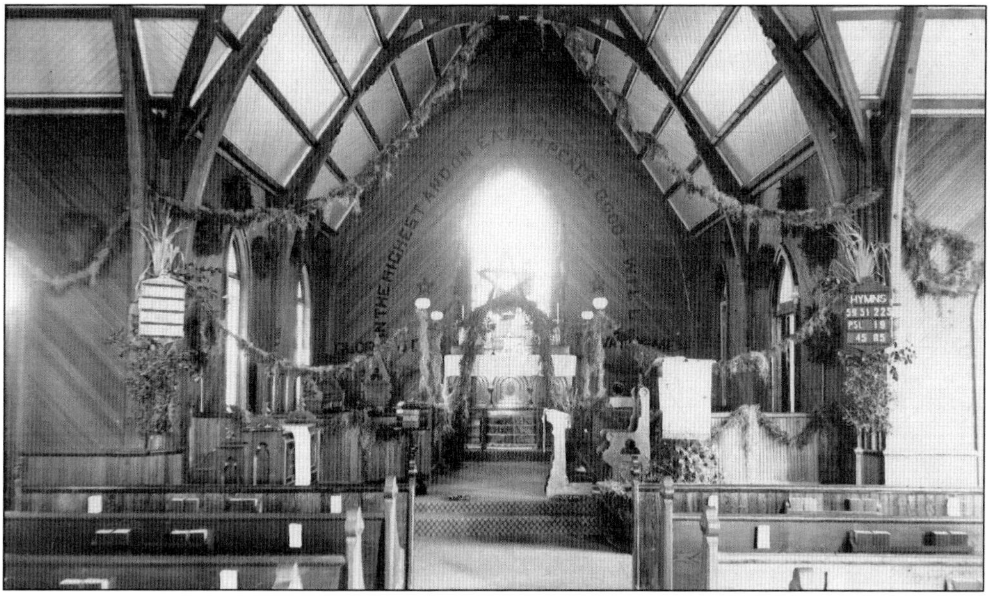

Denison's oldest house of worship still in use is St. Luke's Episcopal Church. That structure, currently holding pews for the congregation, was completed in 1876, along with a home for the rector. Located at the northeast corner of Woodard Street and Fannin Avenue, St. Luke's was later enlarged to accommodate a growing membership. More recently, the church built and operates St. Luke's Parish Day School. (DHH.)

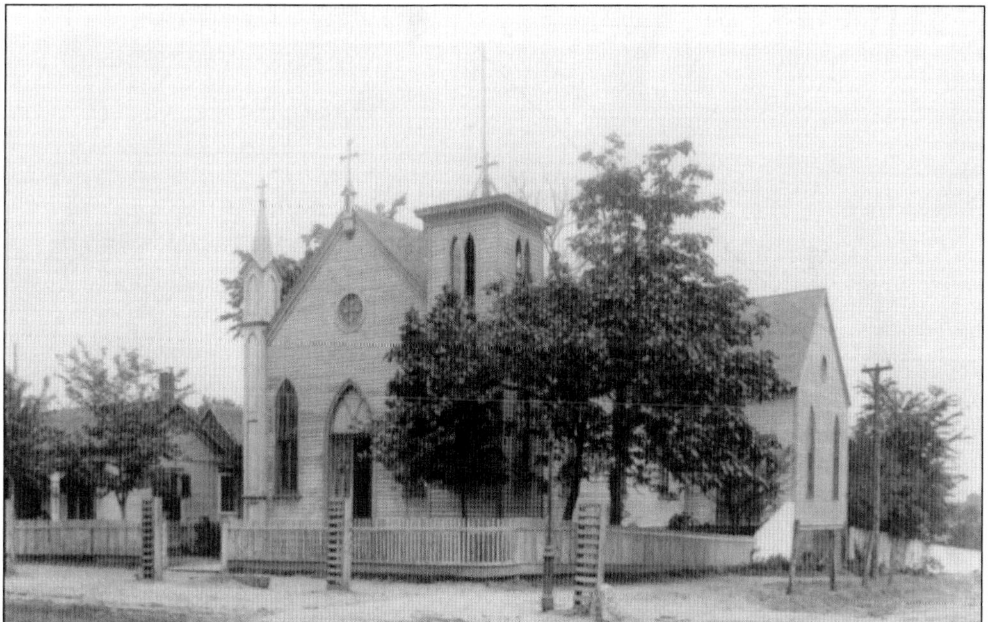

St. Patrick's Catholic parish was established in 1872 by the Roman Catholic bishop of Galveston, Charles Marie Debuis, who sent Fr. Joseph Martiniere to the new Denison mission. The first church building, a small frame structure, occupied the northwest corner of West Sears Street and Rusk Avenue in July 1873. In 1877, it was replaced by a second, larger frame church at 314 North Rusk Avenue, seen here around 1894. (AWGC.)

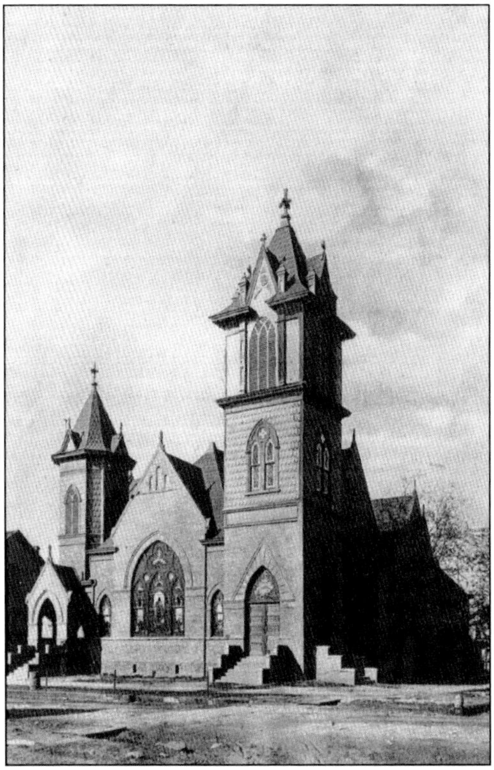

The First Presbyterian Church was founded about a week before the first MKT train arrived in Denison. In 1911, Cumberland Presbyterian Church, founded here in 1901, merged with First Presbyterian. The original church building, completed in 1874 and remodeled in 1900, burned in 1902 (below). Its original bell, used as the town's fire alarm, was donated to Denison's first public school, the Educational Institute; the bell later was transferred to the 1914 Denison High School, where it served for generations. Seen at left around 1930 is the second church building that was erected in 1903. Dr. Alex W. Acheson donated a large bell in 1932. It was not until 1966 that this structure was replaced by the present one designed by architect Donald Lee Mayes. All three church buildings have stood at 213 North Burnett Avenue at Gandy Street. (Left, DHH; below, HD.)

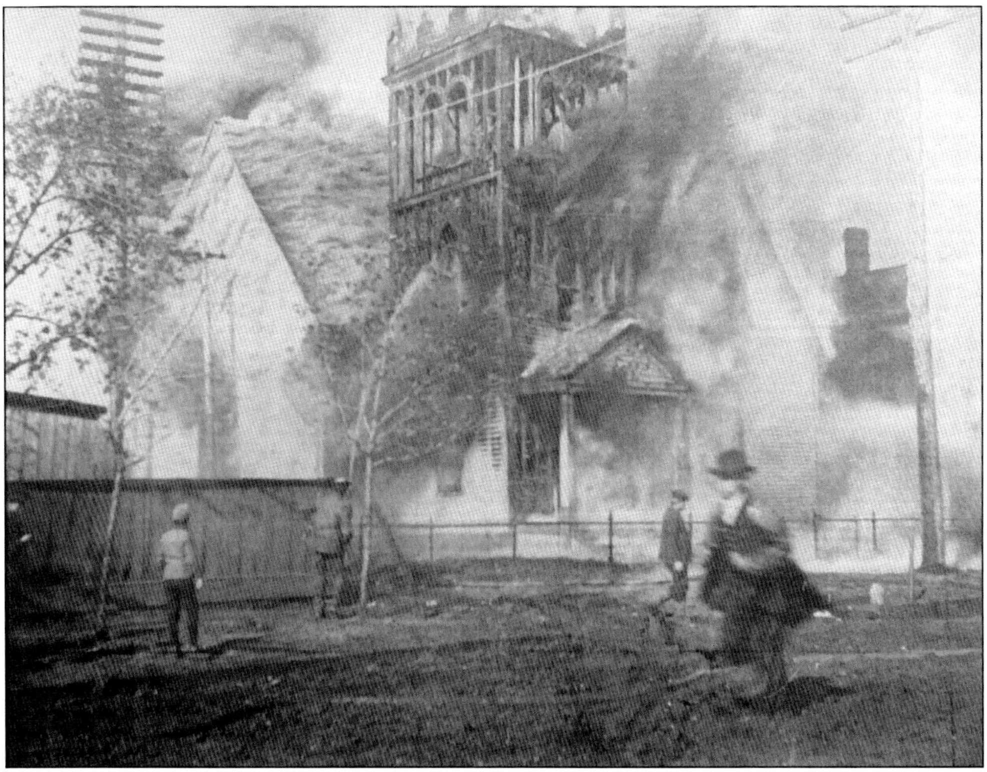

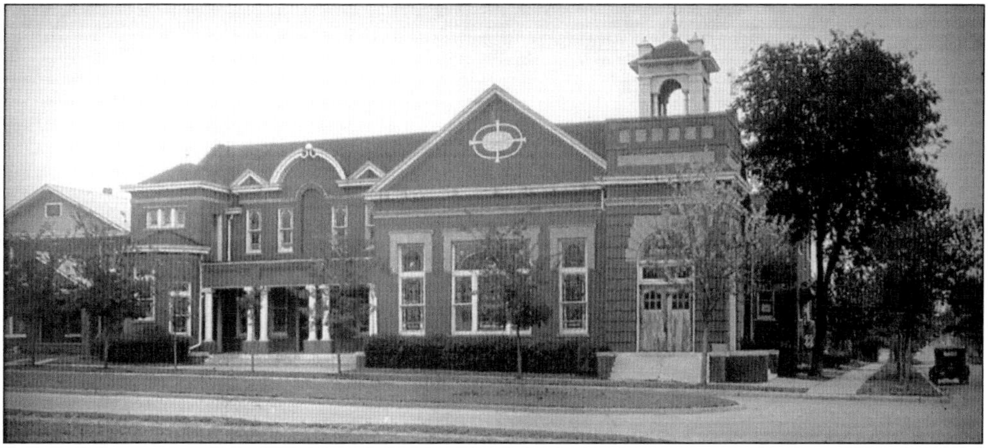

The First Baptist Church of Denison was formed in 1874 by the merger of two earlier Baptist churches. The congregation's first edifice, at 631 West Main Street, was destroyed by a windstorm in 1883. Two years later, a new structure was dedicated at the northwest corner of Woodard Street and Mirick Avenue. In 1907, a new redbrick church—seen above around 1930—replaced that one, serving until 1958. (DHH.)

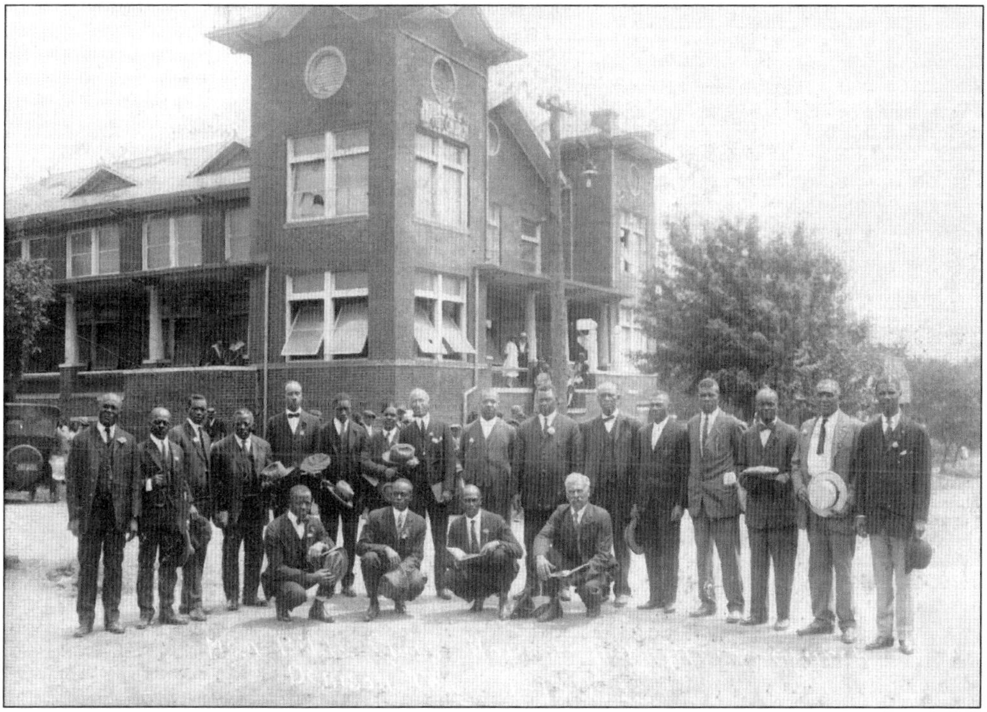

Hopewell Baptist Church was founded in 1874 by African Americans from the Preston Bend area. In 1922, a new brick structure was erected at the northeast corner of Bond Street and Mirick Avenue. The Men's Bible Class is seen here a year later. US Supreme Court justice Thurgood Marshall spoke here in 1950. A new church was dedicated across the avenue in 1995, and the first building was demolished in 2007. (MAB.)

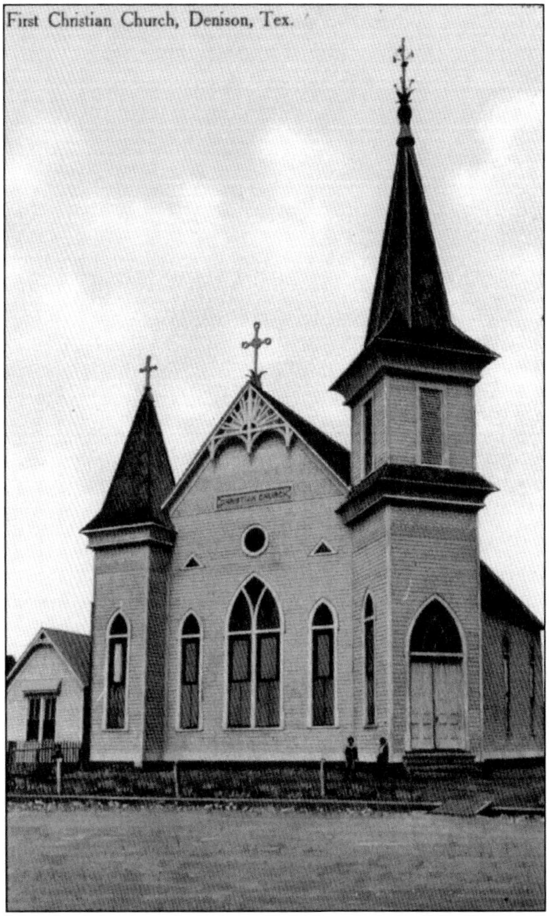

The First Christian Church held its inaugural services in Denison on March 16, 1873. An early leader was elder Caleb S. Burns. After utilizing one small church, the congregation in 1911 purchased the Bethany Cumberland Presbyterian Church (left), located at 800 West Woodard Street at the corner of Armstrong Avenue. Two years later, that white frame church burned. A new Mission Revival–style Denison High School was going up across Armstrong Avenue. It made sense to build a new church in the same style (below). It was dedicated on July 26, 1914. The building served until being demolished in 1947 to clear the way for the church that still serves the congregation. (Both, DHH.)

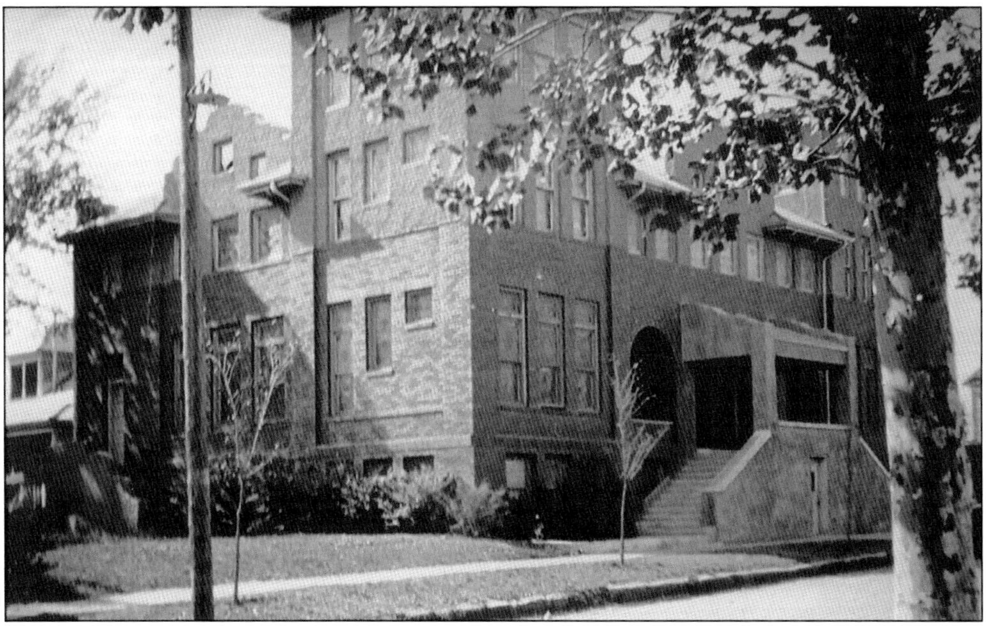

Four

WATER HERE, WATER THERE

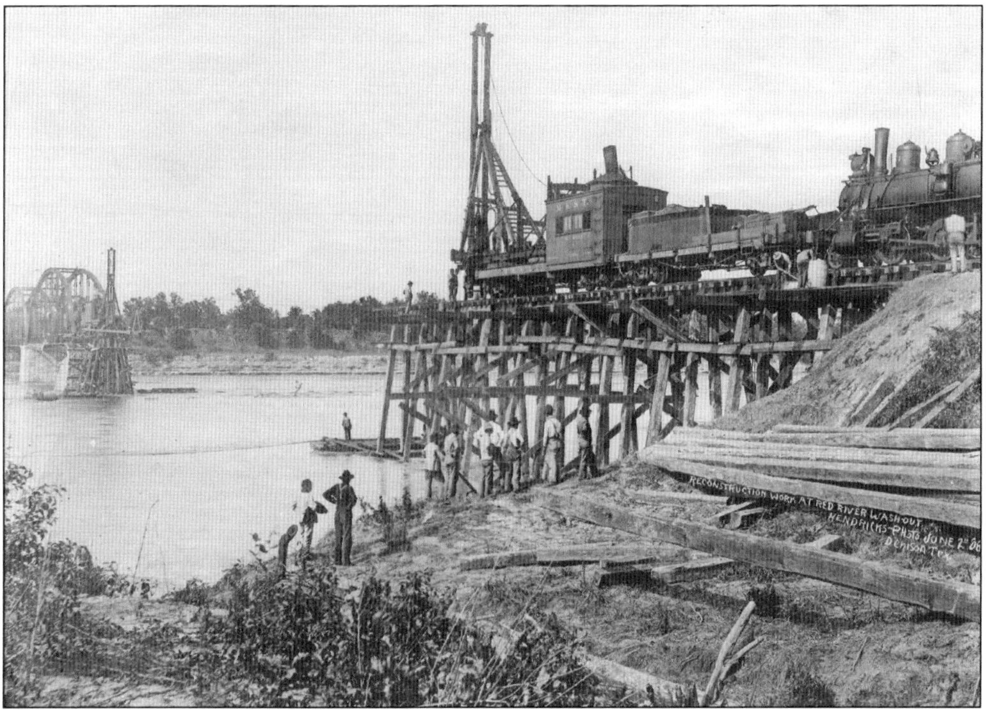

Workers with the MKT Railroad rebuild a bridge across Red River on June 2, 1908, after what became known as the "Great Flood" destroyed the earlier train bridge. Construction workers are on the Texas side of the river, where railroad ties have been stacked. The flood struck on May 26, 1908, and was called the largest national catastrophe in Texas. Fourteen lives were lost. (Hendricks, in MAB.)

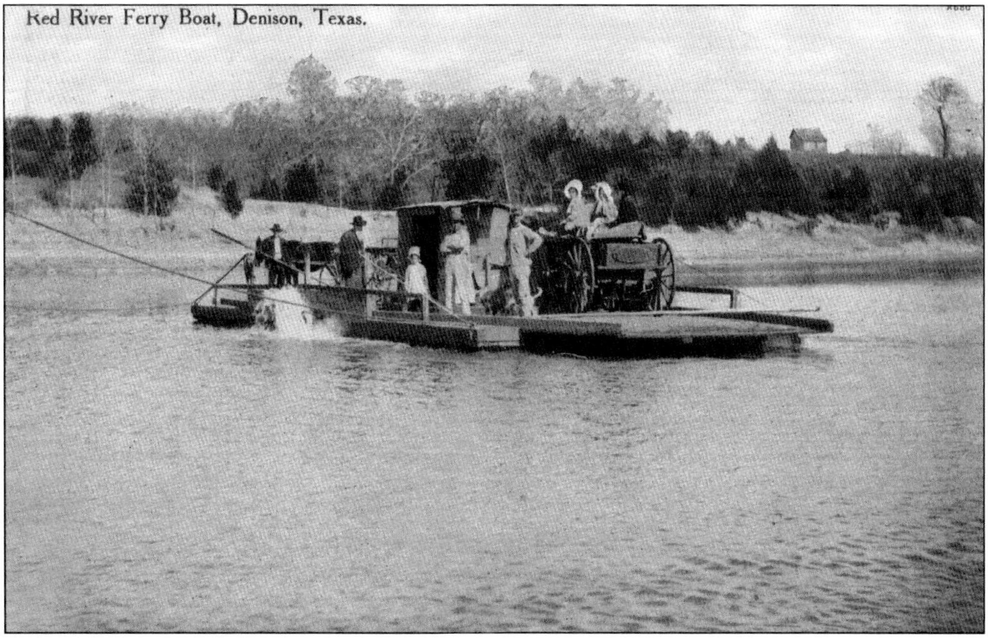

In the years before bridges were built, crossing the Red River was only a small problem. Ferries like the one pictured here were available in several places to move wagons, horses, and travelers between Oklahoma and Texas. This postcard could depict a ferry at Colbert or Rock Bluff, the Thompson ferry at Preston Bend, or any of several others that operated a useful service for a very small fee. (DHH.)

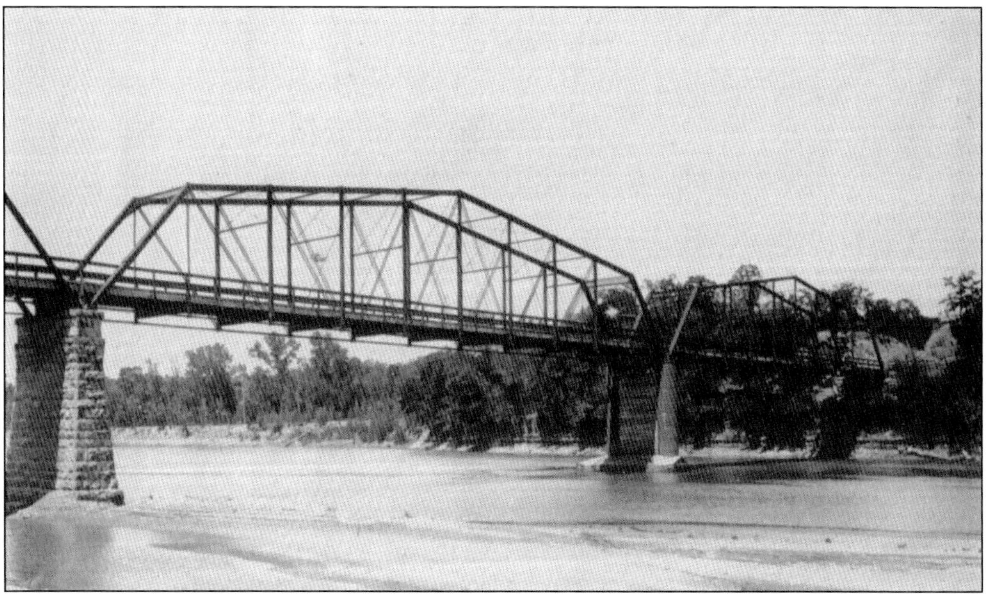

When road bridges were built over the mighty Red River between Texas and Oklahoma, a big problem was solved for travelers. However, the bridges created a larger problem for ferry operators, who soon were put out of business. This well-built bridge was used by individuals in wagons, on horseback, and eventually in automobiles. (AWGC.)

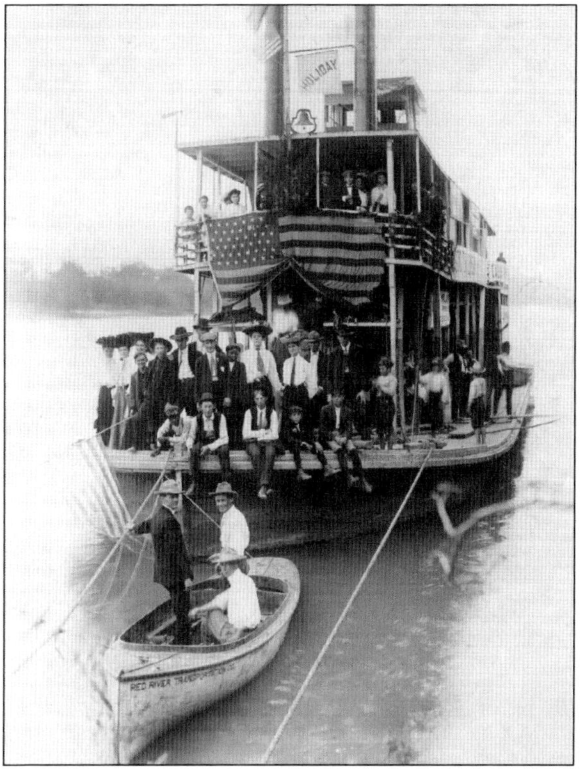

After landing at Riverside Park north of Denison, the *Annie P* steamboat rests at anchor. Eager personnel from the Red River Transportation Company move in for a closer look at the first boat to navigate the Red River from New Orleans. It is loaded with passengers and merchandise. Town leaders came to hear speeches, including one by Dr. W. Alexander Acheson, who had earlier proclaimed the Red River navigable. (HD.)

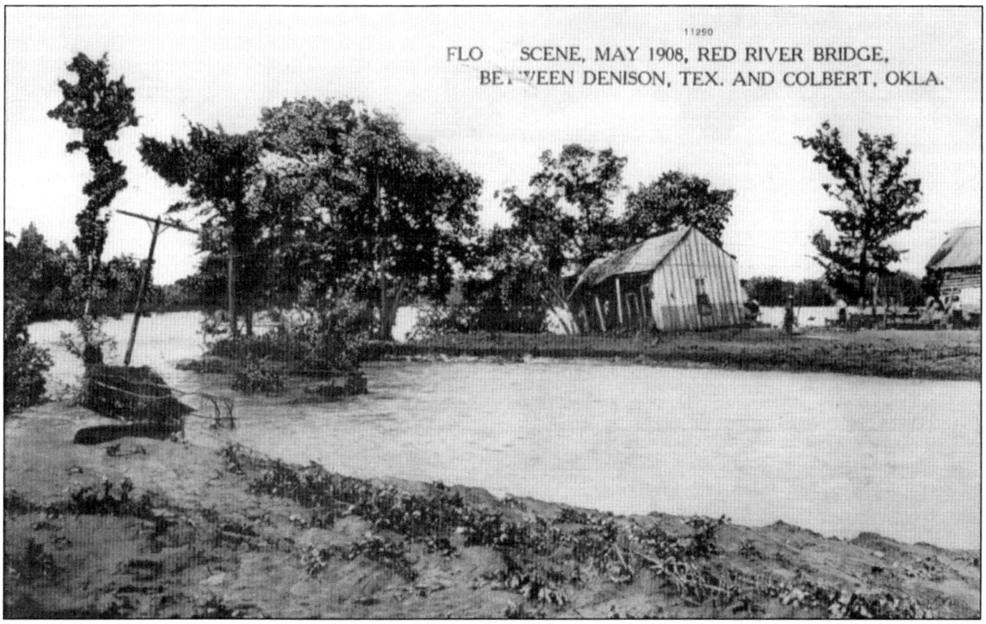

This postcard, stamped August 10, 1908, shows the lasting damage inflicted by the May 26 flood that year. The water destroyed property in North Texas and downed a railroad bridge over the Red River. Fourteen people lost their lives in the catastrophic flood. This scene was located between Colbert, Oklahoma, and Denison. Eventually the Denison Dam between Cartwright, Oklahoma, and Denison put a stop to such floods. (DHH.)

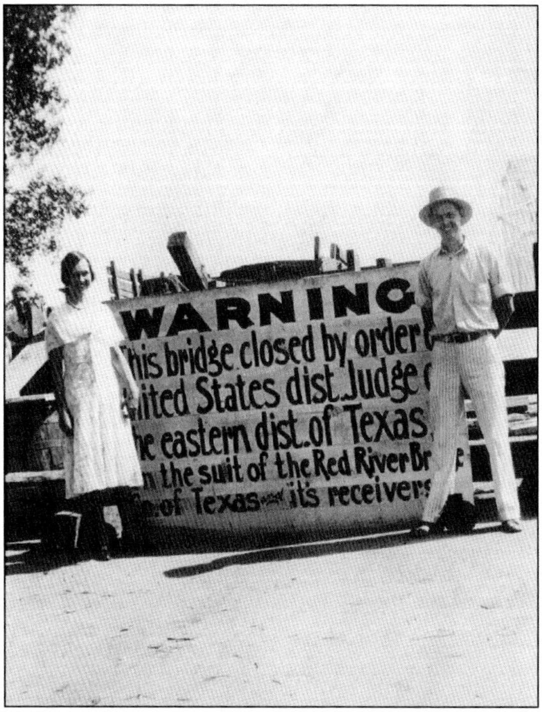

A young couple poses beside a sign posted at the entrance to a free bridge that Texas had constructed over Red River. When a dispute arose between Texas and Oklahoma, a Texas district judge closed the bridge for 10 days until the dispute was resolved. The event has been called the Red River Bridge War, although no shots were fired. The barriers came down on July 25, 1931. (DHH.)

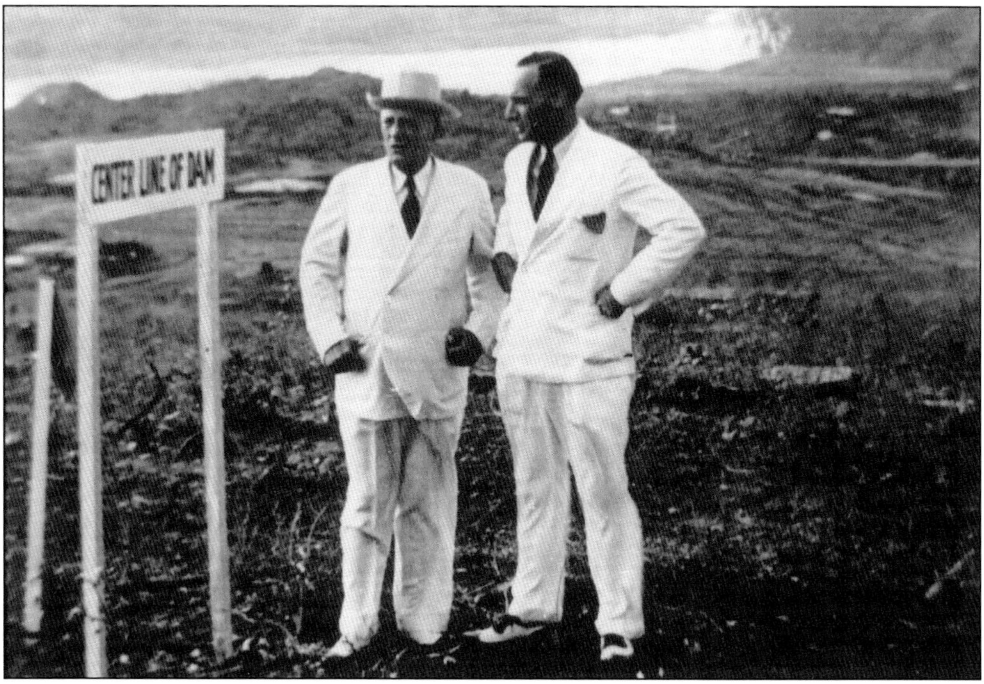

US congressman Sam Rayburn of Bonham and Gen. Lucius Clay, project manager for the US Army Corps of Engineers, stand at the centerline of the Denison Dam. Completed in 1944 for flood control on the Red River, the dam created Lake Texoma. The lake has a boundary of about 726 miles and is located northwest of Denison. Texoma has become a popular resort area in the two states. (HD.)

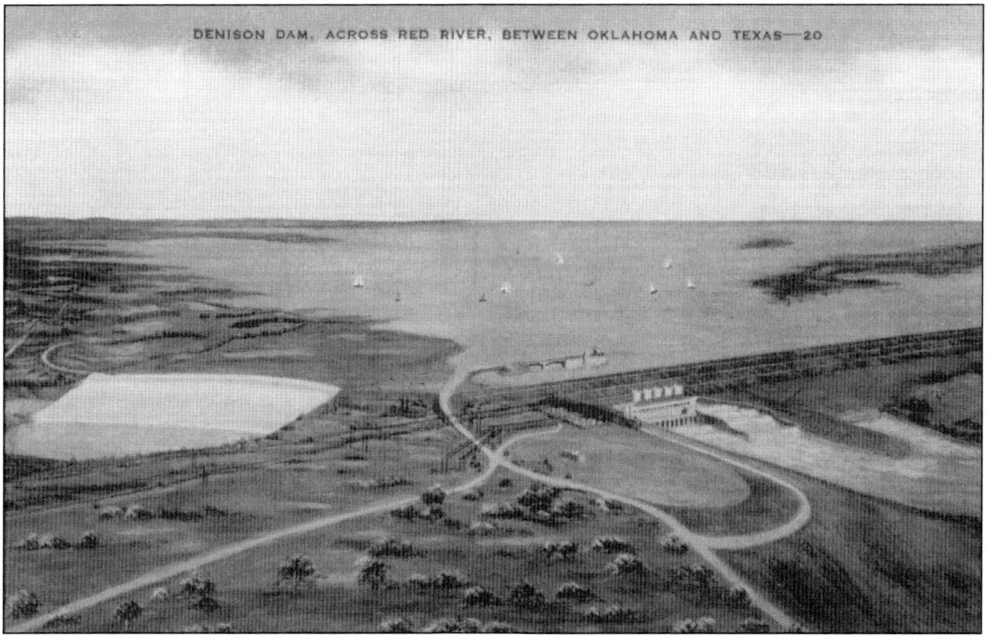

Swift water flows from the powerhouse to produce electricity, one of the main purposes of the Denison Dam. Eighty-four feet of the 15-story powerhouse is below ground. The structure was dedicated on July 1, 1944. When built, the dam was the second largest earthen dam in the world and cost $55,250,000. It extends three miles across Red River into Oklahoma. (DHH.)

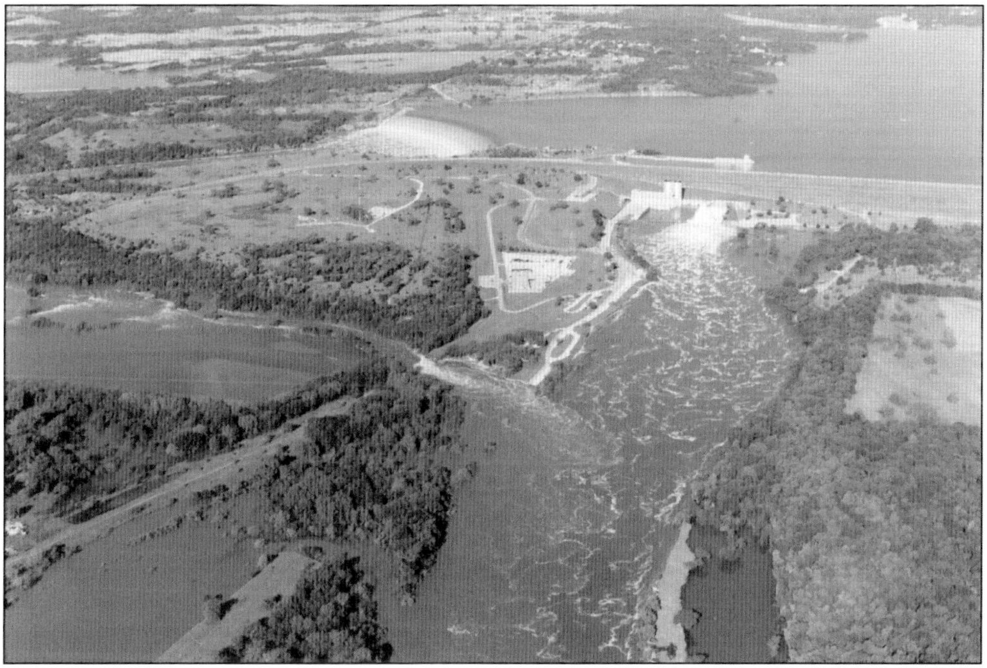

It was said that Lake Texoma, created by the Denison Dam in 1944, might flood only once in 100 years. In 1990, however, water flowed freely over the spillway, washing out Highway 75-A, then cutting back into Red River below the dam. Floods occurred all along the river's banks. The first overflow that caused flooding was in 1957, and a third one occurred in 2007. (DHH.)

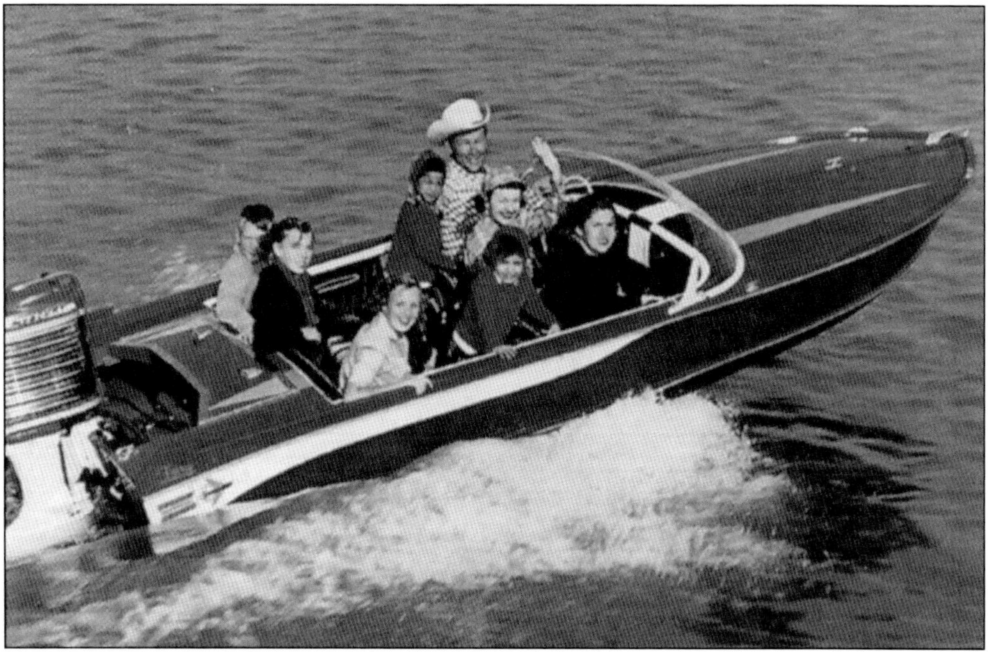

Western movie star Roy Rogers takes his family for a spin around Lake Texoma while visiting the Yellow Jacket Boat plant in Denison. In 1953, Rogers became a partner with R.A. McDerby in manufacturing the wooden boats. Flying across the water with Roy in his Yellow Jacket boat powered by a Mercury motor is actress Dale Evans and their children, Sharon, Linda, Marion, Debby, Dotty, and Dusty. (HD.)

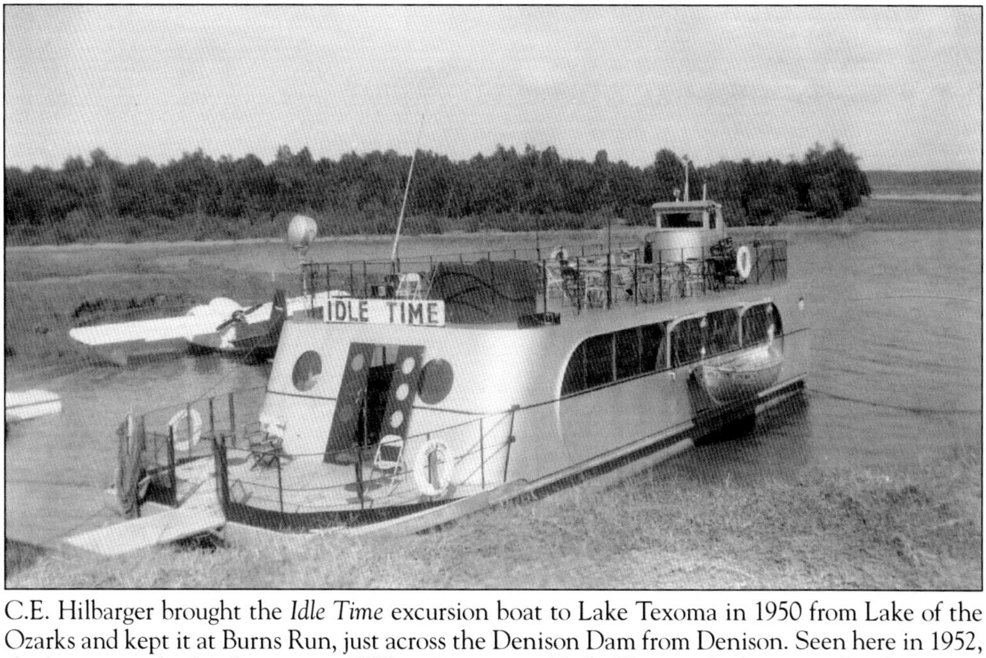

C.E. Hilbarger brought the *Idle Time* excursion boat to Lake Texoma in 1950 from Lake of the Ozarks and kept it at Burns Run, just across the Denison Dam from Denison. Seen here in 1952, the boat ran scheduled cruises to Willow Springs and Lake Texoma Lodge; in its heyday, it was in demand for chartered dinner-dance events. When popularity waned, it anchored at Willow Springs Resort, where it sank. (MAB.)

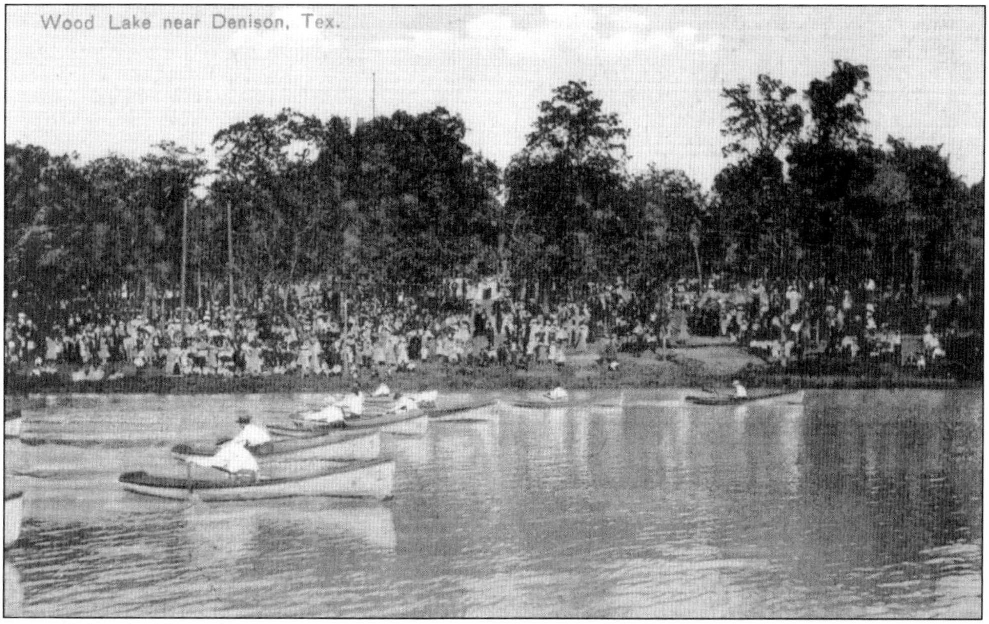

Woodlake, halfway between Denison and Sherman, opened on May 1, 1901. Rides on the interurban were free that day. The entertainment included boat rides, a zoo, swimming pool, penny arcade, and casino, as well as special events and educational programs. Canoe races took place in boats rented for 25¢ an hour. A loud bell indicated when it was time to return to the pier for the boat ride back. (DHH.)

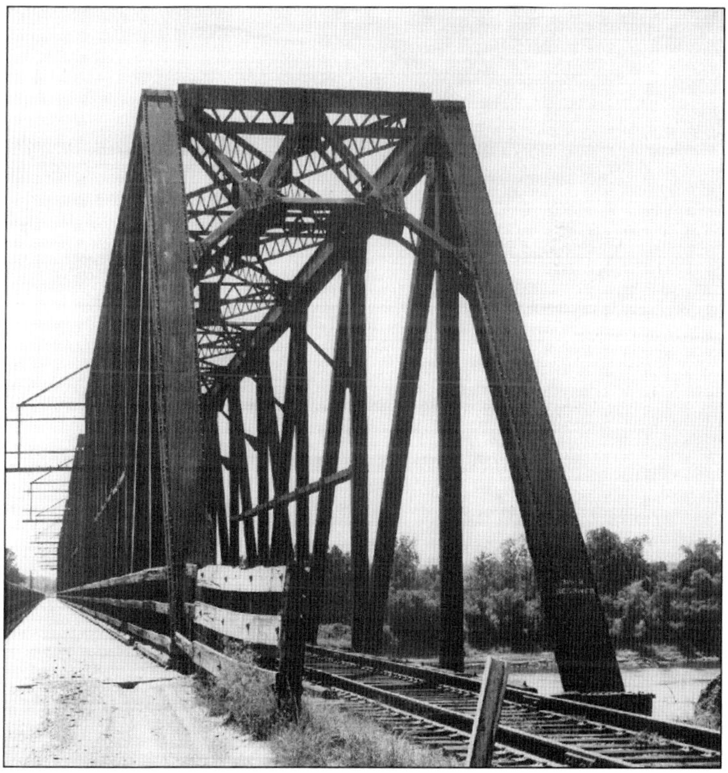

Construction of the Carpenter's Bluff Bridge, east of Denison, began in 1910. The bridge, seen here from the Oklahoma side, became known as "Texas's back door." Today, hundreds of people still cross daily, coming to Texas to work or shop and then return home to Oklahoma. Trains once crossed Red River on this bridge, while wagons, horses, and cars crossed on a side bridge. The tracks were removed, and vehicles now use the iron bridge. (HD.)

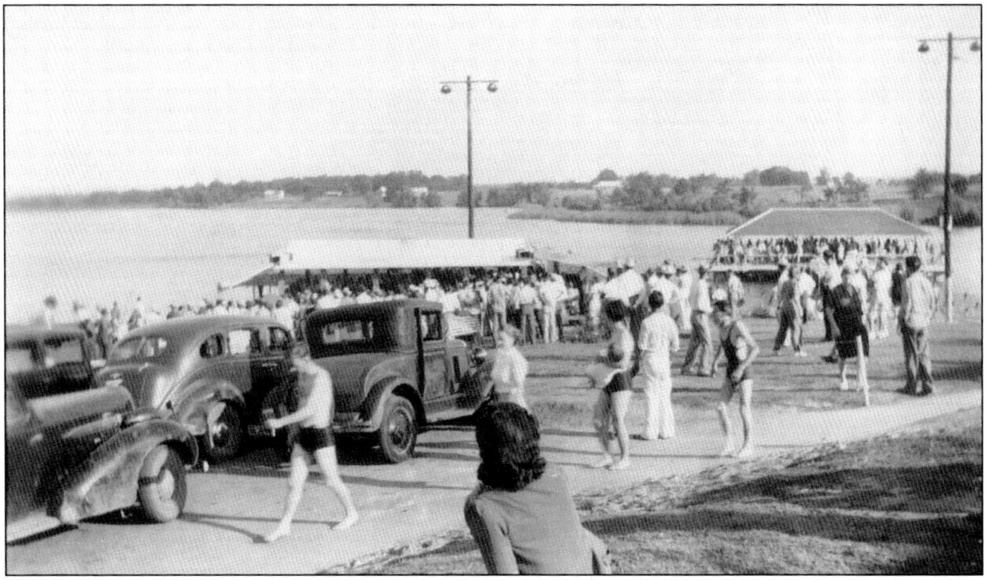

Loy Lake Park was built in 1935 by workers of the Civilian Conservation Corps, which set up a camp there. When the 40-acre lake was completed, the park (controlled by Grayson County Commissioners) became a place for fishing, swimming, camping, dancing, and political speeches. It also houses Frontier Village, a museum composed of numerous pioneer structures, and mounts a free Christmas lighting display every December. (DHH.)

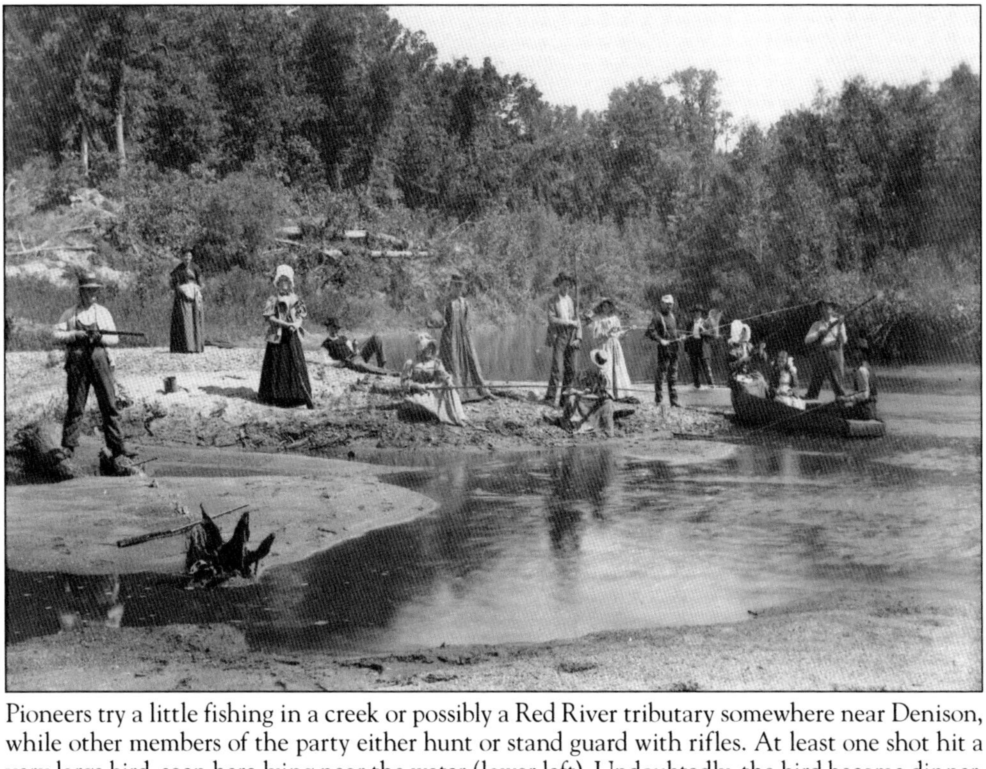

Pioneers try a little fishing in a creek or possibly a Red River tributary somewhere near Denison, while other members of the party either hunt or stand guard with rifles. At least one shot hit a very large bird, seen here lying near the water (lower left). Undoubtedly, the bird became dinner, along with fish that the men and women may have caught with their cane poles. (DHH.)

Five

Growing the Town

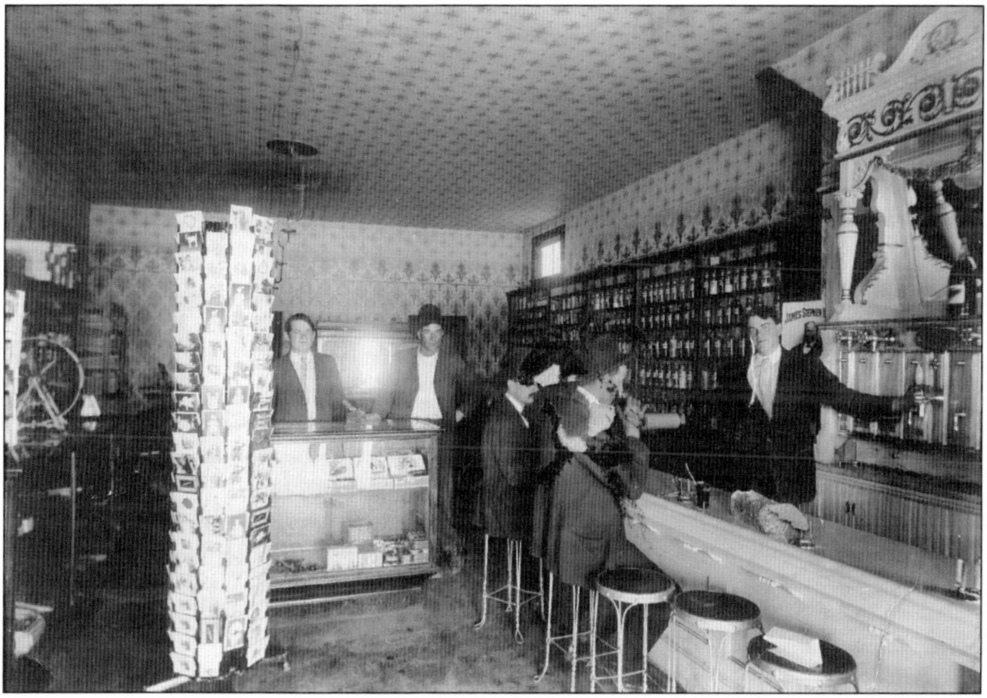

Highlighting an ornate soda fountain, this Denison business (precise location unknown) also features shelves of bottled flavorings, herbs, and other ingredients. Perhaps they will be mixed into refreshing drinks. On the counter sit metal holders for full glasses labeled "Coca-Cola." Patterned wallpaper enhances the welcoming atmosphere. Cigars, a rack of postcards, and stacks of magazines tempt customers. And what about that toy Ferris wheel for the kids? (MAB.)

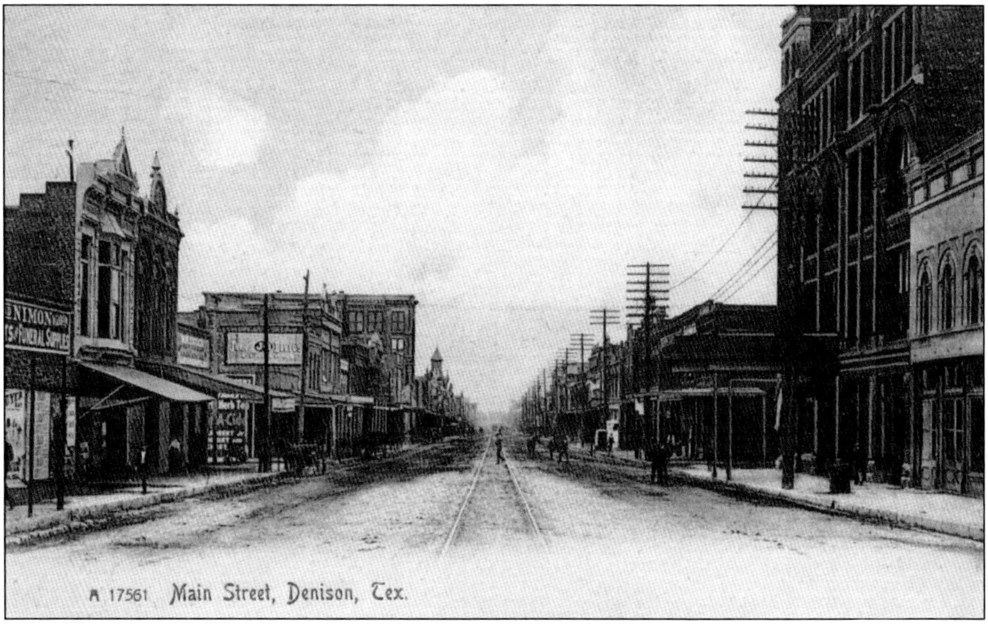

This view looks east from the 500 block of West Main Street in the first decade of the 20th century. Tall utility poles lined the street soon after electricity became available. Trolley tracks facilitated travel within Denison. Charles Nimon previously worked as an assistant to Isaac Lindsey in his undertaking business at 508–510 West Main Street. Here, Nimon has set up in business for himself across the street. (MAB.)

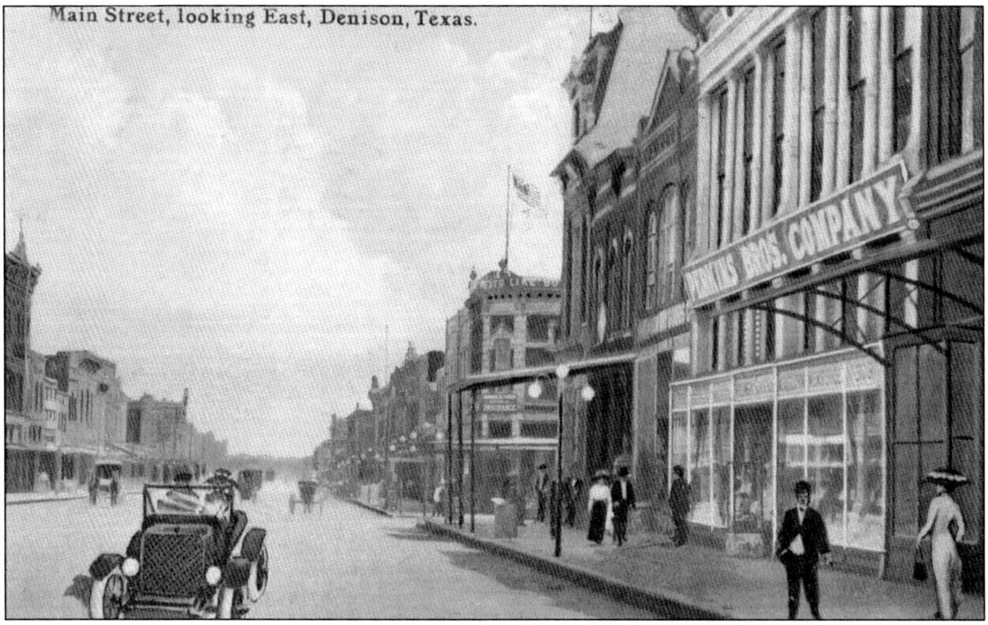

Perkins Brothers Company, with its elegant storefront at 306–308 West Main Street, sold "dry goods, clothing, shoes, etc." In this c. 1911 view looking east, two corner banks face each other across Rusk Avenue. The State National Bank ("Ladies are provided with every facility and courtesy") occupies 300 West Main Street; the National Bank of Denison, flag waving, is at 230 West Main Street. Early motorcars share the street with horse-drawn vehicles. (DHH.)

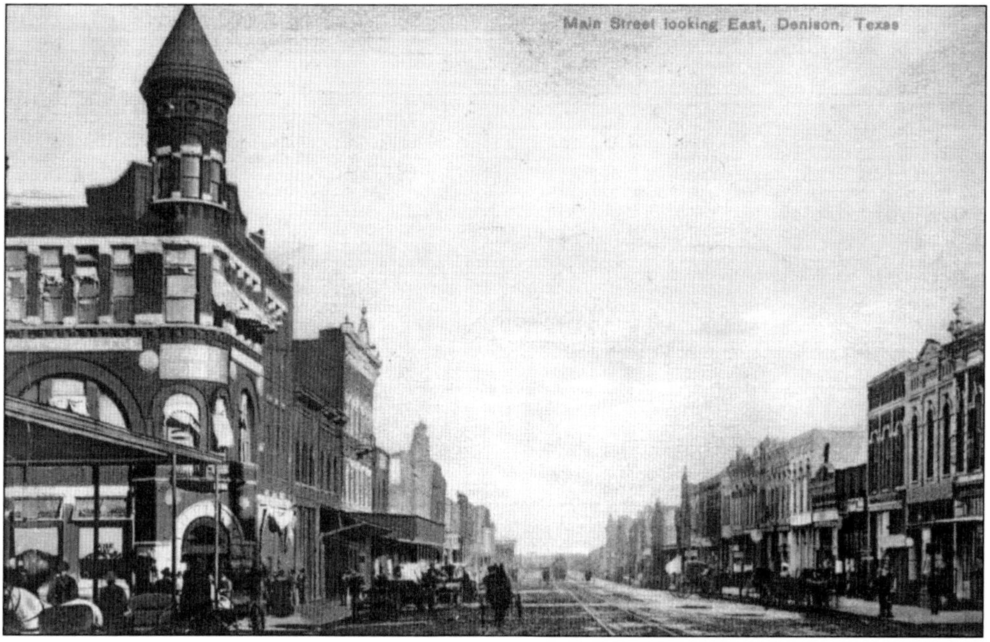

Around 1910, Main Street stretches east from the 200 block, seen here. Automobiles have not yet replaced horse-drawn carts and buggies. Draughon's Business College occupies prime space in the First National Bank/Ford Building at 231 West Main Street at Rusk Avenue. The round tower will be removed later, possibly when the Citizens State Bank takes over the location in 1921. Three doors east stands the McDougall Opera House constructed in 1881. (DHH.)

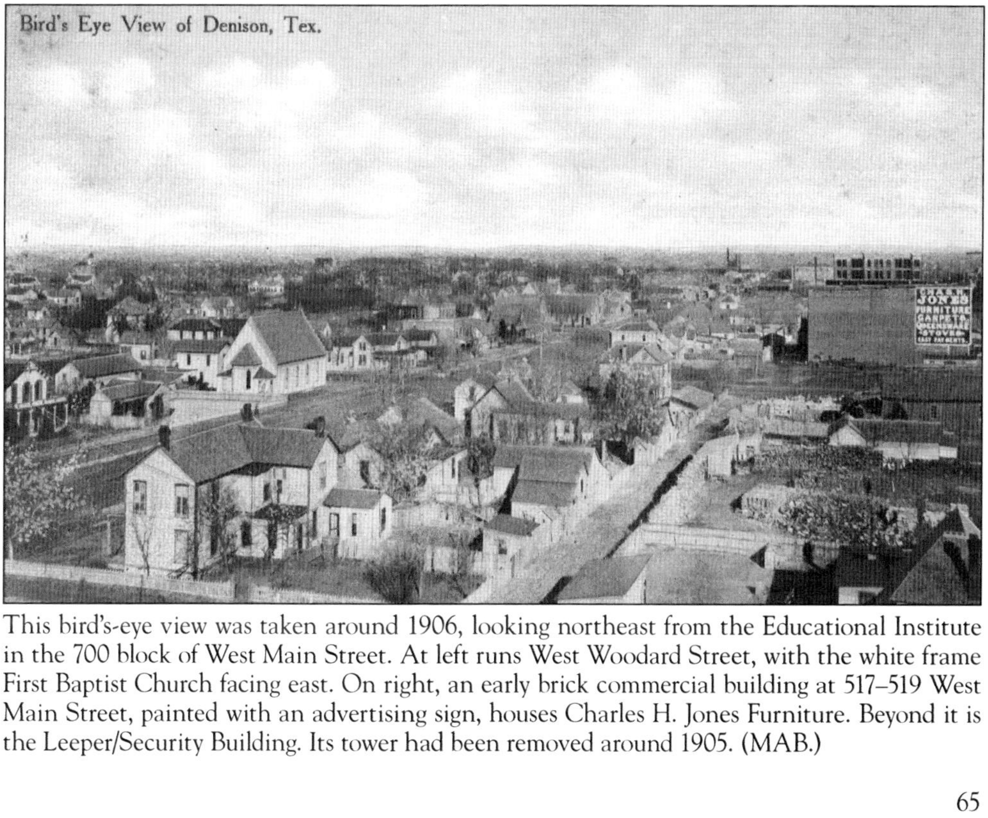

This bird's-eye view was taken around 1906, looking northeast from the Educational Institute in the 700 block of West Main Street. At left runs West Woodard Street, with the white frame First Baptist Church facing east. On right, an early brick commercial building at 517–519 West Main Street, painted with an advertising sign, houses Charles H. Jones Furniture. Beyond it is the Leeper/Security Building. Its tower had been removed around 1905. (MAB.)

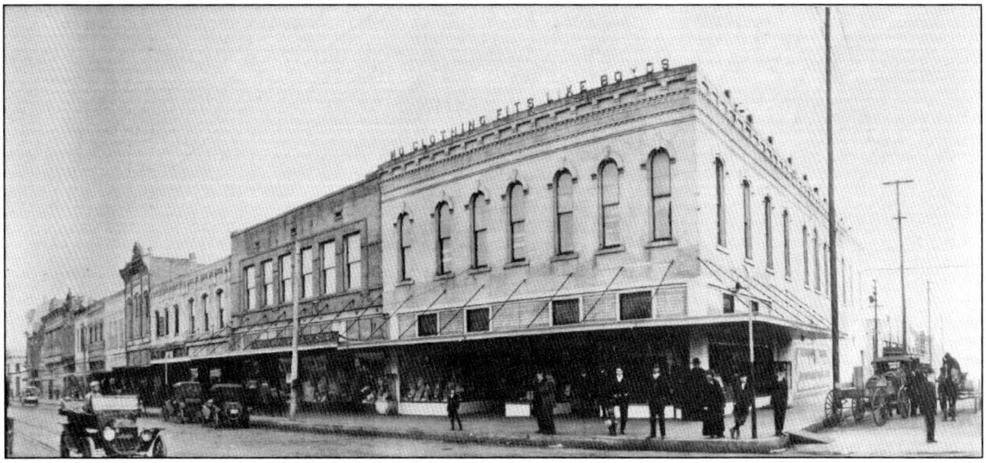

Two halves of a 1916 panoramic photograph by Kelley Studio depict the south sides of two key blocks of West Main Street. In the image above, dominating the 300 block, is James Boyd, Gents' Outfitters, at 328–330 West Main Street (note lettering atop store). Boyd's store began in a primitive rural setting near the Red River. He came to Denison by 1886; six years later, he and Levi Lingo formed Boyd and Lingo at 230 West Main Street. Later, Boyd alone moved to the location shown here, where he prospered until 1929. In the image below, two hotels—the Palace (left) and the turreted first Denison Hotel (far right)—bracket the 400 block of West Main Street. Scott and Jennings Furniture was the first of four Jennings furniture stores on Main Street. The tall hotel/college building perished in a horrific fire on January 24, 1920. (Both, MAB.)

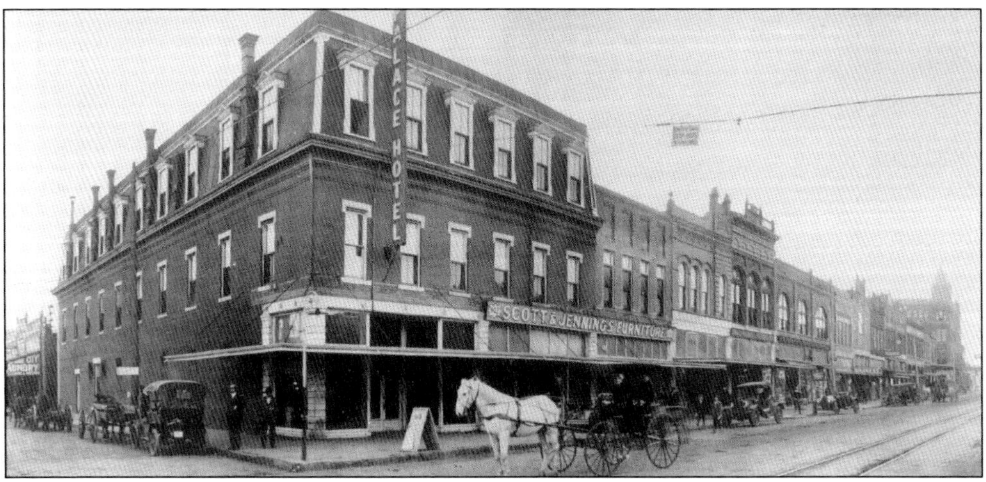

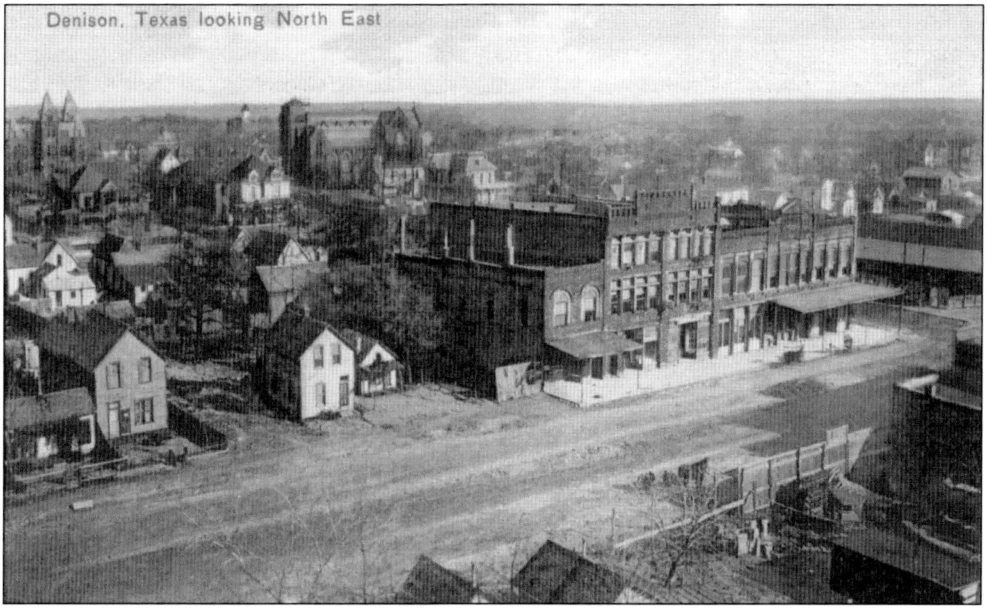

Shortly after 1900, Denison had expanded dramatically. This view shows the 300 block of West Woodard Street and nearby residential blocks, seen looking northeast from a tall Main Street building. The Munson Block stands proudly in the foreground. Numerous prominent businesses were housed in this redbrick strip. St. Patrick's Catholic Church and St. Xavier's Academy are the tallest buildings visible, at upper center and upper left, respectively. (MAB.)

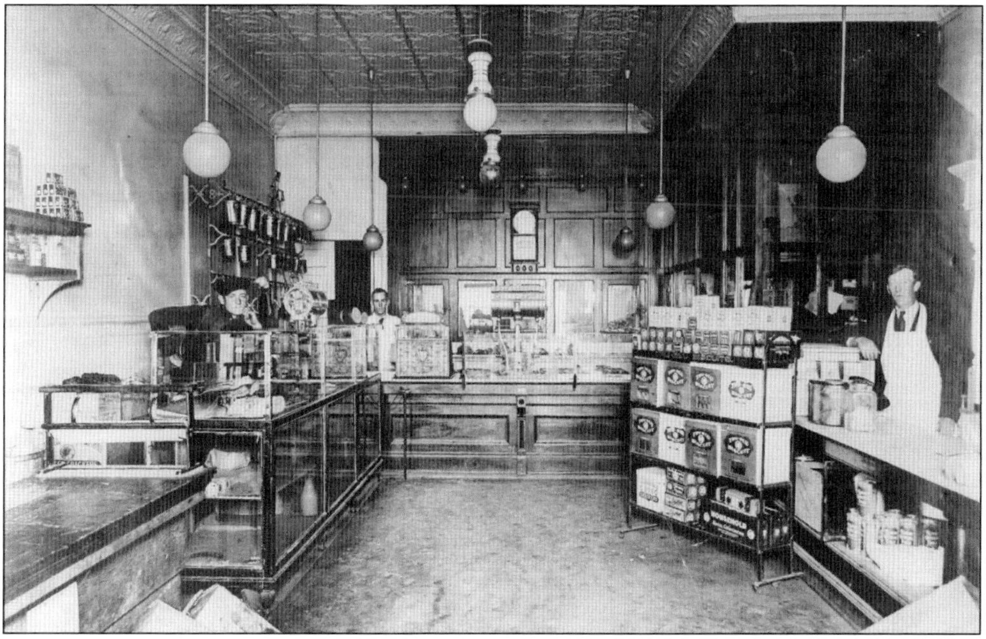

This grocery store may have been at 421 West Main Street. Three young clerks preside over fine counters, display cases, cold storage (at left and back), a cash register, scale, and clock. Note the paneled back wall and fancy tin ceiling. The stock of food, however, seems sparse. Household soda crackers, Royal Crystal Salt, and Tru-Blu Biscuits (made by a company operating in Spokane, Washington, around 1915) are prominently displayed. The floor appears to be dirt. (MAB.)

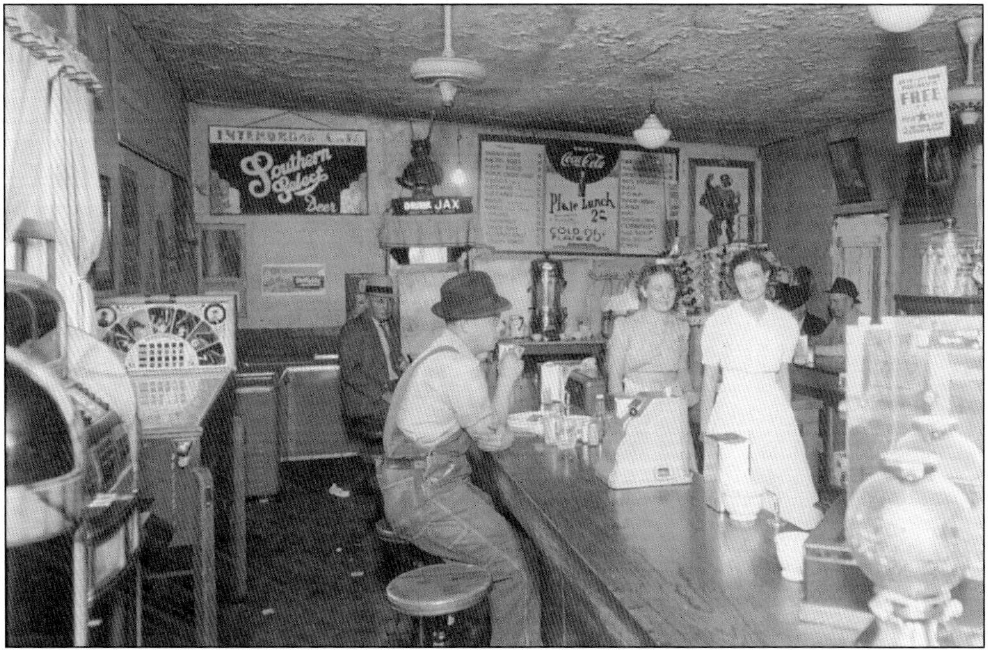

Ouida Cordell (right) operated the Interurban Café near the interurban garage on North Houston Avenue. Breakfast was just 30¢, and a plate lunch only a quarter. The café was a favorite, not only with interurban passengers and workers but also those at the Katy Depot just across the avenue. If a diner got a red star on the cash register receipt, the meal was free. (Betty Ferguson Johnson.)

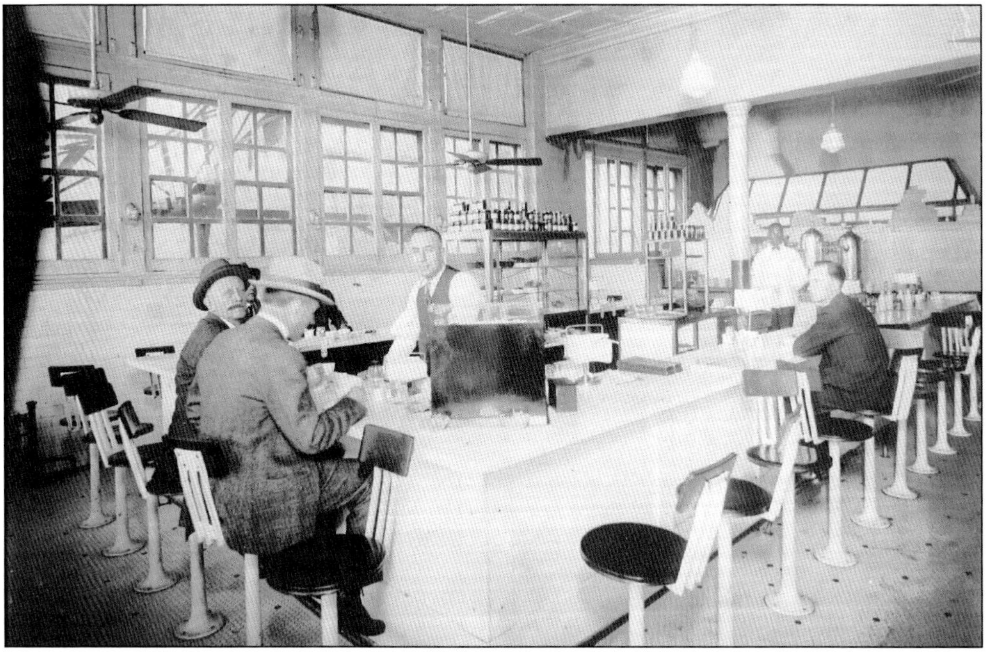

The Palace Hotel at 400 West Main Street had a popular coffee shop, the Palace Grill, with a lunch counter at the rear. The café's entrance was at 109 South Burnett Avenue, while the entrance to the hotel itself was north of the café. The front half of the hotel's first floor was mercantile space. Here, note the fire escape in the alley, visible through the windows. (MAB.)

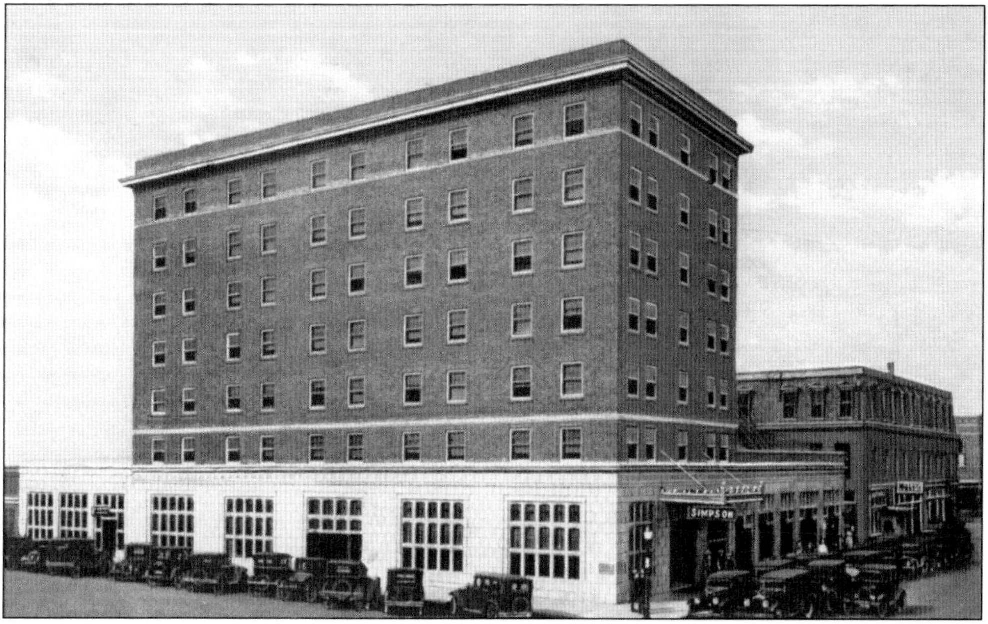

In 1922, after the first Denison Hotel burned to the ground, the town needed a luxury hotel. Brothers W.E. and Arthur Simpson joined Joe M. Crumpton to organize a hotel venture. The resulting Hotel Simpson, with 110 rooms on seven floors, was a matter of civic pride after it opened on October 1, 1924. Every room had a telephone next to the bed. The main dining room (below) was a spacious ballroom fit to host the town's most elaborate functions. At the ballroom's west end was a massive fireplace with a mantle imported from Salerno, Italy. Two noiseless elevators opened into the lobby. Among the noteworthy guests was Harry Houdini, famed escape artist, who signed the guest register two weeks after the hotel opened. Room rates were $2 and $3.50. Later, the name was changed to Hotel Denison. (Both, MAB.)

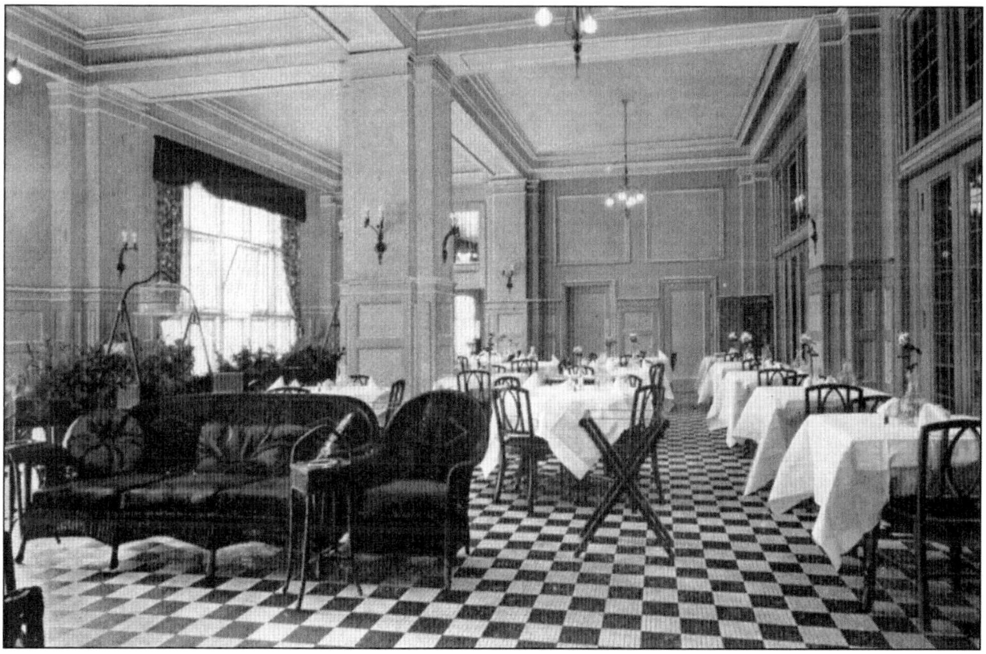

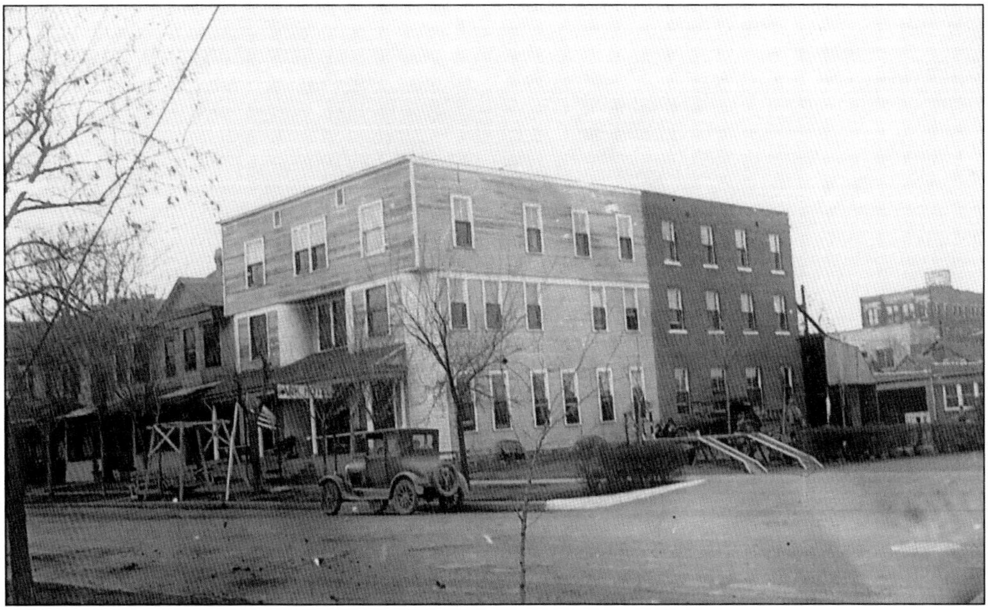

The Park Hotel was the preferred lodging for theatrical and circus performers playing Denison in the early decades of the 20th century. Located opposite Forest Park at 309–311 Crawford Street, the hotel was operated by Peter and Mary Lucille McDaniel. They kept a large cage of birds, squirrels, and other small animals out on the sidewalk for the amusement of guests. The hotel closed about 1957. (DHH.)

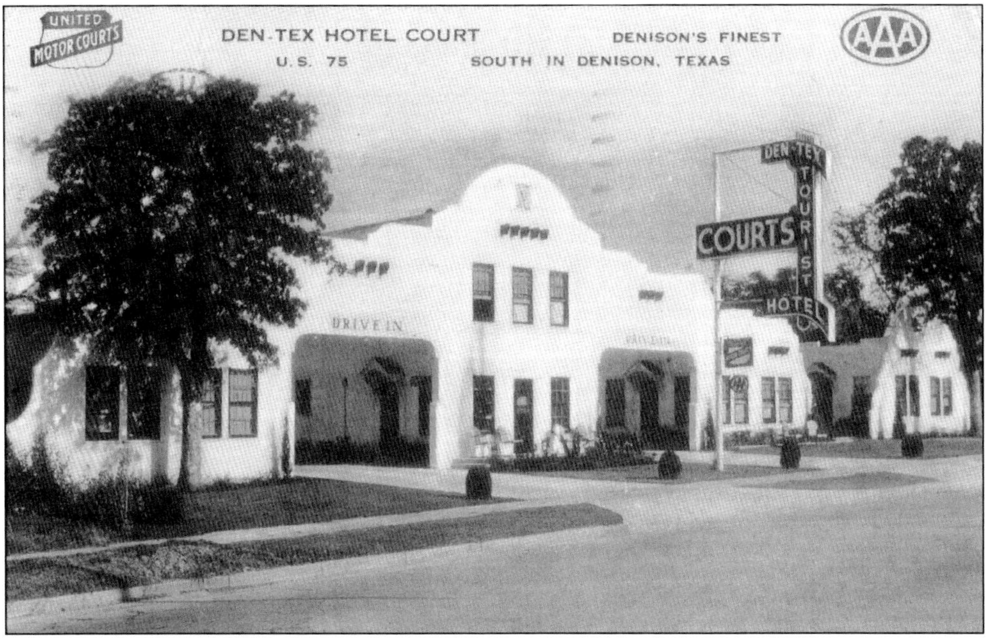

The Den-Tex Courts Tourist Hotel on Armstrong Avenue once sat on the main highway through Denison. Evoking memories of San Antonio's historic Alamo, the two-story Mission-style facade was designed to catch the attention of passing motorists. The comfortable courts were built around 1940 on property once owned by the family of a local school principal, Gordon Rutledge. The Den-Tex was long the only AAA-approved motel between Dallas and Tulsa. (MAB.)

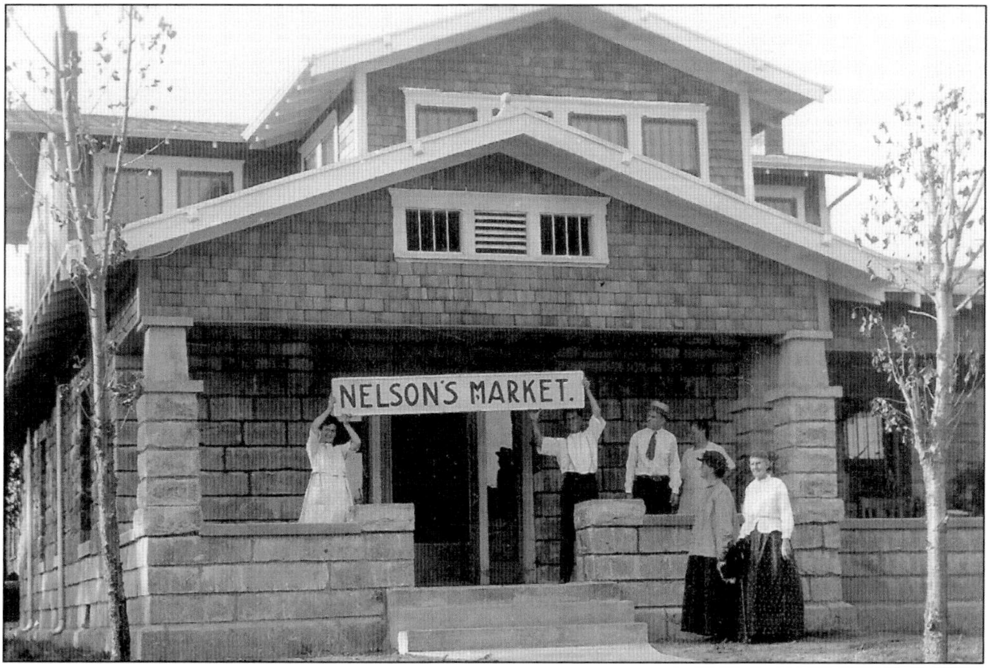

Born in North Carolina, Littleberry B. Nelson (1833–1890) moved to Arkansas as a young man and then on to Grayson County, expecting to farm. Soon, however, "Berry" was living in Denison. He operated a meat market at 931 West Main Street (above); its steps and other construction material were said to have come from the town's first school, which was two blocks east. Around 1945, the building housed Grace Lutheran Church. Subsequently it was demolished, and the American Bank of Texas was erected on the site. Reportedly, the son of Berry and his wife, Mary Catharine Taylor Nelson, was the first white male baby born after Denison was incorporated. The proud parents named him Denison (1875–1945). "Den" is buried in Oakwood Cemetery. In the c. 1900 photograph below, Denison—an avid photographer—is caught in front of the camera amusing himself by riding the family mule. (Both, DHH.)

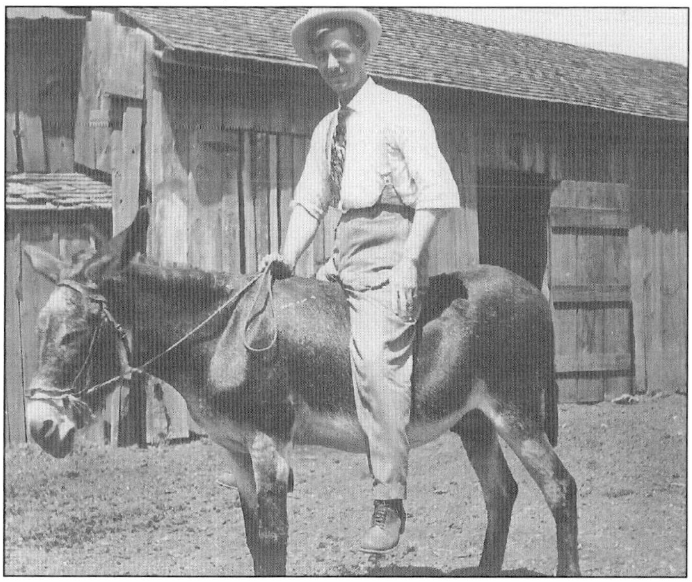

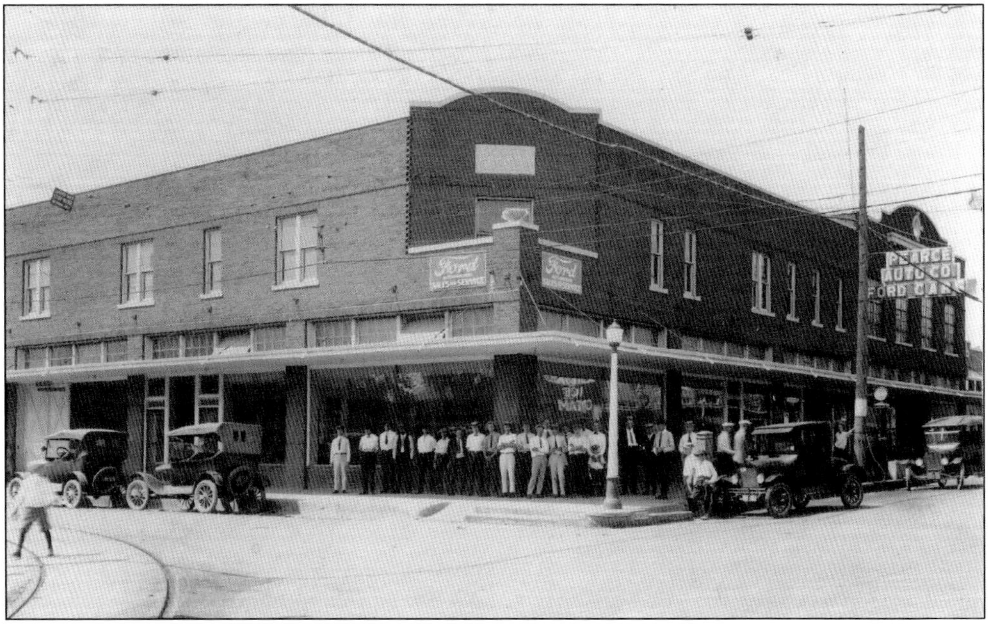

In 1908, Ford produced its first Model T. By 1924, one in seven Americans owned an automobile. Henry E. Pearce gambled on the trend. At age 30, he was a traveling agent for Denison Grocer Company. By 1915, he had created Pearce Auto Company at 116–120 South Burnett Avenue. Two years later, he opened this sales room, garage, and repair shop at 600–608 West Main Street. (Bobby Blankenship.)

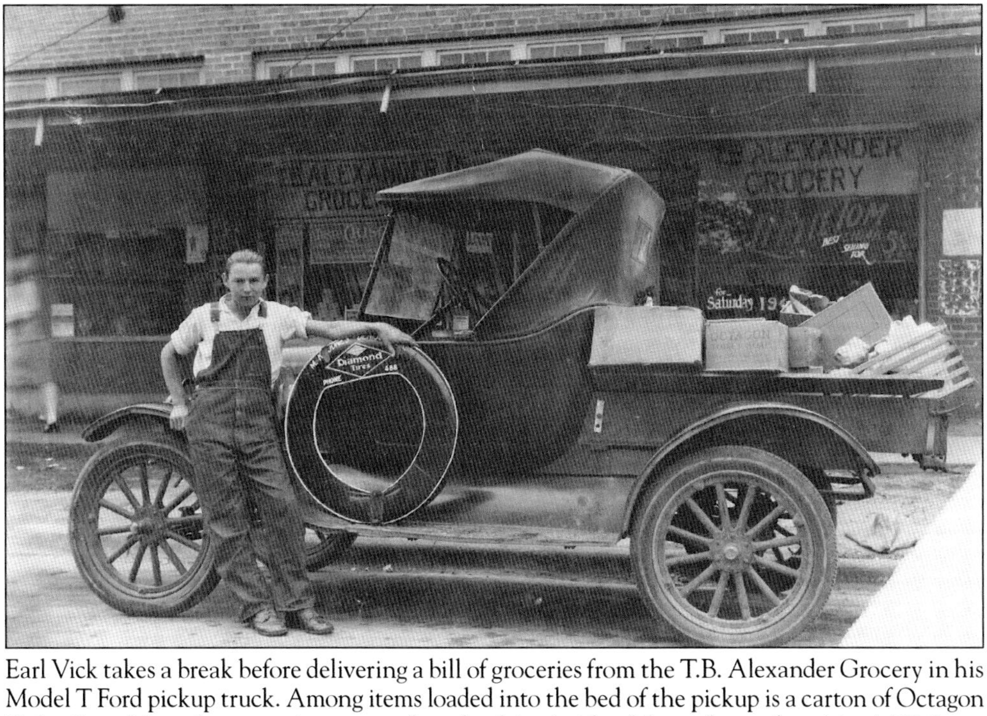

Earl Vick takes a break before delivering a bill of groceries from the T.B. Alexander Grocery in his Model T Ford pickup truck. Among items loaded into the bed of the pickup is a carton of Octagon Toilet Soap. Note the spare tire mounted on the driver's side of the pickup, advertising M.K. Jones Tires and Batteries at 306–308 West Chestnut Street; the firm sold Diamond Tires. (DHH.)

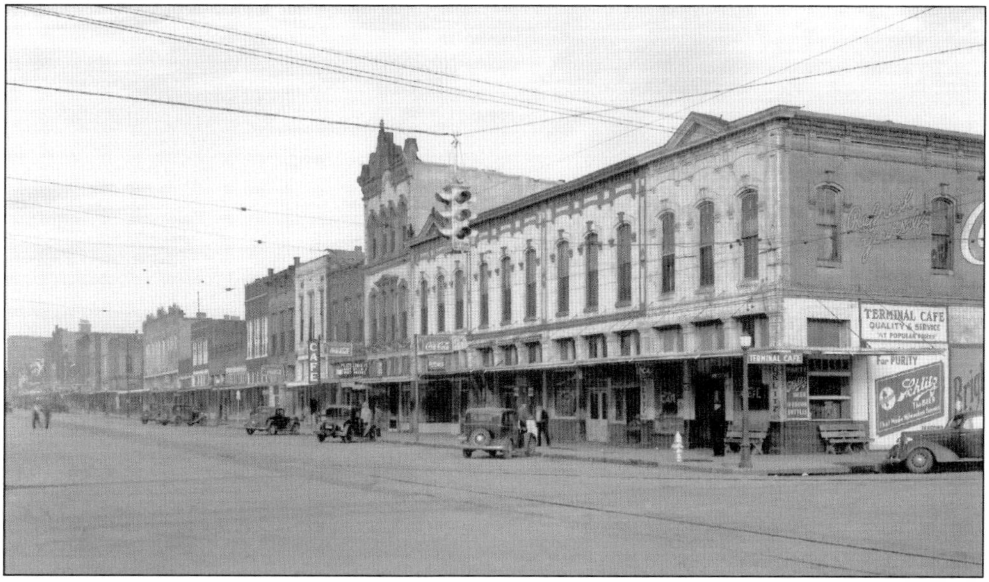

The Terminal Café, seen in this c. 1925 photograph of the northwest corner of Main Street and Houston Avenue, was one block from the Katy Depot. Railroad workers could grab a bite to eat here on a stopover in Denison. Rooms were for rent upstairs in most of the buildings in the block. Coca-Cola and Dr. Pepper soft drinks and Schlitz Beer in brown bottles were advertised on almost every building. (WPL, in MAB.)

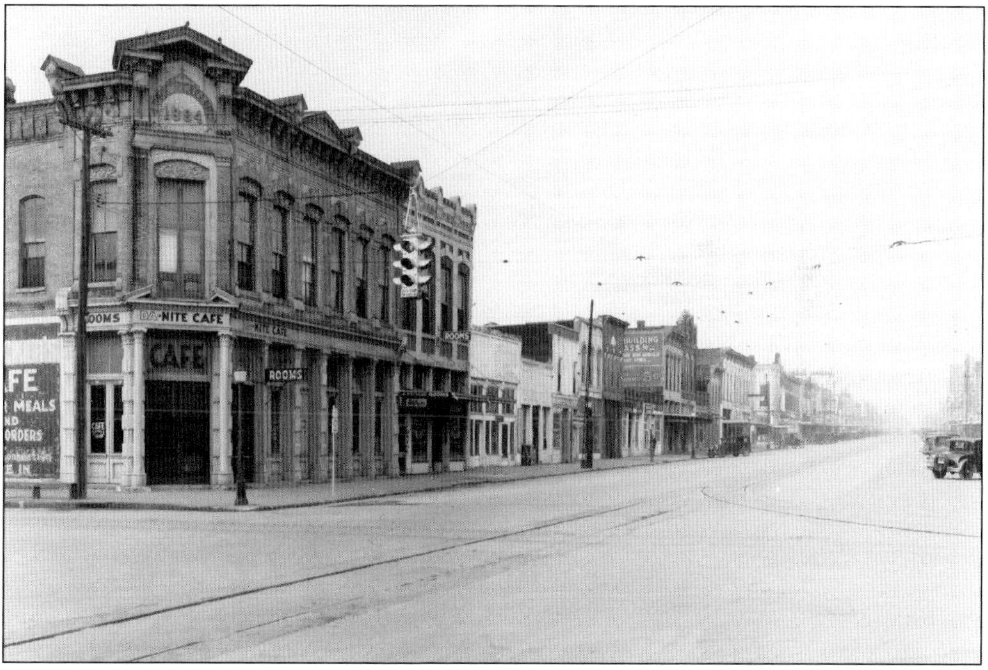

The Lebrecht Building (1884) dominated its corner location at 100–104 West Main Street for more than 70 years. Louis Lebrecht, a two-term mayor who came to Denison in 1873, operated a wholesale tobacco business. His sons inherited the property upon his death in 1902. During the Depression, they established the Da-Nite Café and lived upstairs. Son Walter P. Lebrecht took this photograph looking west around 1934. (WPL, in MAB.)

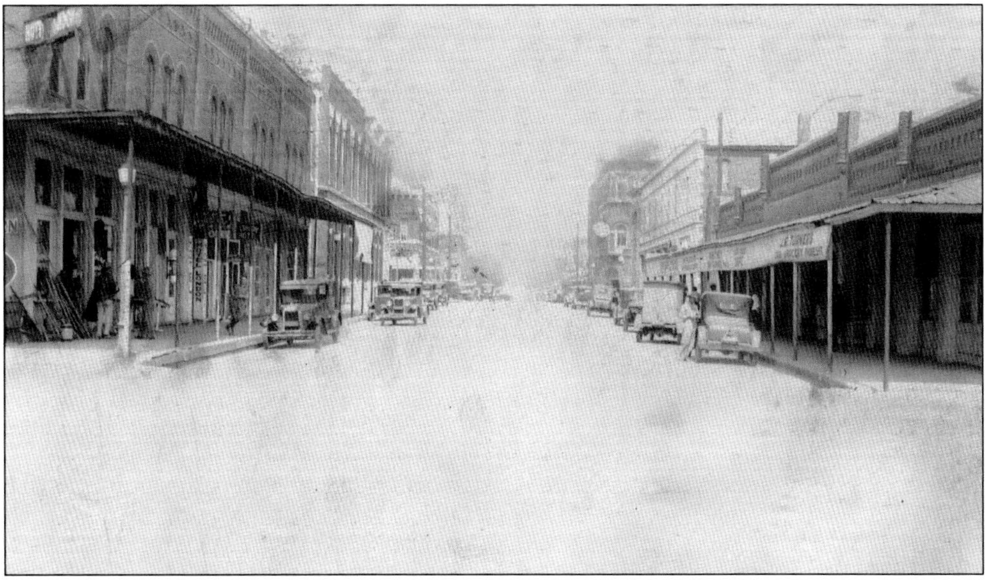

The avenues off Main Street housed modest stores, service businesses, hotels, saloons, and eateries. This photograph looking north through the 100 block of South Rusk Avenue was taken around 1930. On the west (left) side are a hardware store, the Hotel London, a café, Shorty's Barber Shop (with pay phone), and the State National Bank. On the east side are Turner's Grocery, a café, and a dry cleaning establishment. (WPL, in MAB.)

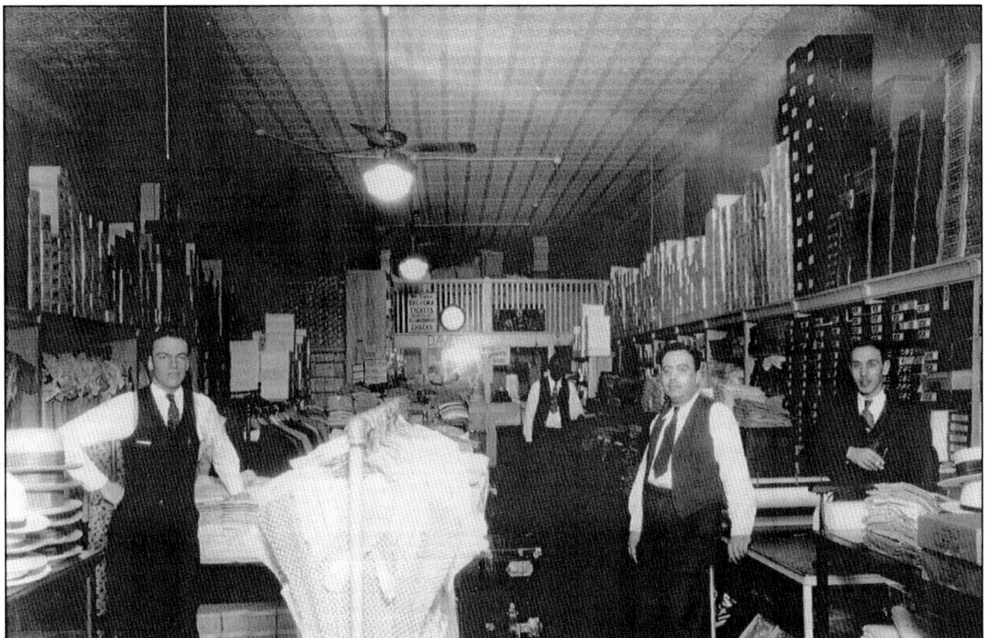

C.J. McManus (1915–1998, at left) founded his first Dad and Lad's store in 1935 at 213 West Main Street. In this photograph, signs in the back proclaim terms of purchase: "We take RFC and CWA tickets and cash. US government checks." The Civil Works Administration (it closed in 1935) and Reconstruction Finance Corporation were New Deal programs. Both men's and women's goods are stacked to the tin ceiling. (DHH.)

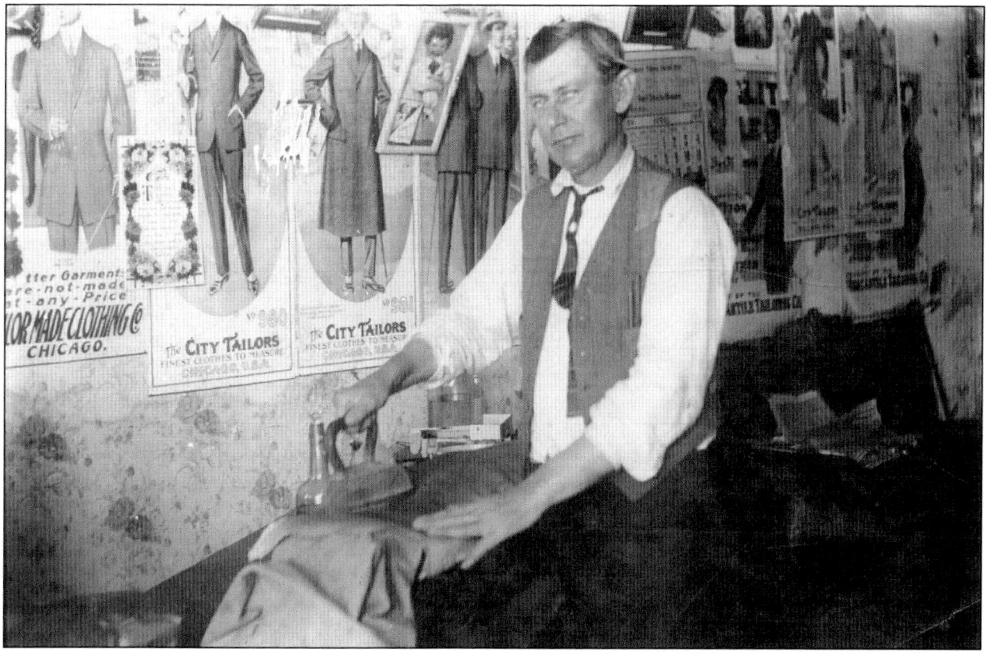

Early in the 20th century, Denison's city directories always listed several merchant tailors. Such tailors stocked cloth, advised customers, took measurements, cut, stitched, and made final adjustments. The skills of tailoring, dry cleaning, pressing, and alterations are closely linked. In the image above, William E. Cross seems to be hard at work pressing a garment in such a tailor's establishment around 1914. Born in Kentucky in 1870, he and several siblings followed his father, a grocer, to Denison before 1900. In the image below, Colie Coe Odle (1882–1964) was a men's tailor in Denison by 1910. Six years later, he owned C.C. Odle's Cleaning and Pressing Shop in the 200 block of West Main Street. Later, he operated Better Dry Cleaning, seen here at 110 North Rusk Avenue. In later decades, he returned to tailoring. His son was Judge Charles F. Odle. (Both, DHH.)

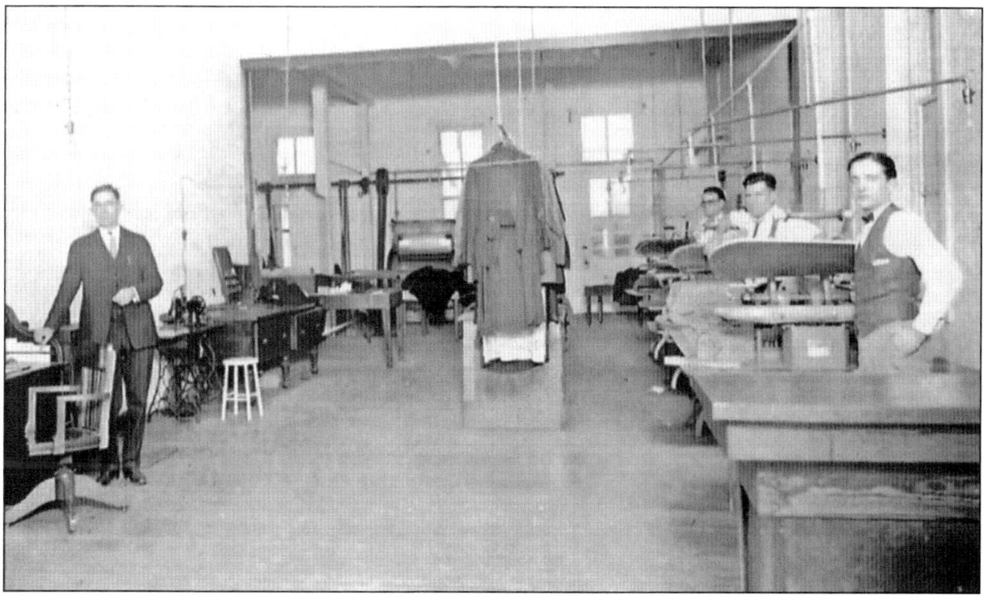

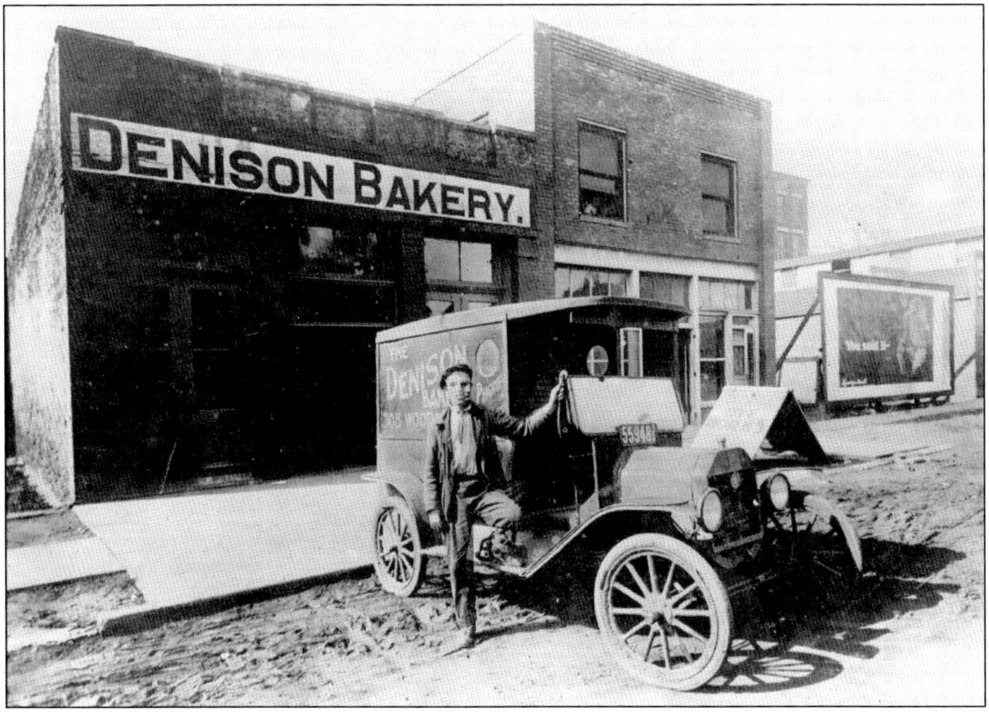

The Krattiger family brought its baking skills from Switzerland to Denison around 1890. Over the next 15 years, father Jacob (1832–1928) and son John (1869–1936) worked at the McDougall Hotel, Hallenbeck's Gate City Bakery, and Carlat's Confectionery. When Hallenbeck's closed after 1900, the son joined another Hallenbeck baker, Constantine "Mack" Christman (1874–1925) in forming the Home Steam Bakery at 610–612 West Main Street. Jacob Krattiger opened his own Denison Bakery (above) at 308 West Woodard Street. Bakeries were profitable in the days before stores stocked sliced bread. By 1915, an aging Jacob had taken Martin Groezinger, a young German butcher, as partner. Around that time, posing with the Home Steam delivery truck (below) are, from left to right, a grocer, Alfred M. Cross; his brother Alonzo E. "Lon" Cross; and his grandsons Willard B. and Forrest Cross. (Above, MAB; below, DHH.)

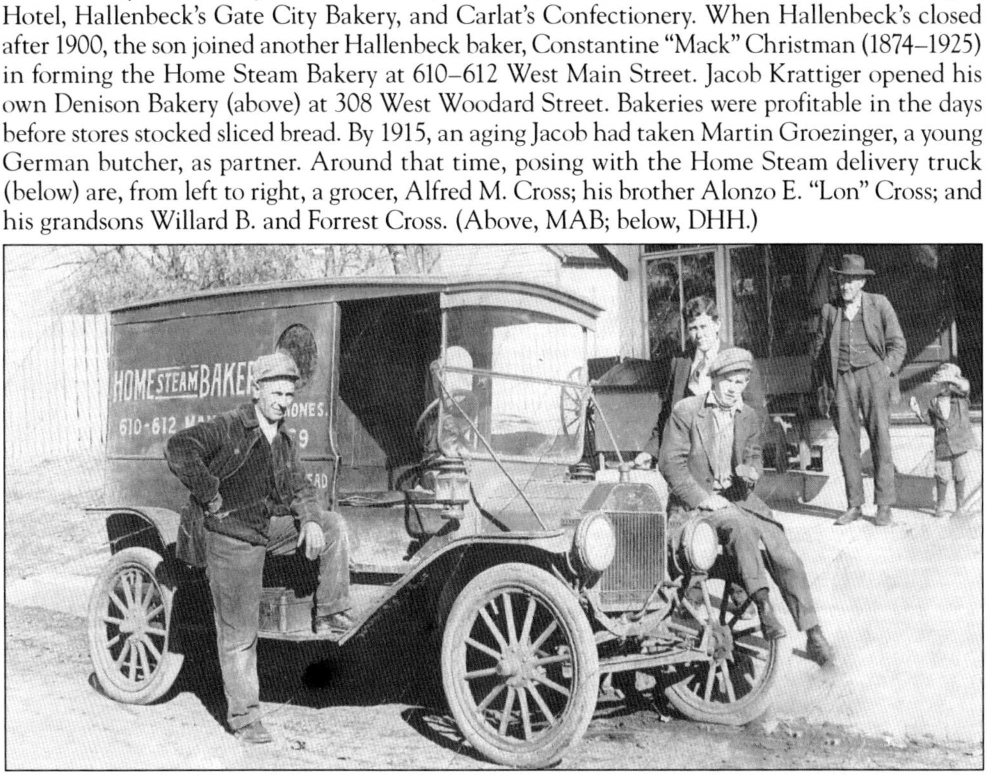

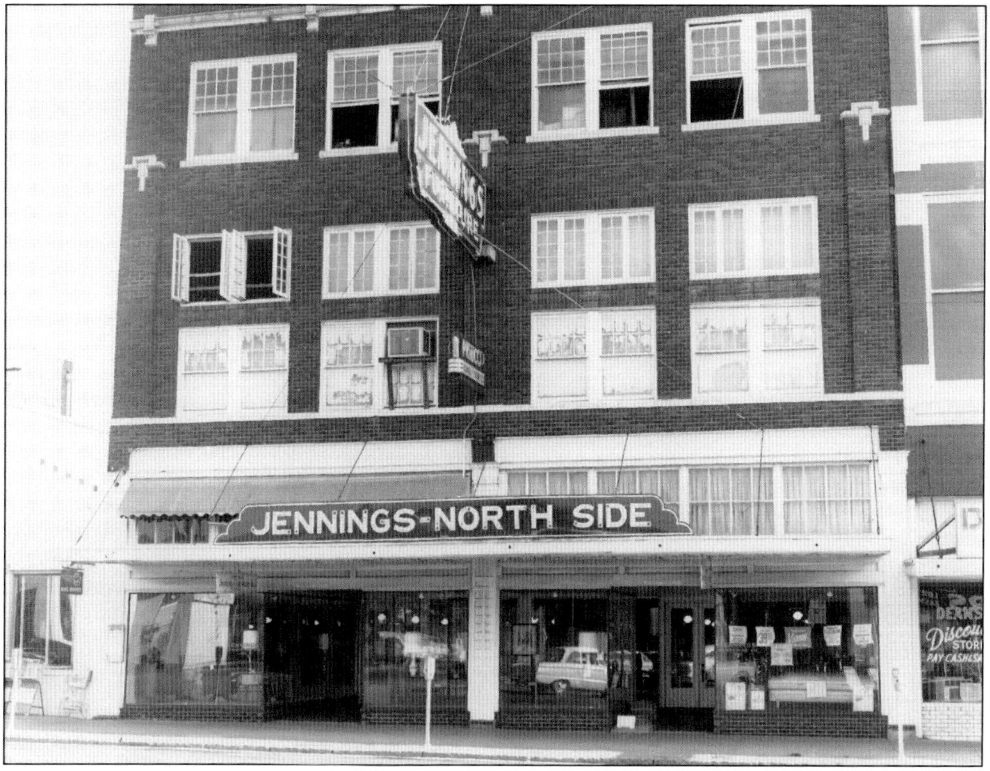

At one time, four furniture stores were owned and operated by members of the Jennings family. Jennings–North Side at 517–519 West Main Street was owned by Frank Jennings in 1953. Noel Jennings and Paul Jennings were managers. At 500 West Main Street was Walter Jennings Furniture, while the 400 block was home to Household Furniture owned by Fred Jennings and Home Furniture, owned by Henry Jennings and Cecil Newland. (MAB.)

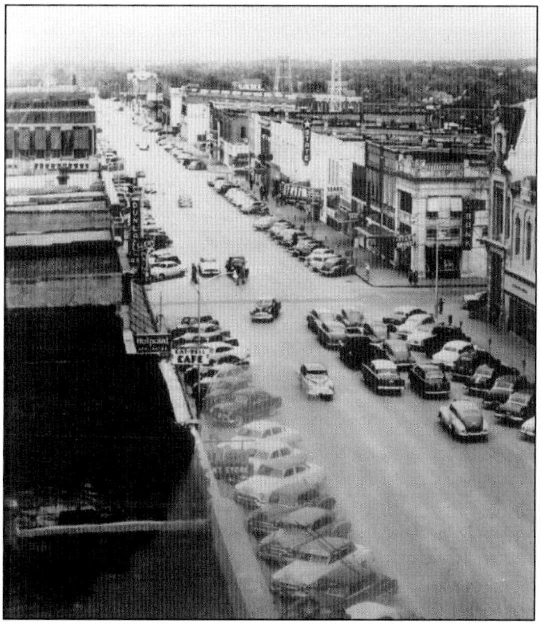

In 1954, just before the Leeper/Security Building (331 West Main Street) was demolished, this photograph was snapped from its top floor. In the 300 block (at left), Dunlap's has succeeded Madden's Department Store, but the Eat-Well Café survives. On right, the 200 block contains Bear Drug; Sears, Roebuck, and Co.'s catalog office; and the State Theater. In the distance stands the Traveler's Hotel was built in 1893 and expanded significantly in 1909. (MAB.)

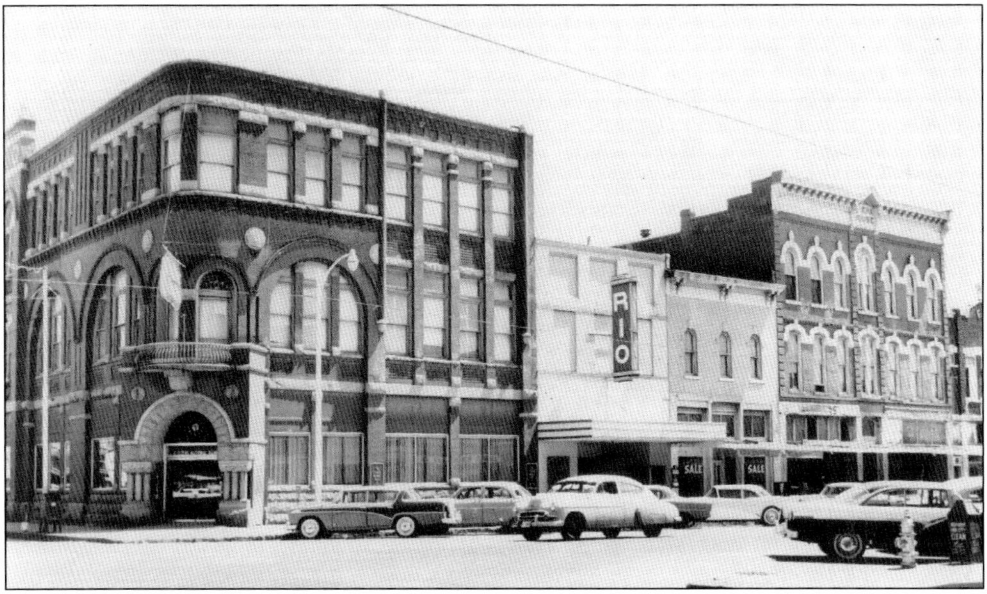

After this photograph was taken in 1959, the north side of Main Street's 200 block was totally transformed. On the far right is the former McDougall Opera House. The Rio Theater, which operated from 1940 to 1956, delighted crowds with "B" westerns. On the left corner is the Citizens National Bank that was founded in 1925. All were razed in 1959 to make way for a new, modern, larger Citizens Bank. (Claud Easterly, in MAB.)

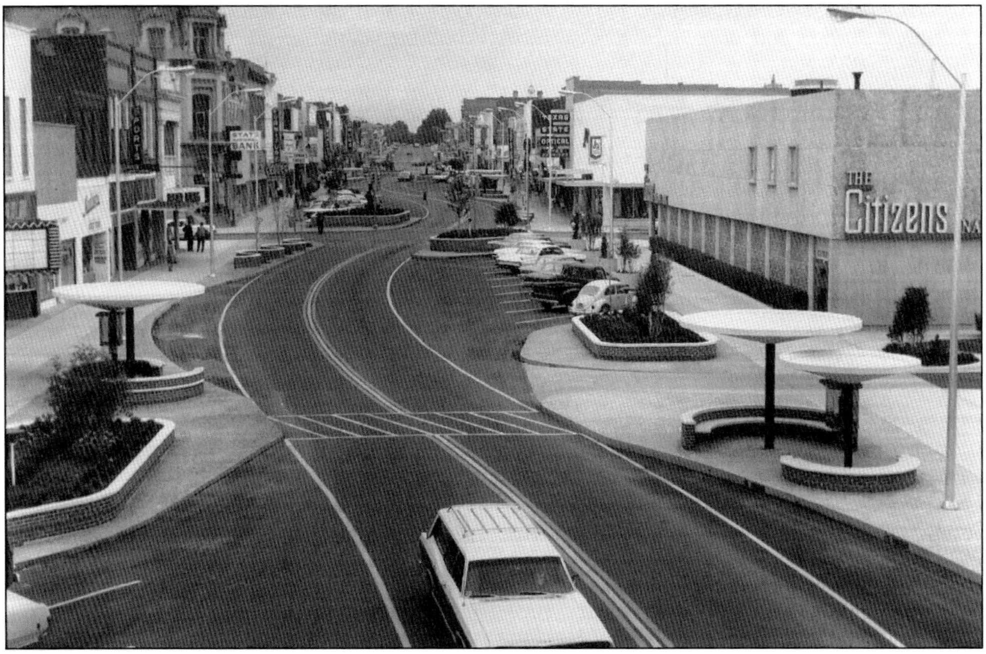

In 1968, Main Street merchants saw their business declining alarmingly. After much research, they raised private funds to replace the straight form of Main Street with a curving, serpentine configuration that slowed traffic. Extensive plantings and seating invited shoppers. Much parking was moved to new lots behind the stores. This photograph, looking west, shows the 1960 Citizens National Bank (231 West Main Street) designed by architect Donald Mayes. (HD.)

Six

WORK, WORK, WORK

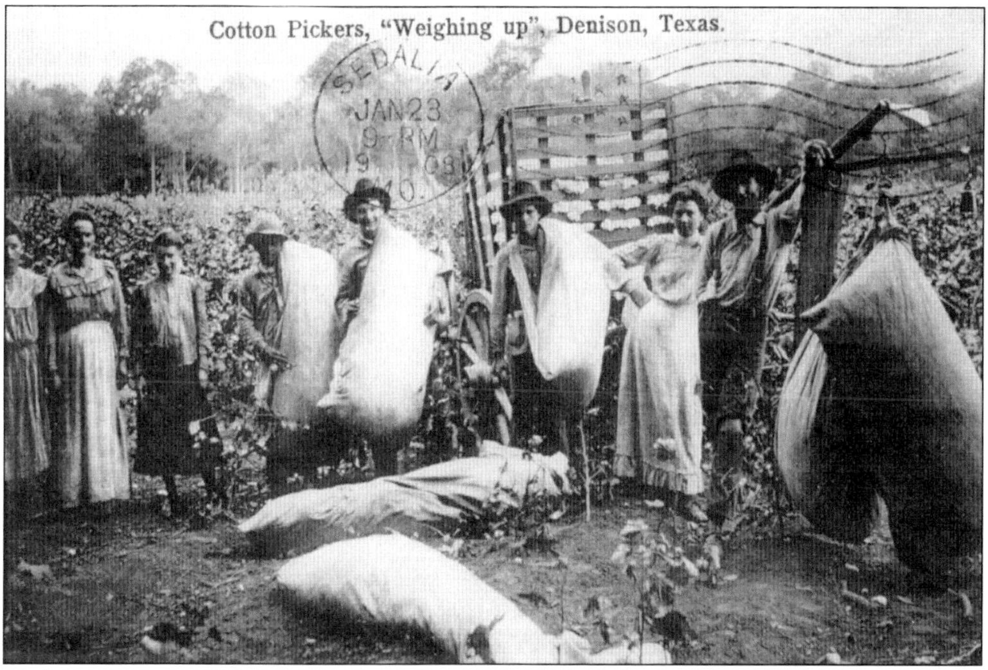

In the early years of the 20th century, cotton was king in the Denison area. Cotton pickers dragged heavy sacks filled with the fluffy white bolls behind them, often with small children in tow. They lined up to weigh their day's pickings and collect the meager pay for their work. The cotton then was hauled by horse and wagon to the cotton gin in Denison. (DHH.)

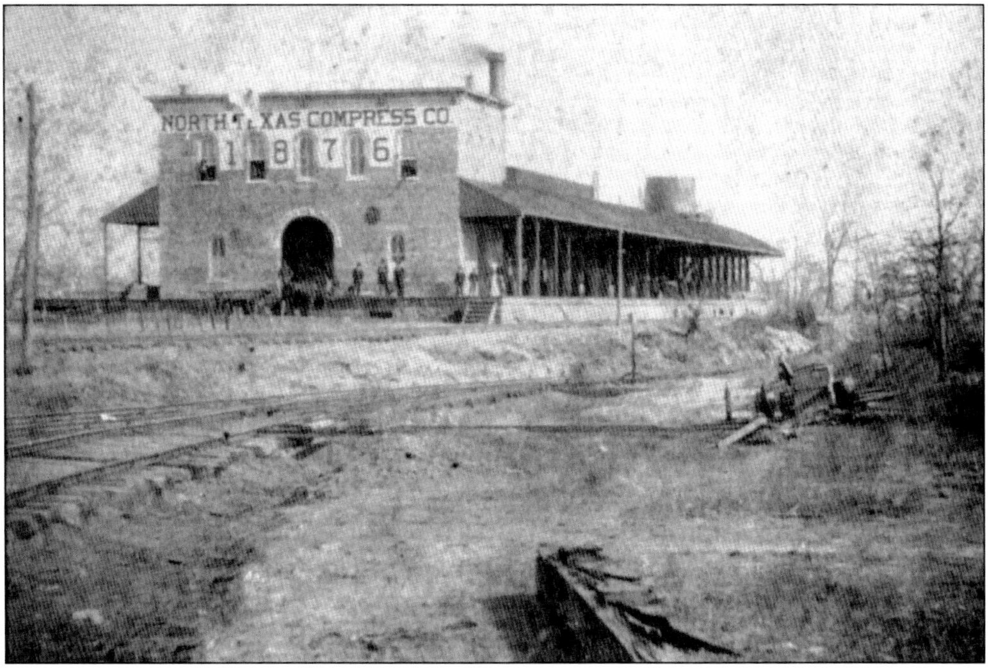

One of Denison's earliest industries, the Denison Cotton Compress (seen in the stereoview above), was operating just north of Union Station in 1876. The company was established by the MKT Railroad in partnership with Patrick H. Tobin, the engineer who brought the first Katy work train to Denison on Christmas eve in 1872. Cotton was hauled by wagon to the compress, where it was processed to be shipped by rail. The firm could turn out 800 bales of cotton a day and had a storage capacity of 5,000 bales. Cotton gin workers (below) are seen stacking cotton that has been baled at the compress, which was rated as one of the finest in the South. Cotton was stored for both growers and buyers. The compress operated until well into the 1940s. (Both, DHH.)

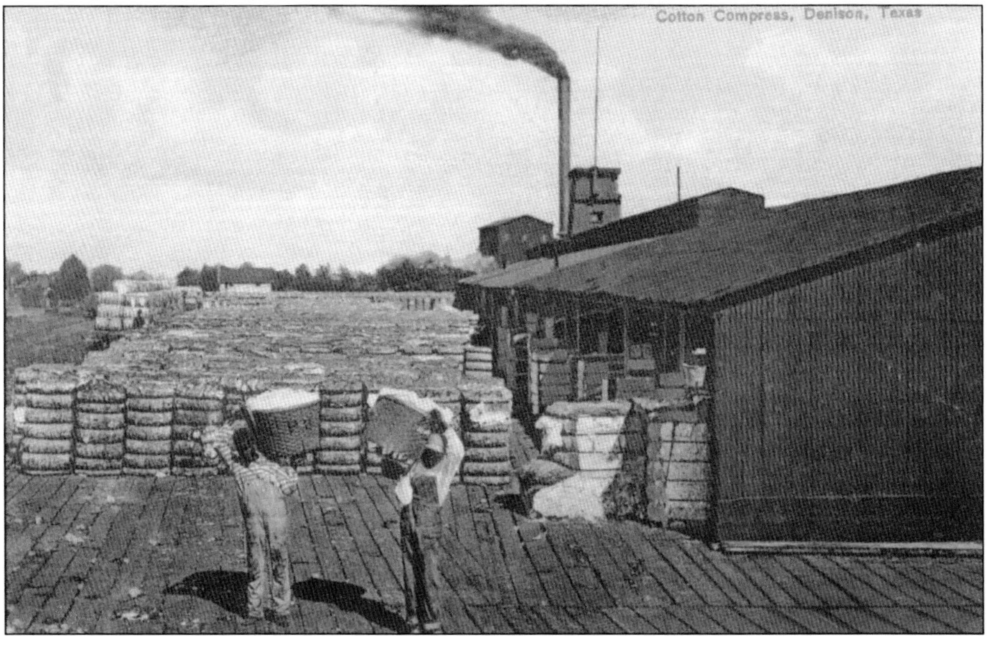

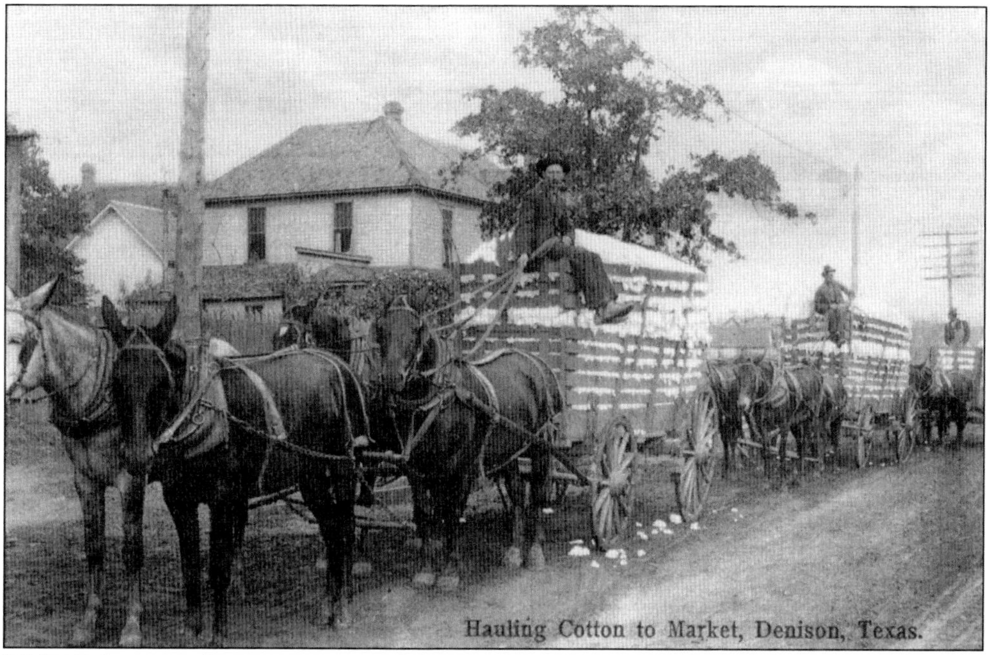

With all the cotton being grown around Denison, getting it to market was accomplished by piling it high aboard horse-drawn wagons. Around 1908, a caravan of three wagons brought a day's worth of cotton picking to market in Denison. With the Denison Cotton Compress located just north of the Union Station, the cotton probably was delivered directly to the compress to be shipped via the railroad. (DHH.)

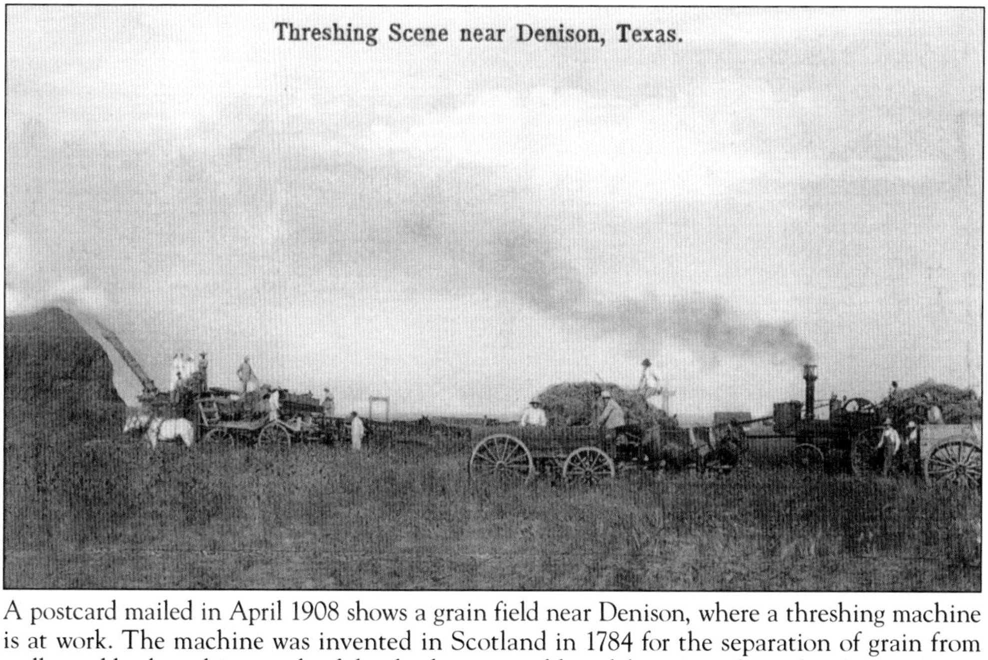

A postcard mailed in April 1908 shows a grain field near Denison, where a threshing machine is at work. The machine was invented in Scotland in 1784 for the separation of grain from stalks and husks, taking much of the drudgery out of farm labor. A working thresher used near Denison in the late 1890s is part of the farm equipment collection at Grayson County Frontier Village. (MAB.)

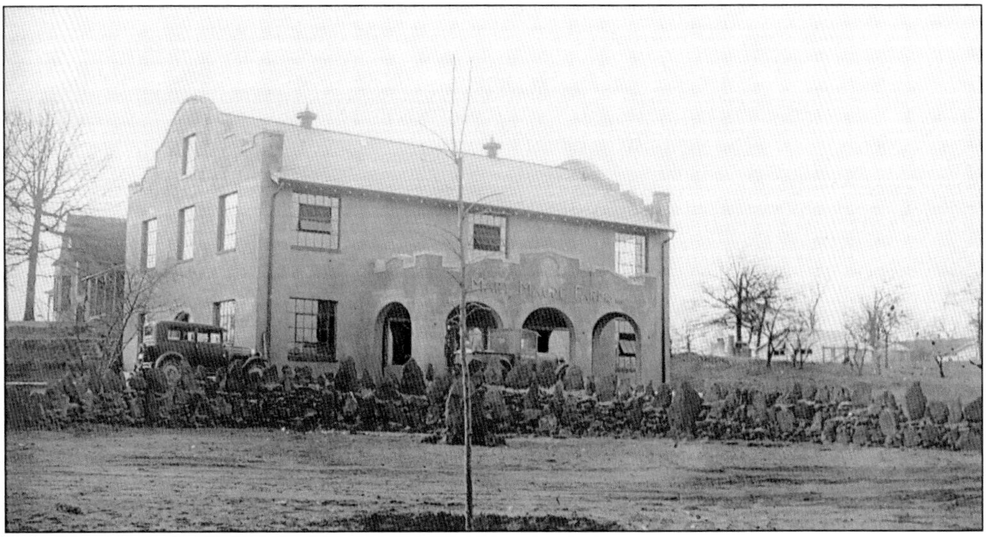

Merry Maud Farm was located on South Armstrong Avenue and was not actually a farm. The two-story building was inserted into a high embankment in the back. The business sold chickens from George Knaur's Chicken Farm on Bells Highway to local residents. In the 1930s and 1940s, the building became Tropical Gardens, a nightclub where crowds came to hear popular musical groups perform. (DHH.)

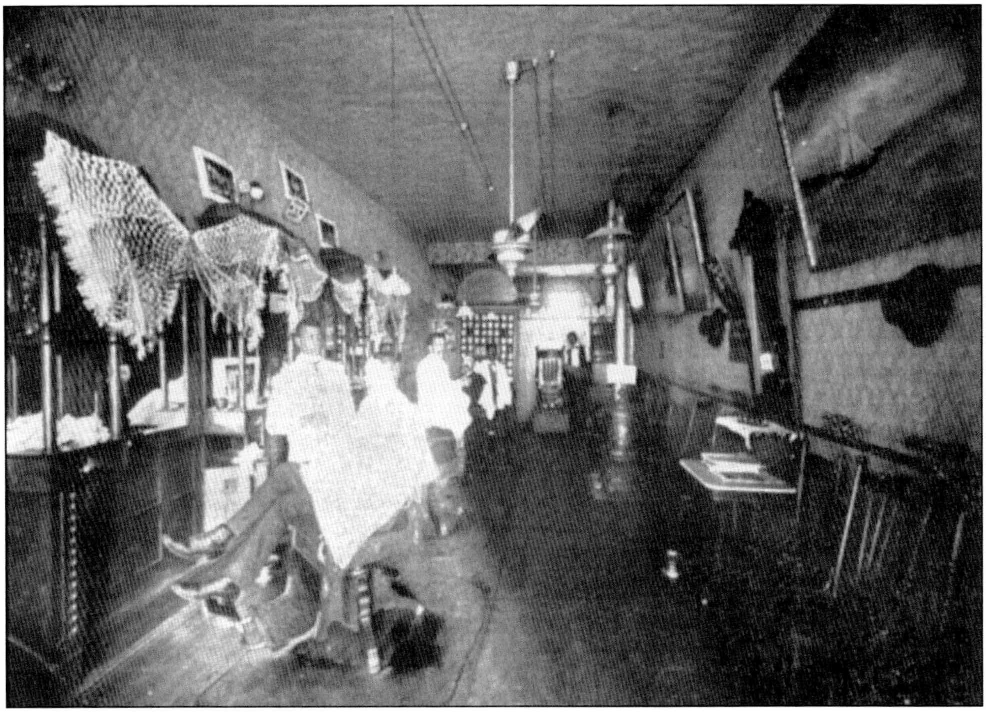

Barbershops and shaving parlors were legion in Denison's early days when cowboys, train crews, and travelers arrived in town badly in need of shaves, haircuts, and hot baths. Beginning around 1895, Edward D. Gentry operated his elegant Palace Barber Shop at 109 East Main Street, seen here about 1909. One of several African American barbers working downtown, he died before 1917, when his widow was matron at the Katy Depot. (IndDen.)

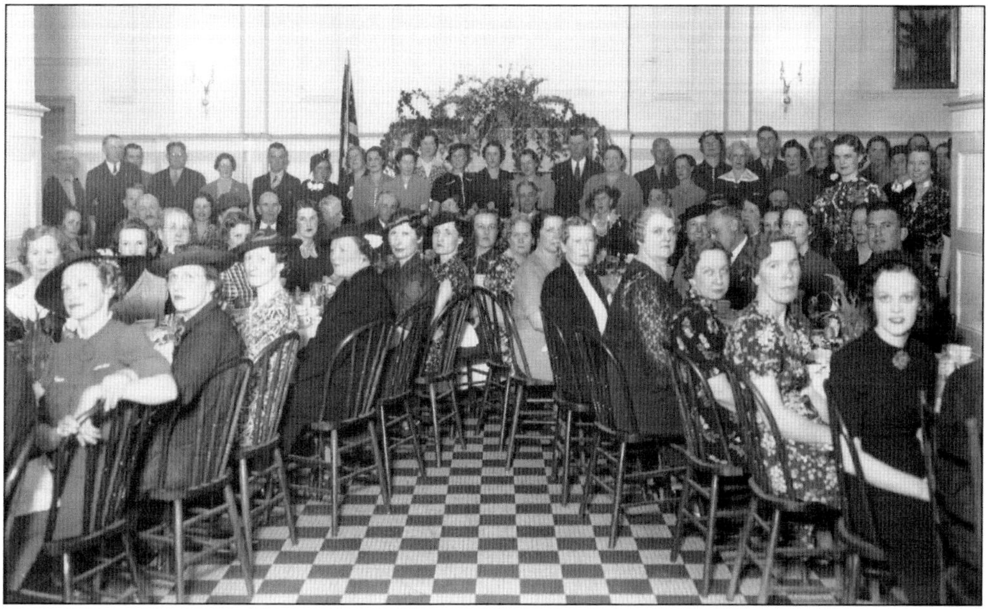

Between 1886 and 1918, Denison had two telephone companies ("old phone" and "new phone"). By 1901, the Southwestern Bell Telephone Company was advertising its service in the *Denison Herald*. In 1923, Southwestern Bell bought the exchange. The number of phones grew from a few hundred in the 1920s to nearly 16,000 in 1972. Here, Denison's Southwestern Bell employees enjoy a dinner in the ballroom of the Hotel Denison. (HD.)

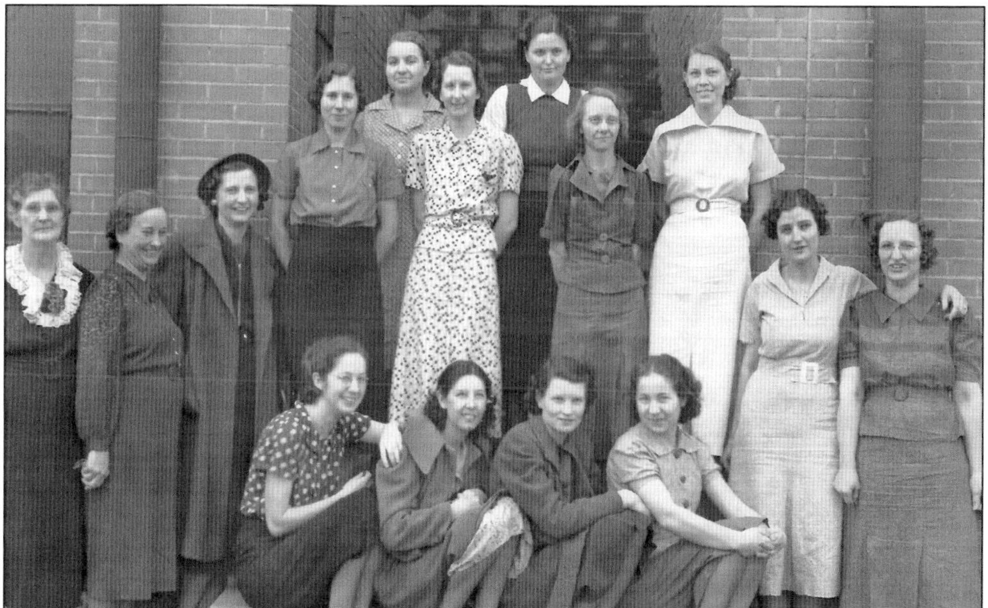

The Denison Peanut Company was founded in 1922 and later became Southern Style Nuts. Located at the north end of the old concrete viaduct, the plant in 1938 was shelling peanuts and shelling and polishing pecans. George Morgan was an early manager. Here, workers in the Peanut Department stand on the plant's steps on February 15, 1938. Second from right is Ouida Cordell McGlothlin. (Betty Ferguson Johnson.)

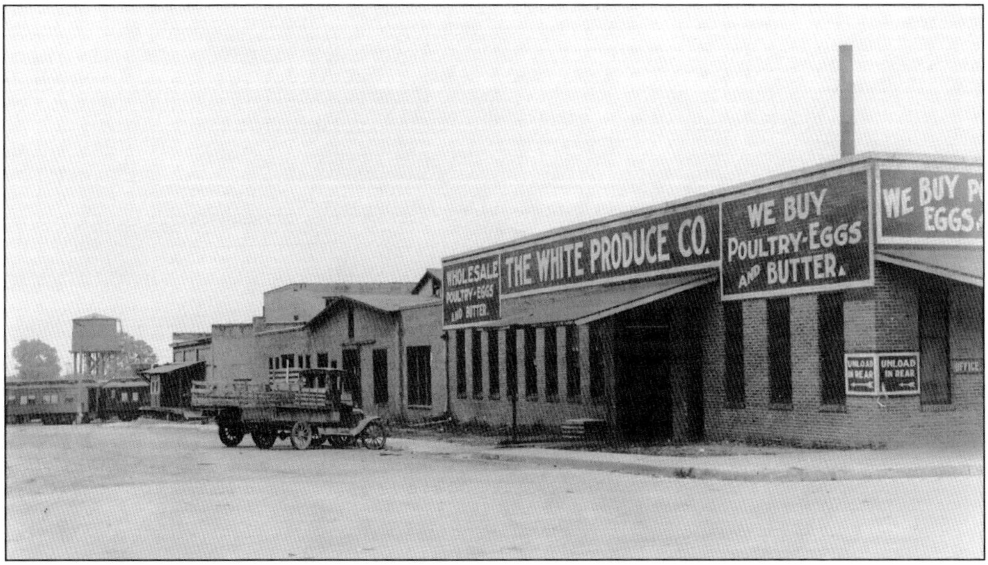

Near the railroad tracks, along North Houston Avenue, arose a number of businesses based on the agricultural riches of the land around Denison. At the corner of East Gandy Street stood White Produce Company, which was built in 1906 and operated until 1925 by William Richard White Sr. (1867–1951). Then this structure hosted several overall manufacturers: Barrow-Johnson (1925), Cowden (1929), Patterson (1933), and, memorably, Levi Strauss and Company (1949–1966). (MAB.)

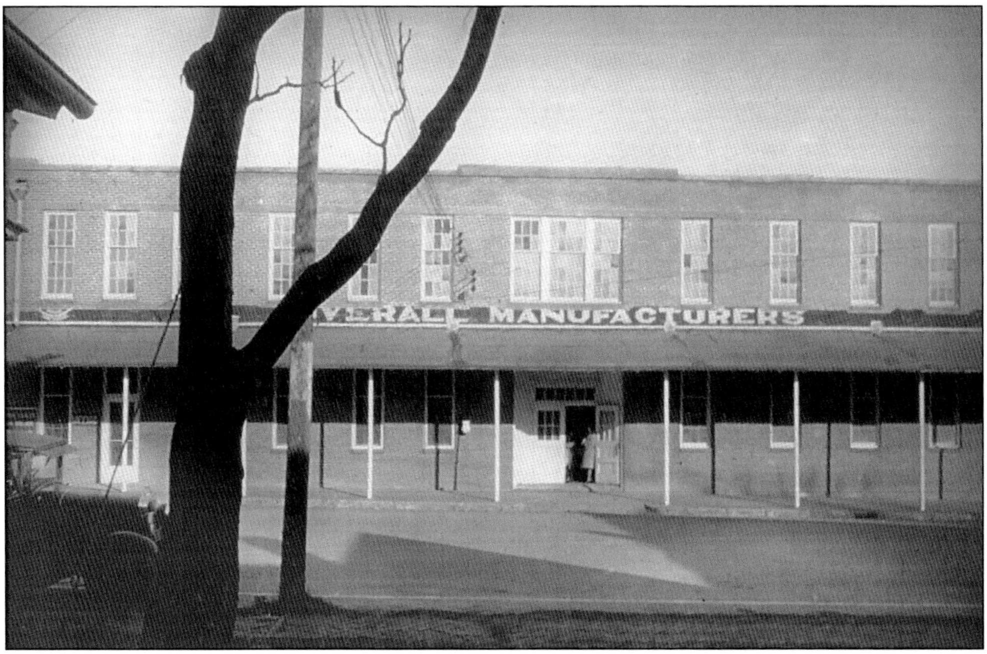

Patterson Manufacturing Company developed its plant at 210–212 North Houston Avenue into a modern and efficient organization by 1938. The firm manufactured Patco-brand overalls and dungarees for men and women and Farmerette suits for women and children. Patterson employed as many as 450 employees, including a night shift. Annual payroll was about $100,000 in 1938. When Levi Strauss came to town in 1949, it leased the vacant building. (MAB.)

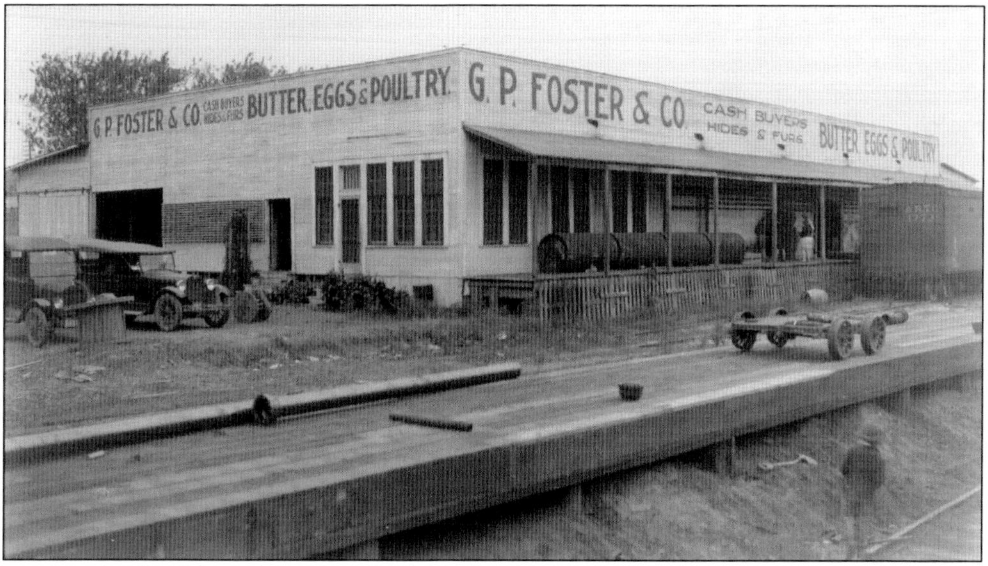

Many carloads of dressed and live poultry were shipped to market in 1927 by the G.P. Foster Company from its warehouse at 129 East Morton Street. By 1934, Foster Pecan Company and the Crescent, a wholesale produce company, occupied the location. Subsequently, by 1938, Denison Poultry and Egg Company, owned by John Raymond Clymer Sr., was in full operation there. (WPL, in MAB.)

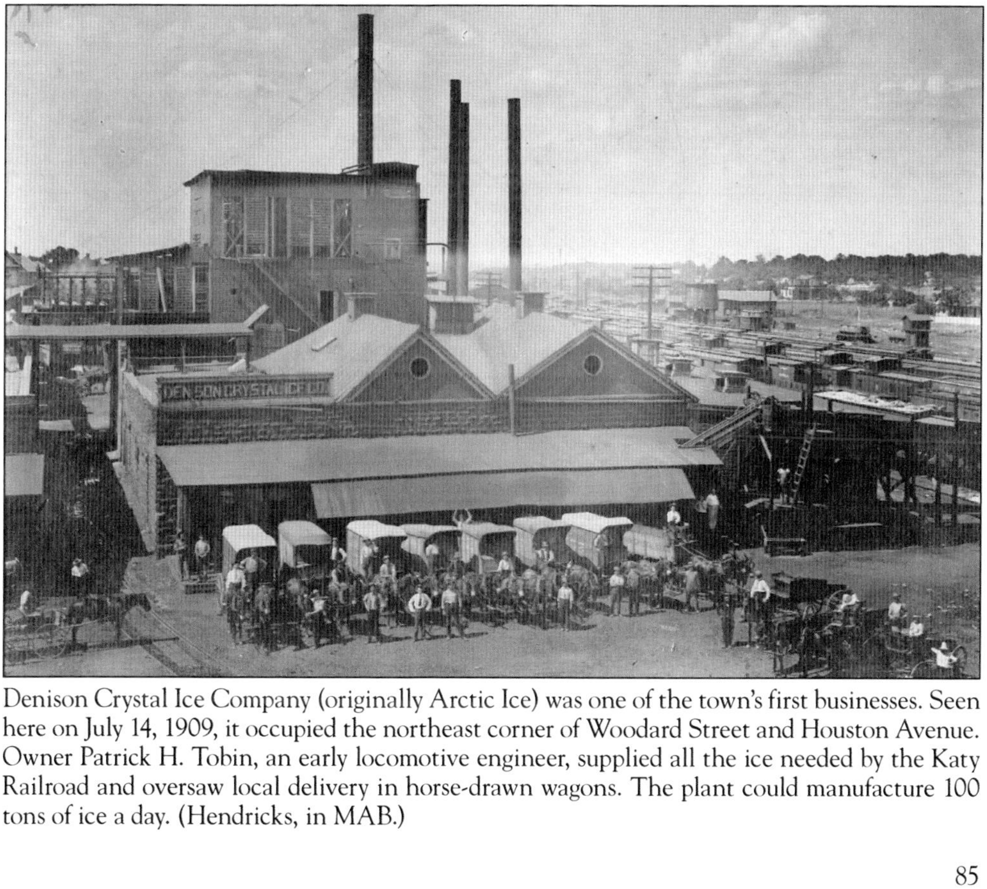
Denison Crystal Ice Company (originally Arctic Ice) was one of the town's first businesses. Seen here on July 14, 1909, it occupied the northeast corner of Woodard Street and Houston Avenue. Owner Patrick H. Tobin, an early locomotive engineer, supplied all the ice needed by the Katy Railroad and oversaw local delivery in horse-drawn wagons. The plant could manufacture 100 tons of ice a day. (Hendricks, in MAB.)

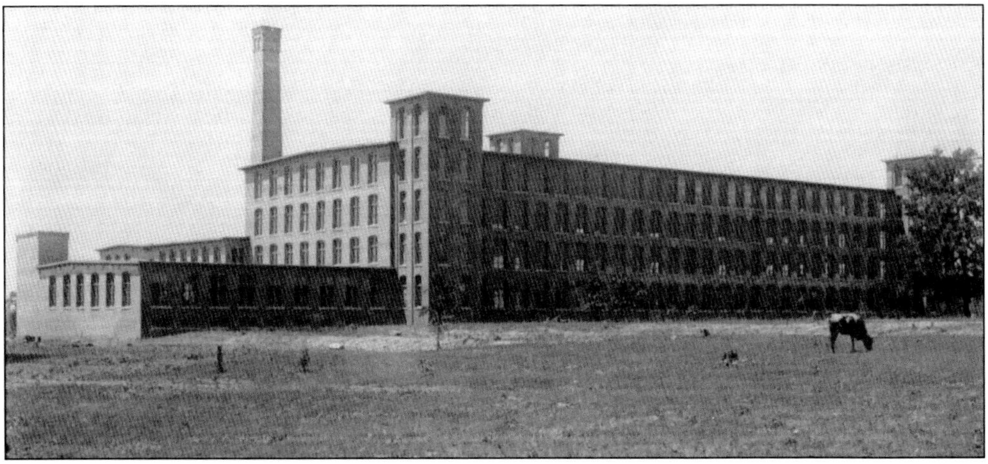

The Denison Cotton Mill, erected in 1890 at 701 West Rice Street, was one of the largest buildings in Texas and the largest cotton mill west of the Mississippi. W.B. Munson Sr. and brother J.T. purchased the mill in 1905. W.B. Munson Jr. became manager in 1912 and was president when his father died. When Munson Jr. died in 1936, his sister Eloise Munson took over. In 1955, W.B. Munson III became president, serving as long as the mill operated. The workforce, varying from 300 to 400 people, had their homes around the mill in South Denison. The area, served by Golden Rule Elementary School, was annexed by Denison in the late 1950s. The mill fell on hard times and closed in 1977. In 1981, the four-story building burned to the ground. (Above, AWGC; below, HD.)

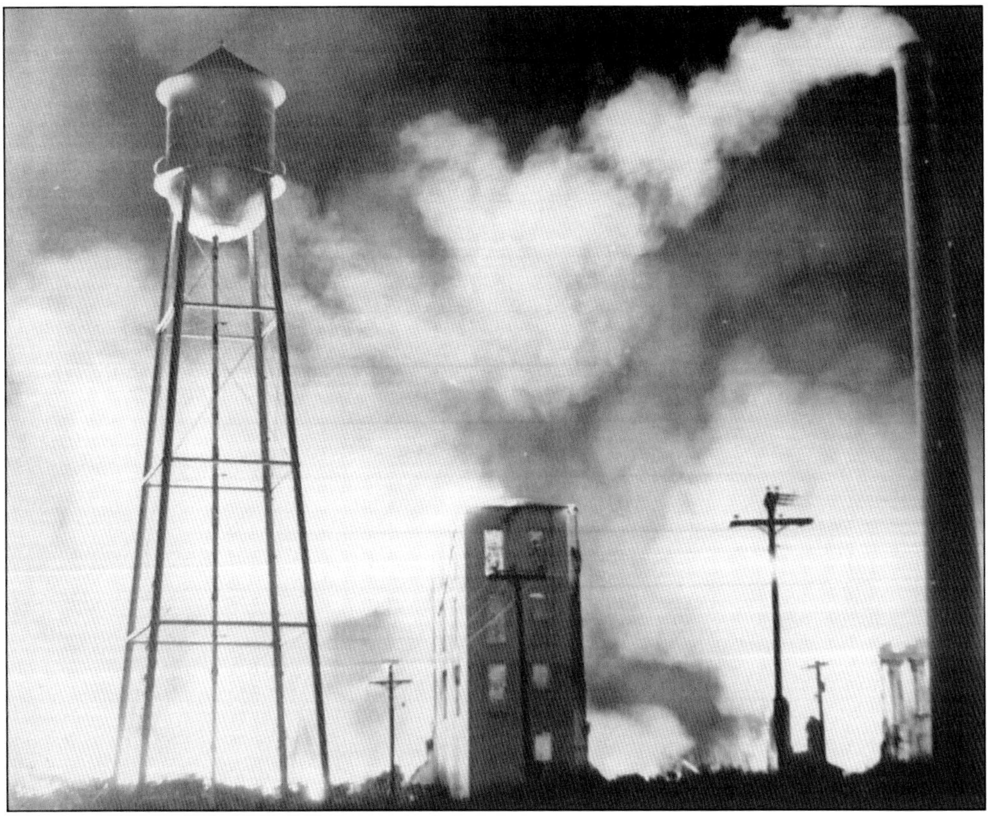

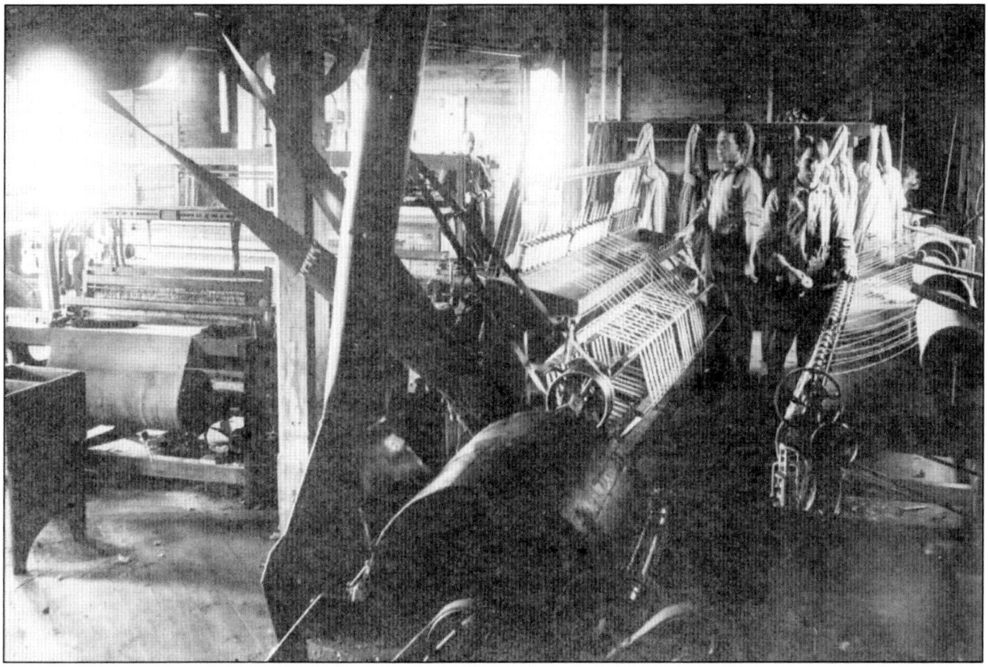

In the 1890s, residents of the community known as the Cotton Mill District, on the south edge of Denison, began toiling over machines at the Denison Cotton Mill. The plant produced cotton duck and other materials. During World War II, after receiving the Army-Navy "E" rating, it provided cotton duck for the American armed forces. The mill closed in 1977. (HD.)

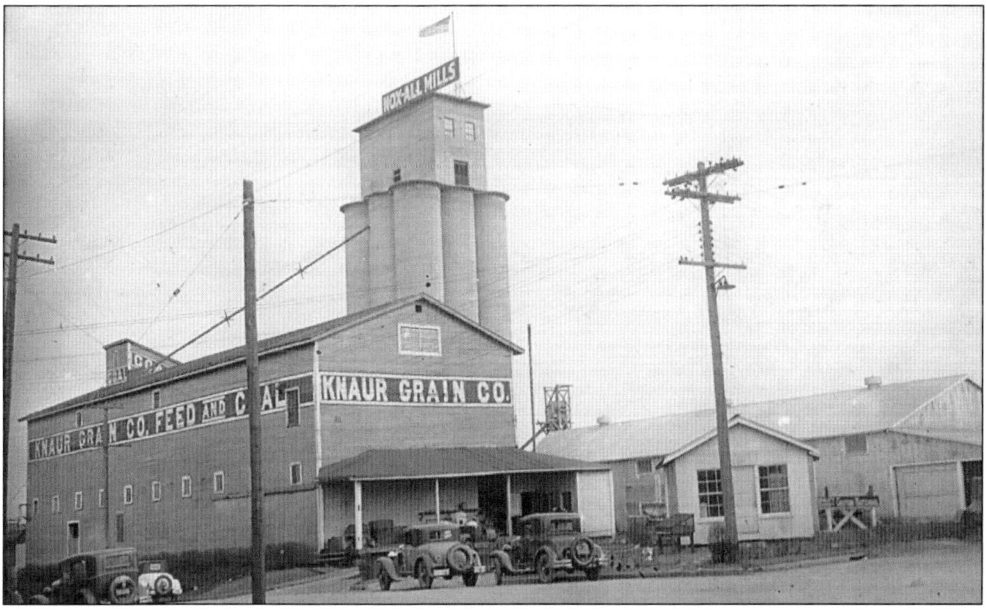

Knaur Grain Company was located on the south side of Crawford Street between Houston and Austin Avenues. The grain elevator and structure housing operations, seen here around 1930, were constructed in 1902. Until 1946, the firm was owned by John Simon Knaur (1858–1933) and his son George C. Knaur (1890–1946). Then Vit-a-Way Company owned it for 33 years. The grain elevator remains an impressive structure today. (DHH.)

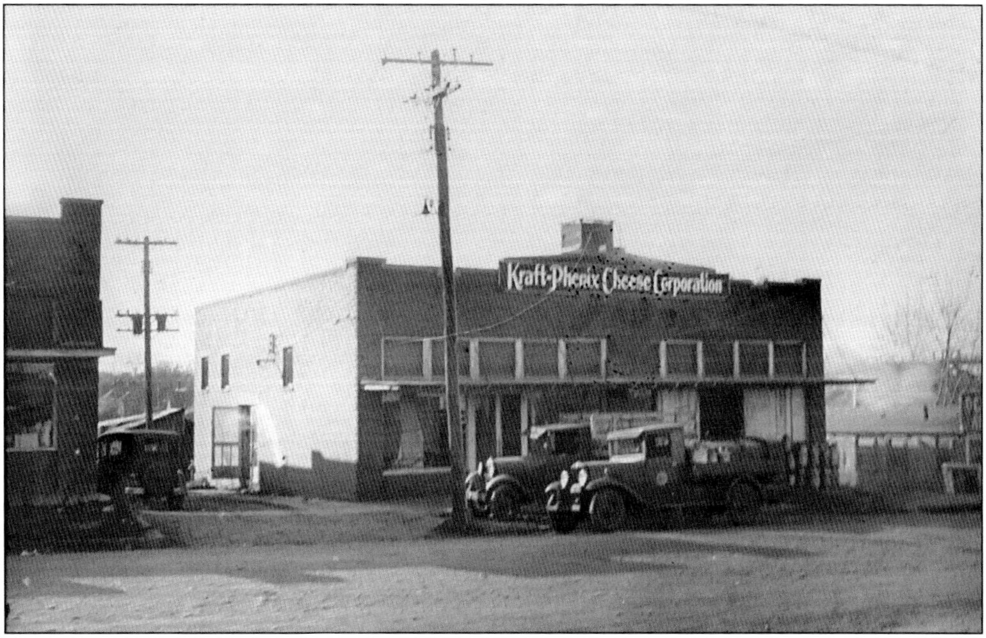

The Kraft-Phenix cheese and mayonnaise factory was located in three redbrick buildings joined into one at 1406 West Washington Street (above). The factory manufactured processed cheese for national distribution. It became one of the country's most modern cheese plants, producing approximately 27 million pounds of cheese annually. In 1929, the operation of 28 plants in eight states, in addition to the major local plant, was directed from the Southwest Division Headquarters in Denison. Arthur Riddle was division manager. In the 1944 picture below, a group is seen in the maintenance area. Jesse W. Neff, a photographer with the US Army Corps of Engineers, took the photograph. In the late 1940s, the federal government offered Kraft a war-surplus plant in Garland, Texas, that was larger and better suited to the operation, so Kraft moved there. (Above, DHH; below, Betty Ferguson Johnson.)

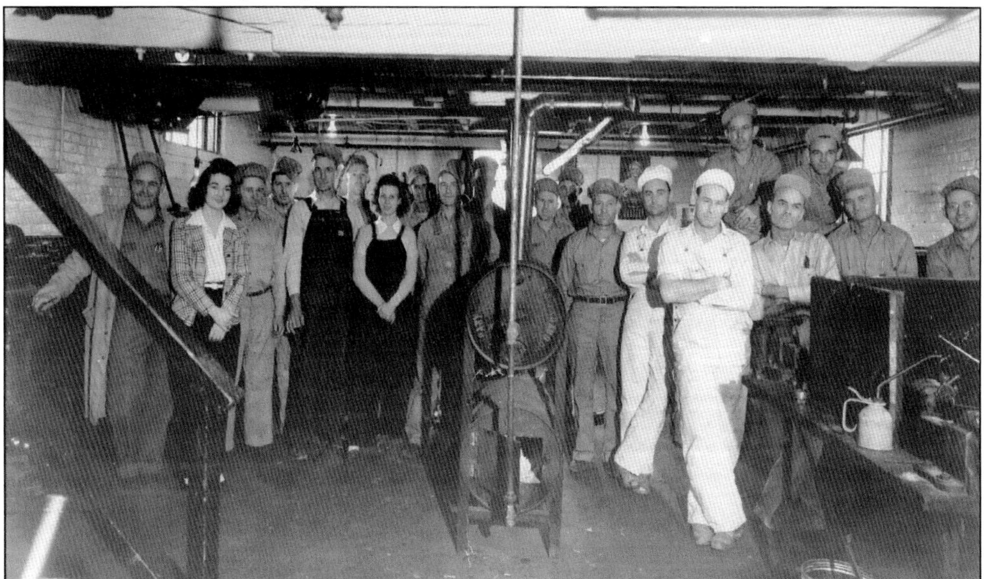

Seven

What Fun It Was

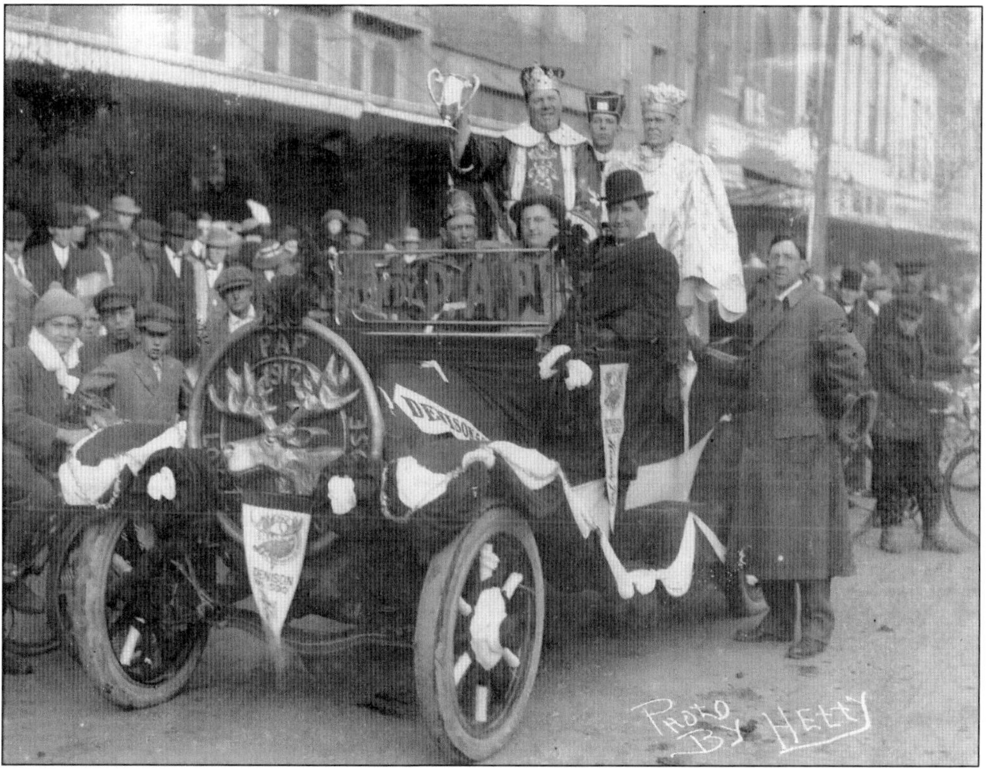

In 1912, members of the Loyal Order of Moose decorated their car and their bodies and won a trophy in a Denison parade. Recently organized, Denison Lodge No. 530 touted the national organization's motto, "PAP: Purity, Aid, and Progress." This image was taken by Hetty Green, a local photographer who was also a baseball pitcher. In March 1913, he left town to begin training with an Indianapolis team. (MAB.)

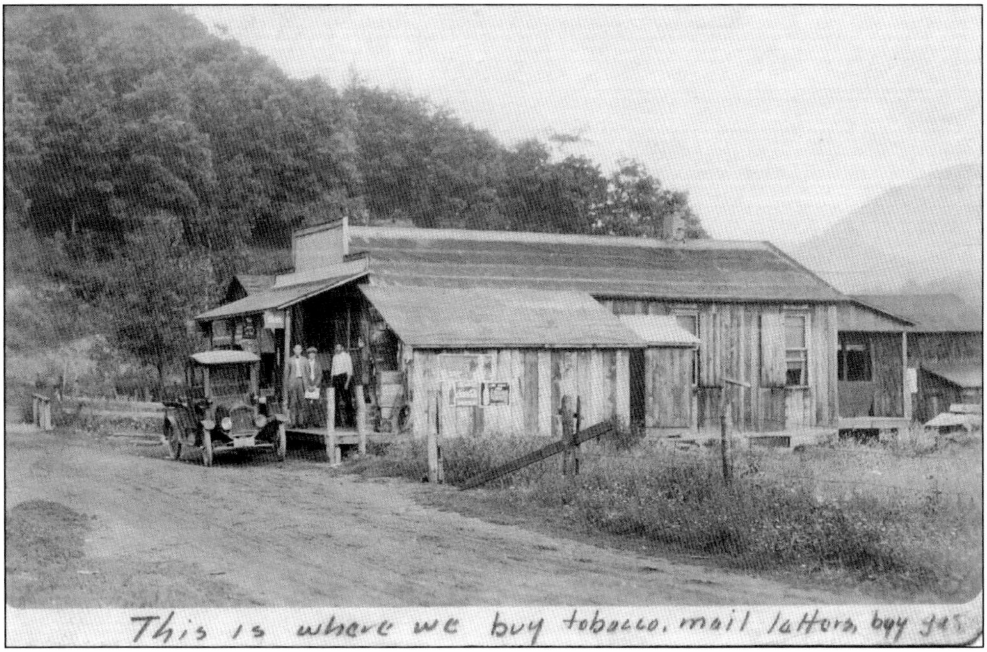

An early-day camp store of sorts made gun shells available for hunters in the Denison area. On December 2, 1922, a visiting hunter bagged an eight-point buck with shells purchased here. A group of 10 hunters made camp nearby but bagged only two deer before breaking camp; they had heard that snow was predicted. The location of the camp store is unknown. (MAB.)

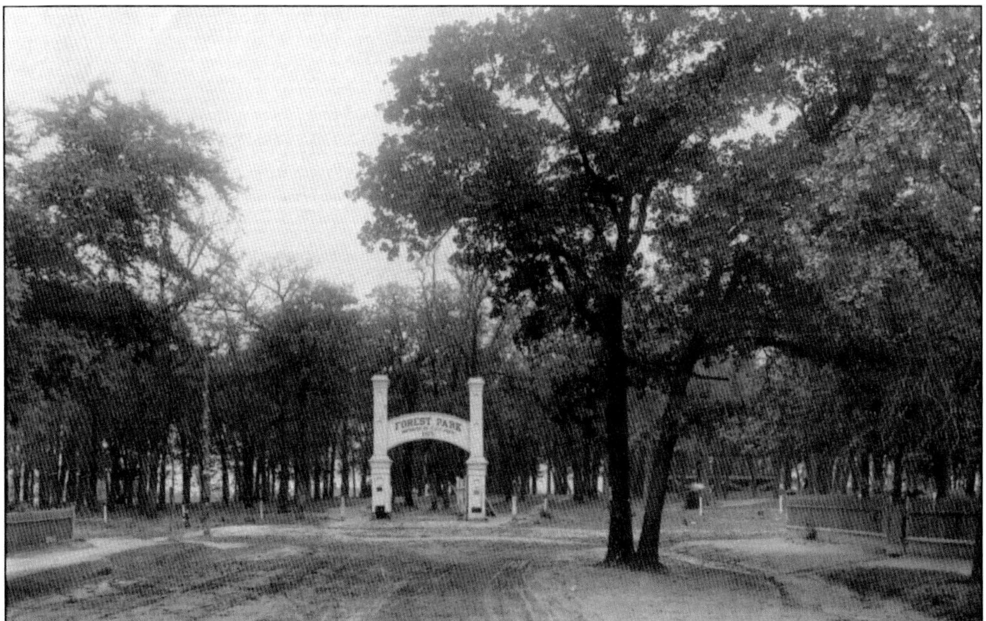

A one-dollar investment in 1882 was the best ever made by the City of Denison. On June 8 of that year, the Denison Town Company deeded four blocks in the center of Denison to the city for a park. Bounded by Crawford and Morgan Streets and Fannin and Rusk Avenues, the area always has been known as Forest Park. (AWGC.)

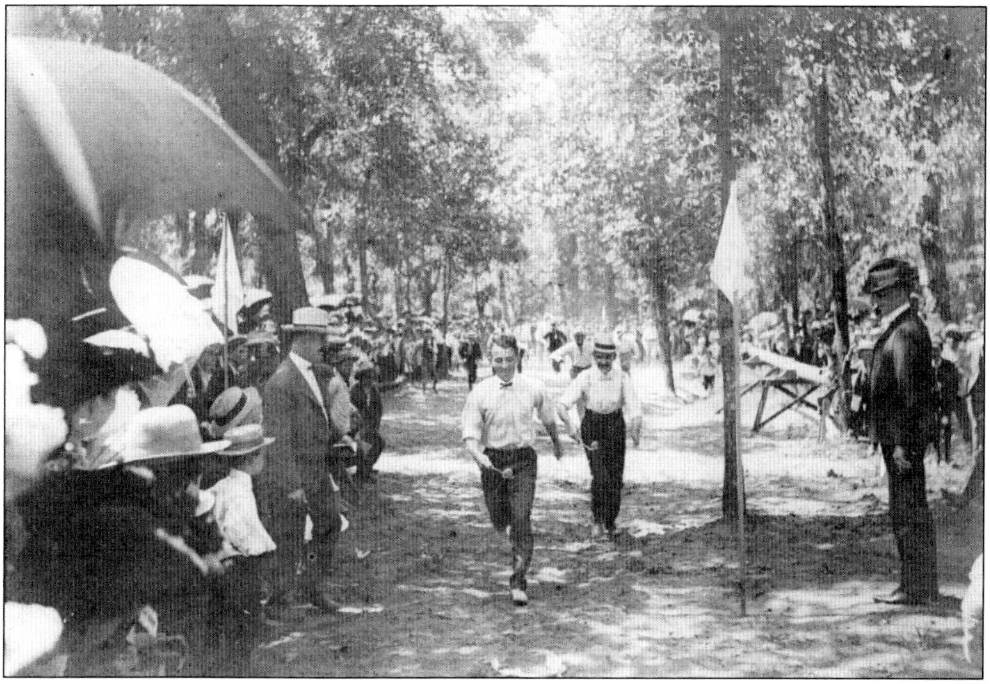

The Fourth of July was a time for fun and frolic in Denison's early days, just as it is today. Here local people are running in a spoon race in Forest Park. Anyone who dropped his egg was disqualified. The crowd egged on its favorites with cheers and jeers. The exact year is unknown but, judging from clothing and the dense trees, appears to be the 1870s or 1880s. (HD.)

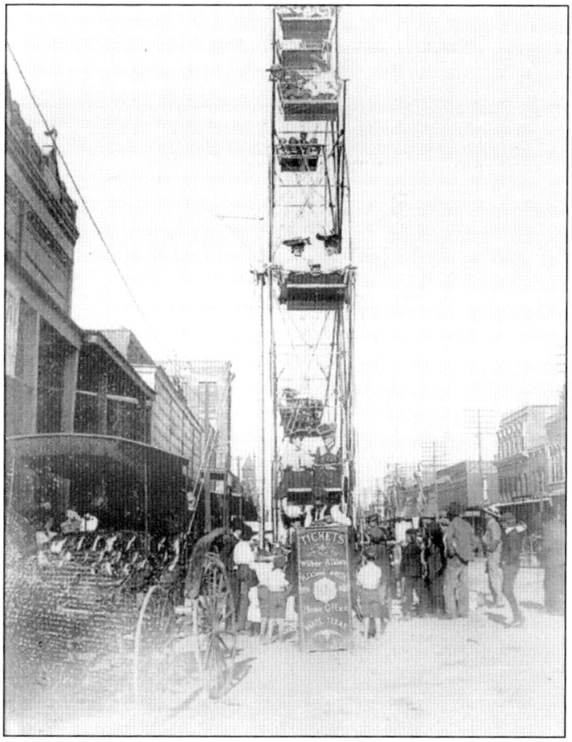

The carnival came to town in 1904 and set up in the 400 block of West Main Street. Children and adults who stood in line to ride the Ferris wheel were delighted. Wilbur Atkins of Paris, Texas, owned the high-flying pleasure wheel seen in this view looking east. The wheel was conveniently situated right in front of a Denison confectionery, in case riding the wheel made patrons hungry. (BCT.)

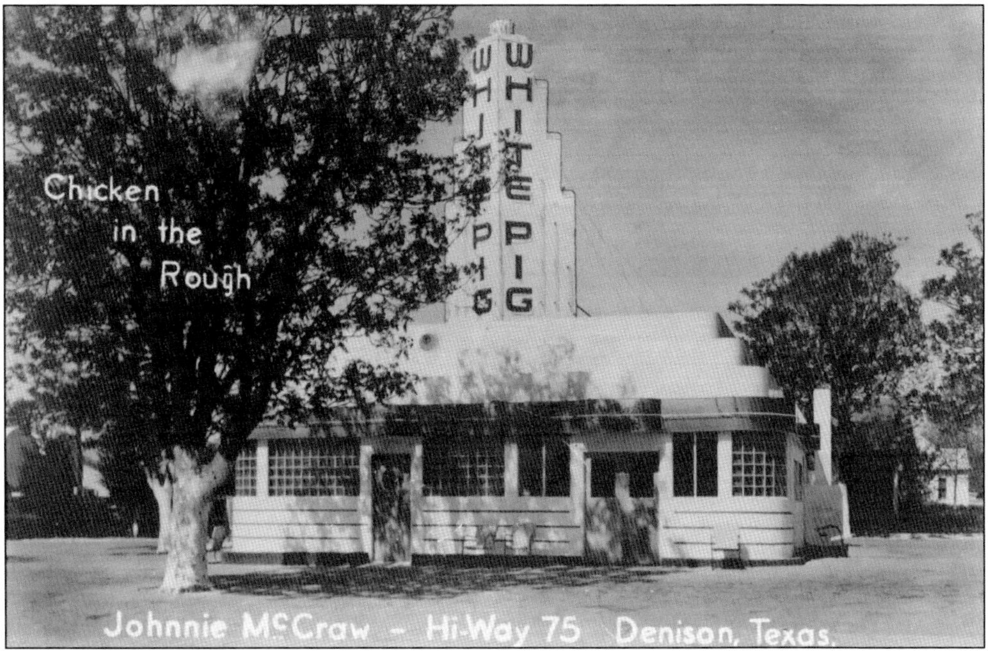

In the 1940s, few people traveled on Armstrong Avenue without stopping at Johnny McCraw's White Pig Stand at 505 South Armstrong Avenue or across the street at the Tom-Tom Drive-In. At either place, one could hang out by staying in the car and having food and drinks brought to the window, sometimes by waitresses on roller skates. With its drumming Native American motif, the Tom-Tom's flashing neon sign—itself a type of drum on top of the building—encouraged customers to stop. That enterprise disappeared many years ago, but the White Pig Stand, which opened in 1936, operated well into the 1960s, and the building still stands today with another business inside. Part of the McCraw family's string of area restaurants, The Pig epitomized the drive-in restaurants of the 1940s or 1950s. (Both, DHH.)

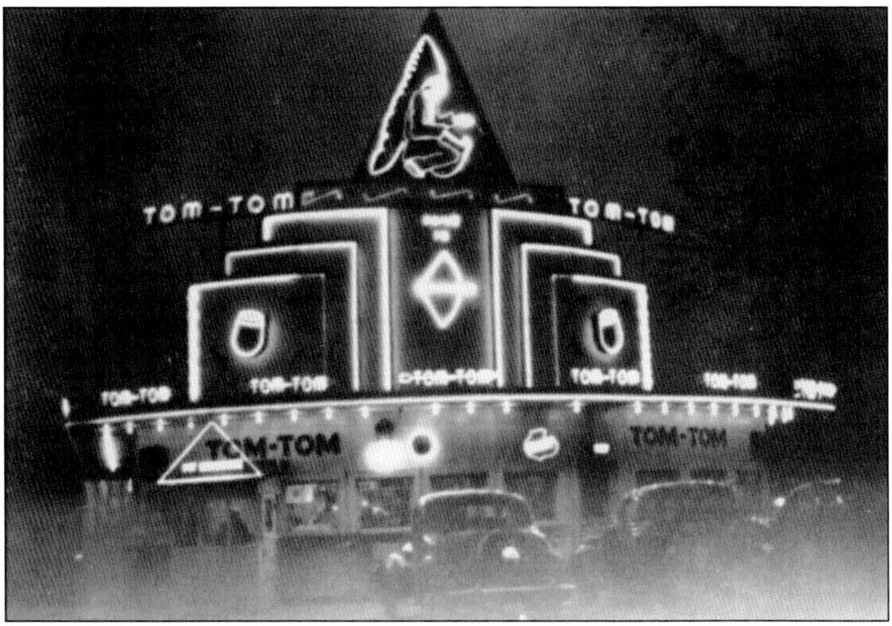

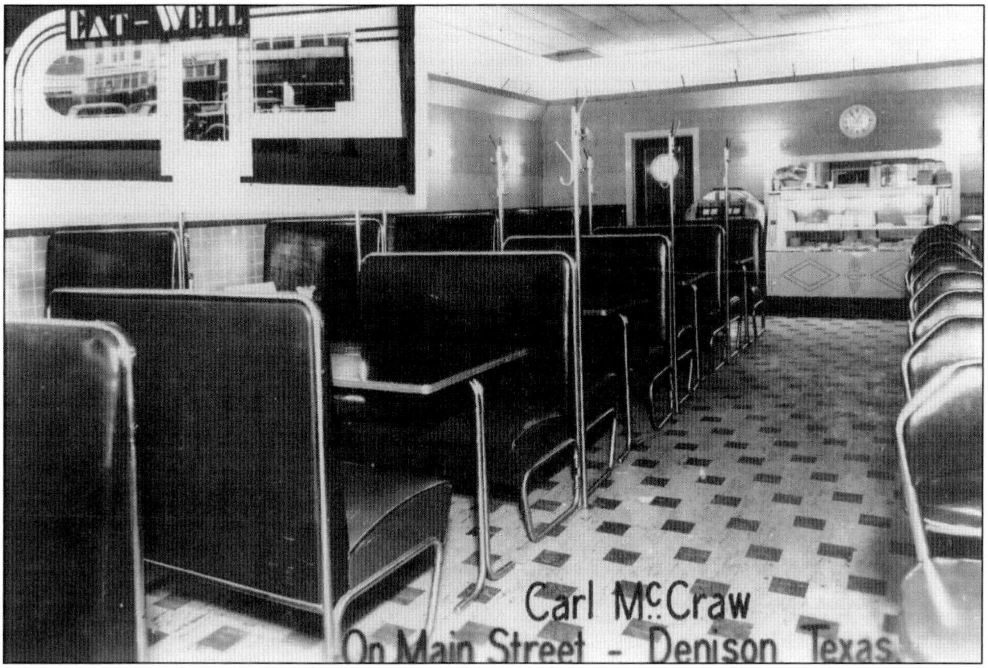

The Eat-Well Café, at 309 West Main Street, owned by Carl McCraw, was the gathering place for downtown Denison store employees at noon every day for many years. The booths would be filled for lunch. A back room could be opened for an overflow crowd. Large windows on the front of the café allowed diners to watch the happenings on Main Street while they ate. (DHH.)

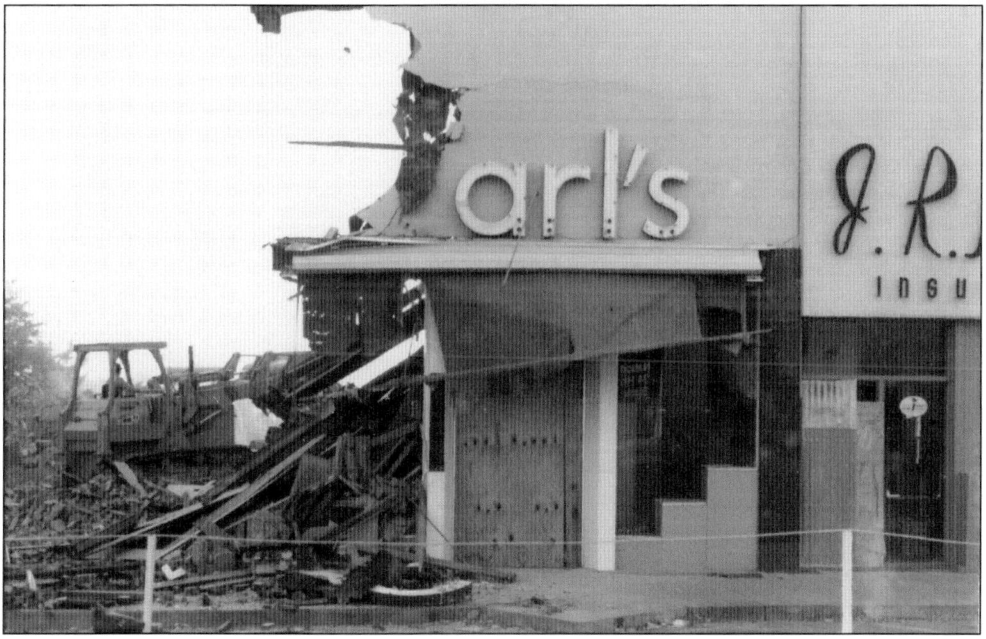

Located at 112 North Rusk Avenue, Carl's Cafe was an institution for 33 years until it closed on May 4, 1979, to make way for a bank parking lot. Peggy Benedict's homemade pies, rolls, and Mexican food drew crowds. Eating at Carl's was like eating at home. Carl's moved to a new location, 203 West Main Street, but it was never the same. (MAB.)

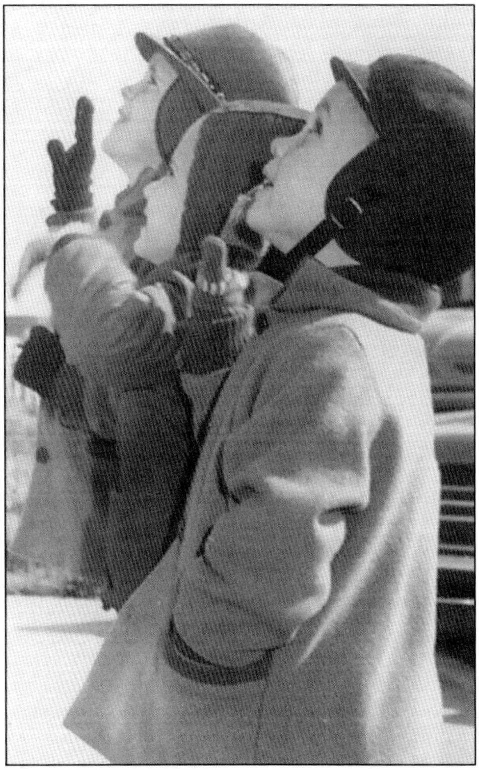

Tedd Riffell was a best friend to Santa Claus and thousands of children in Denison for many years. Every December, Tedd took a month off from his landscaping business to walk the downtown streets wearing his Santa Claus outfit. He posed for pictures with children on his knee, handed out candy, did a lot of waving and shaking hands, rode in his sleigh in the Christmas parade, visited children in their homes, and spread the Christmas spirit everywhere he went. Wide-eyed children waved as Santa Tedd brought up the end of the Christmas parade every year. At left, Robby Hunt, Billy Crawford, and Brian Hunt wave excitedly to Santa as his sleigh passes in the 1965 parade. Below, Santa is pictured soaking his tired feet on the day after Christmas. (Left, John Crawford, in DHH; below, HD.)

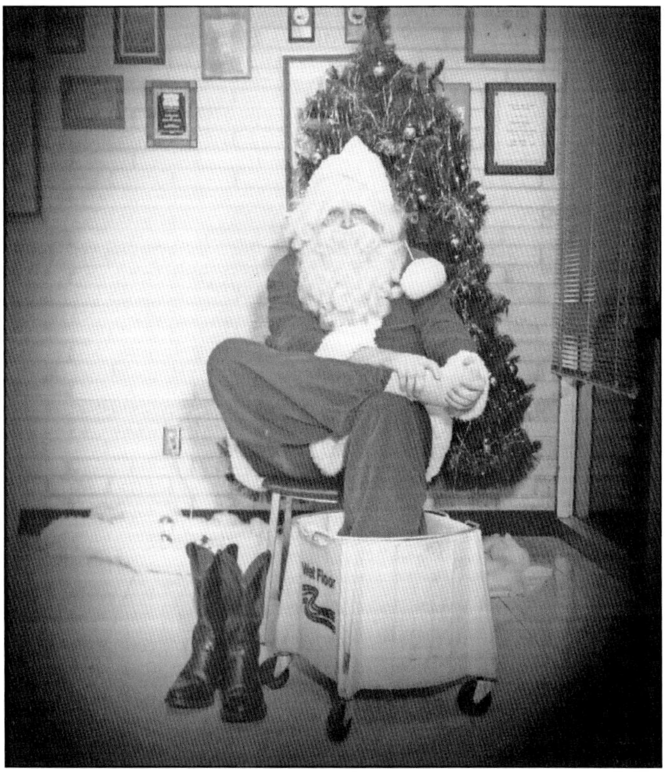

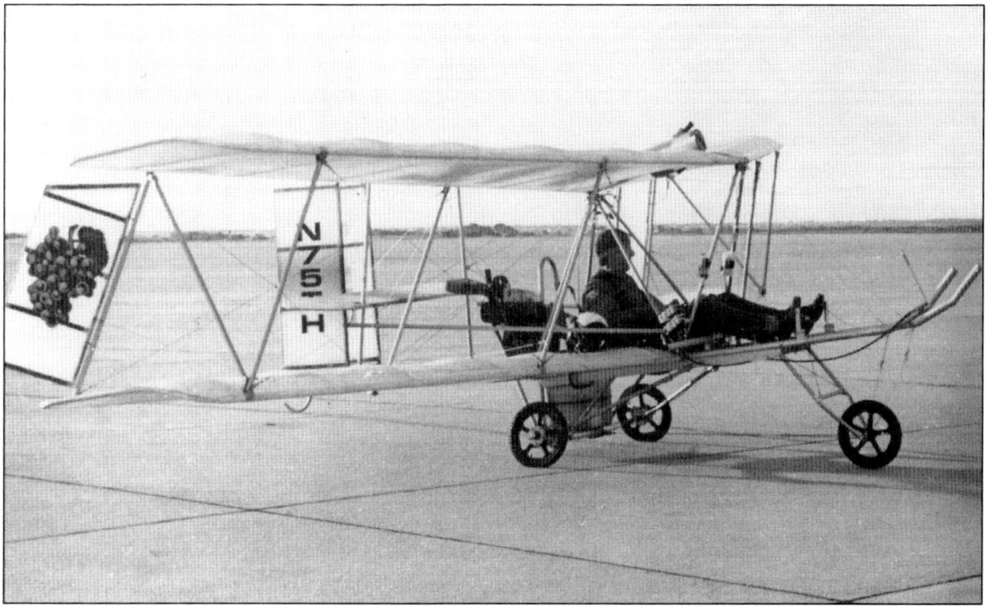

The Vin-Fiz, a box-kite aircraft, was the first plane to pass over Denison. It arrived on October 17, 1911. Calbraith P. Rodgers was on a leg of the first coast-to-coast flight from New York to San Francisco. The plane landed in a field west of Denison for repairs. No photographs recorded the event; this one was taken during a reenactment more than 50 years later. (DHH.)

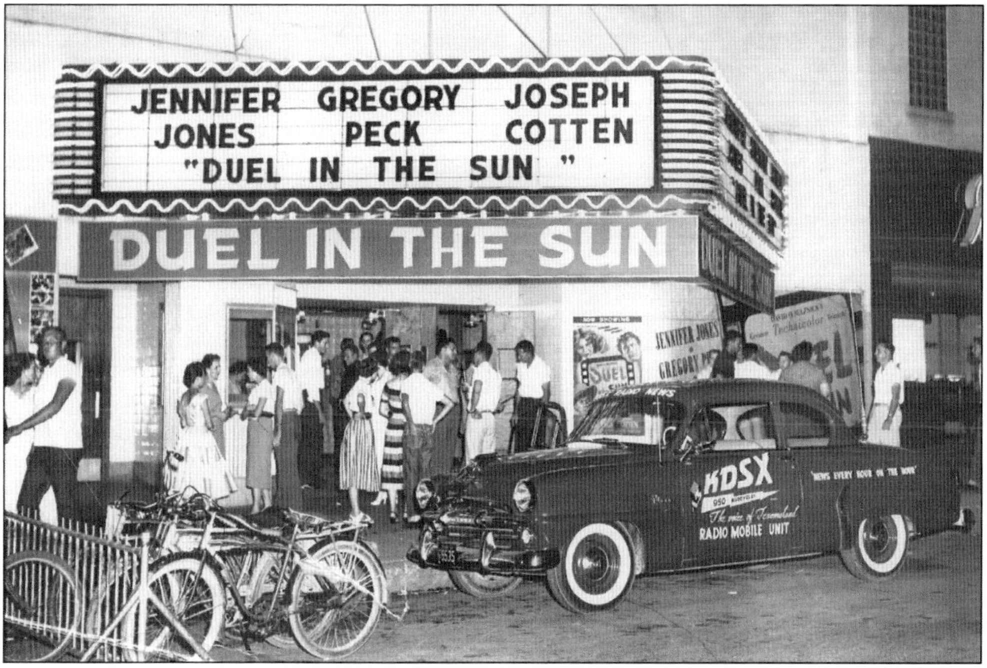

A crowd gathers in front of the State Theater in 1948 when the cinema was at the height of its glory. The Star Theater, which preceded the State on the site, opened in 1913. Here, the movie theater has just been remodeled and renamed, with *Duel in the Sun* as its first featured film. Howard Mayes of KDSX Radio stands by with the mobile unit, ready to broadcast live during the reopening celebration. (Dee Gaines, in DHH.)

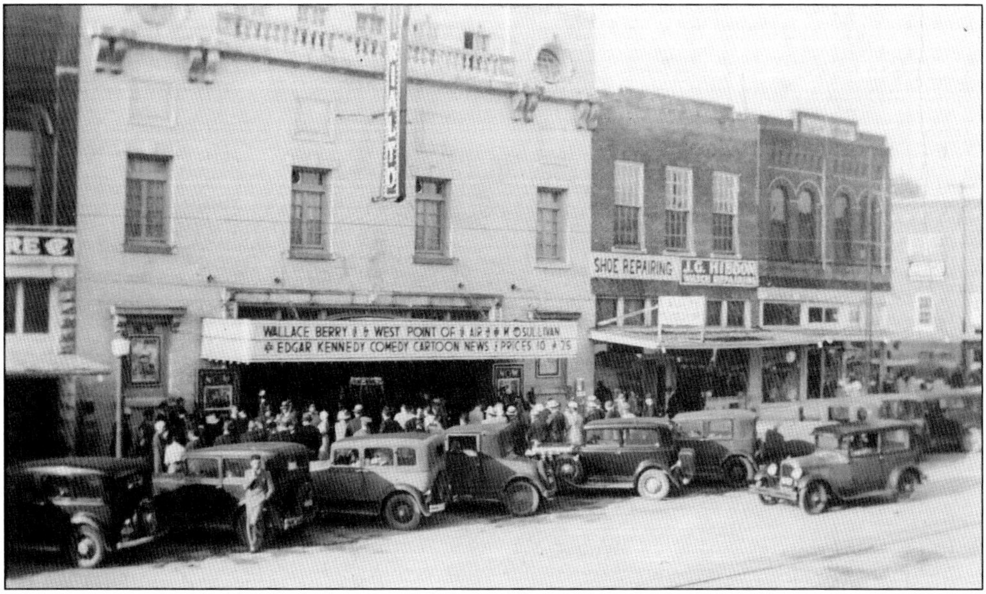

At Denison's Rialto Theater, an eager crowd of moviegoers lines up early on a morning in 1935. The newly remodeled theater is showing Wallace Berry in *West Point of the Air*. Note the ticket prices: 10¢ and 25¢. The theater, Denison's finest, originally opened in 1924 and took the town by storm. Every seat was filled at every showing the first year. (MAB.)

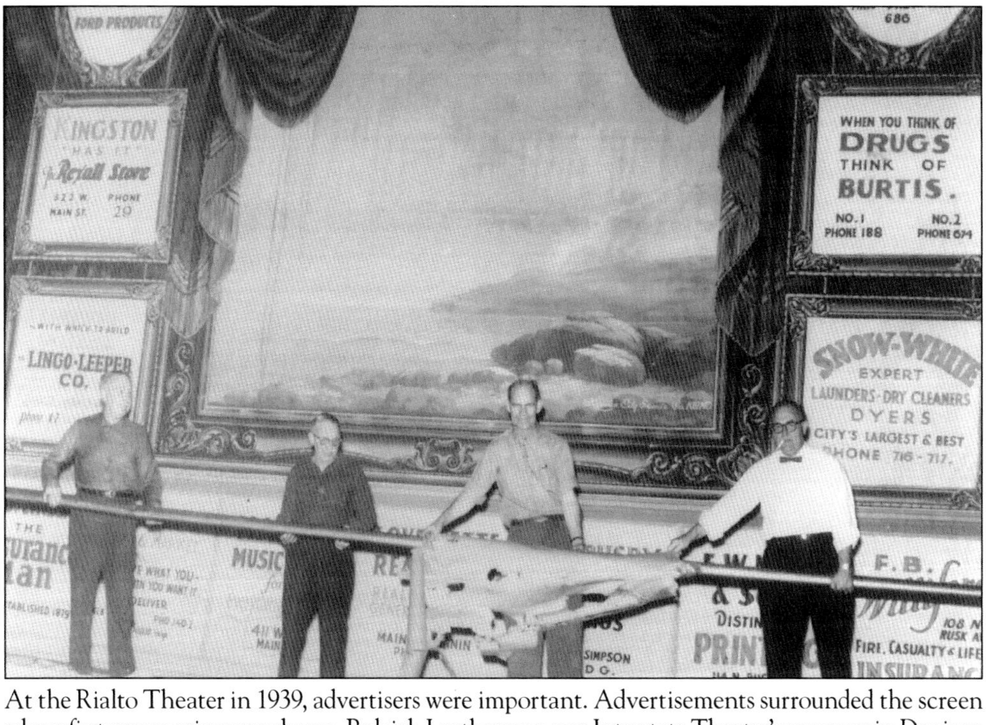

At the Rialto Theater in 1939, advertisers were important. Advertisements surrounded the screen where first-run movies were shown. Raleigh Leatherman was Interstate Theater's manager in Denison from 1935 to 1943. He was followed by Charles Snyder (seen at right). Others pictured include two unidentified persons and J.F. "Dude" Durham (second from right), a stagehand. The Rialto operated as a movie house until 1990 and then as a live theater before closing in 2010. (DHH.)

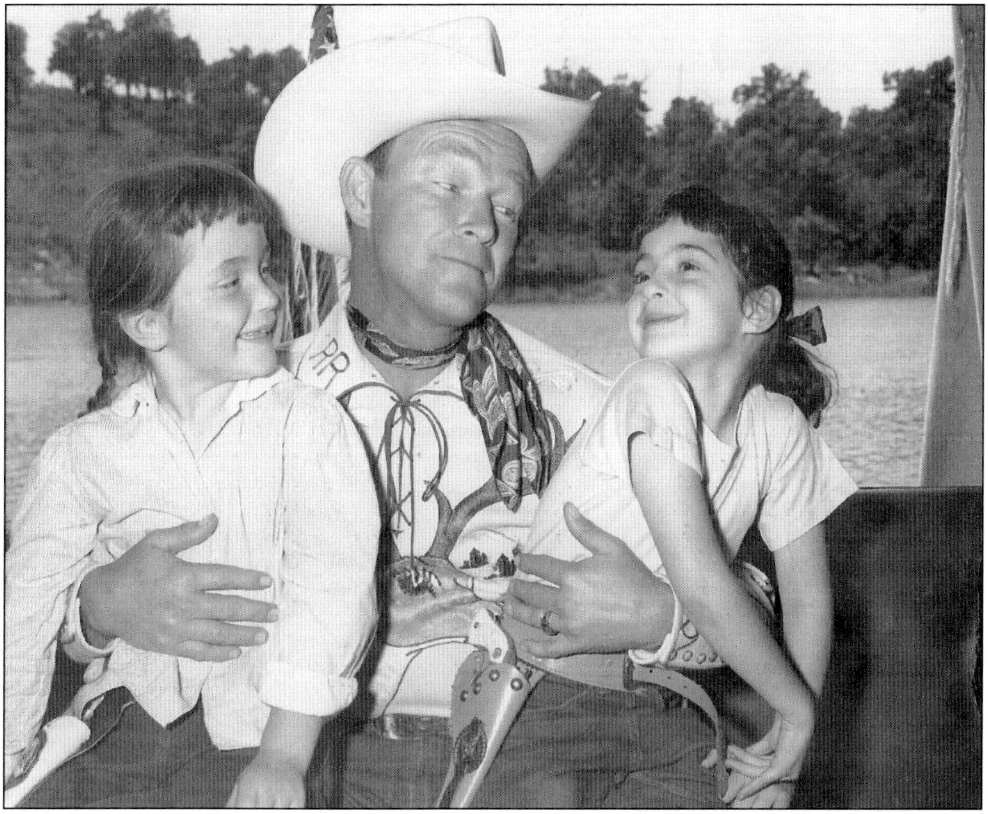

Cowboy actor Roy Rogers poses with two youngsters—Kyra Joan Clift (left) and Mia Marsico—during a visit to Denison around 1954. He was a partner in the Yellow Jacket Boat Company. Rogers and his family were frequent visitors to Denison during the days when the boats were being built. Kyra's father, a *Denison Herald* reporter, snapped this photograph for the girls. (Mia Marsico Munson.)

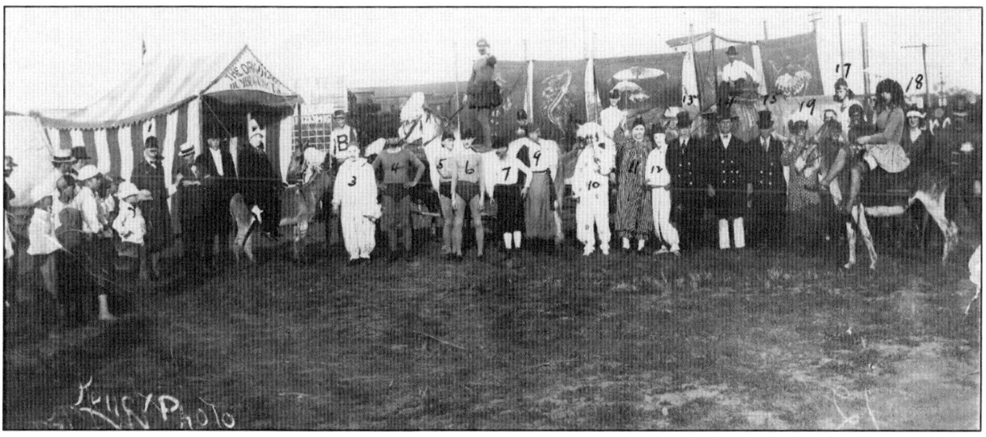

On June 22, 1916, the Denison Elks Lodge staged a Humbug Circus. To the delight of the citizenry, Elks donned costumes and performed. Among them were H.Y. Parrott, Roy Finley (clown riding mule), Lingo Platter (clown in white), Billy Scott, Clarence Scott (standing on horse), Jim Chaffe (clown), Dan Leeper (clown), Will Clymer, Tom Steen, Franz Kohfeldt, Tom Hall (riding mule, right), and Jason Buckman. Note the painted backdrops. (MAB.)

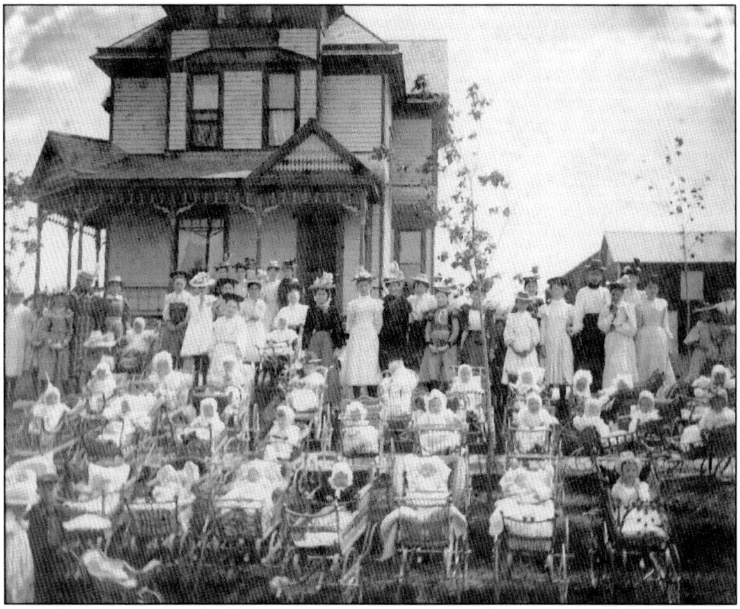

This picture must have been taken on Easter Sunday. All the women and children are wearing their Easter hats, and even the babies in their carriages are all dressed up in their Sunday best: white outfits and ruffled bonnets. The house seen here no longer exists in Denison, but, judging from the very young trees, it must have been relatively new on the day this photograph was made. (MAB.)

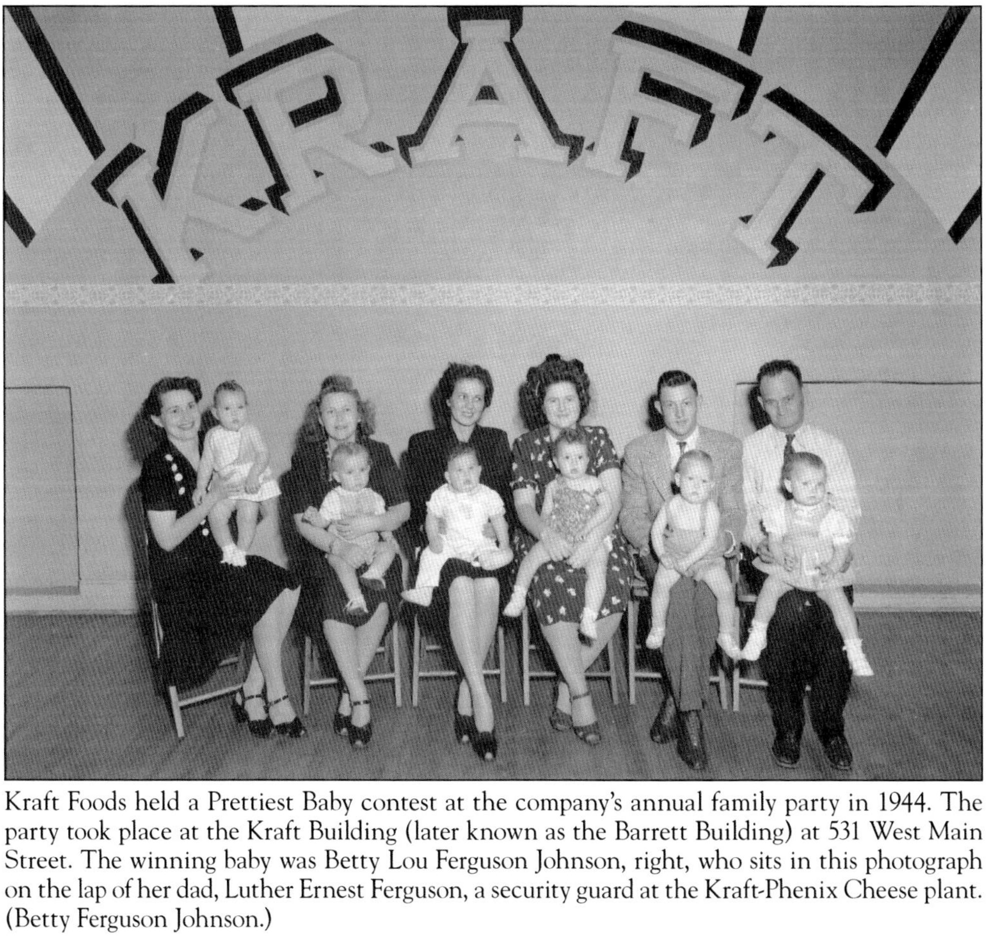

Kraft Foods held a Prettiest Baby contest at the company's annual family party in 1944. The party took place at the Kraft Building (later known as the Barrett Building) at 531 West Main Street. The winning baby was Betty Lou Ferguson Johnson, right, who sits in this photograph on the lap of her dad, Luther Ernest Ferguson, a security guard at the Kraft-Phenix Cheese plant. (Betty Ferguson Johnson.)

Young Blue Birds are bringing a gift for a newborn baby boy. In the process, they learn about infant care. The girls have donned masks so that they will not spread germs to the infant. As the youngest girls in the Camp Fire Girl organization in Denison, Blue Birds was a must organization for little girls in the 1940s and 1950s. The Camp Fire headquarters was at 730 West Sears Street. (MAB.)

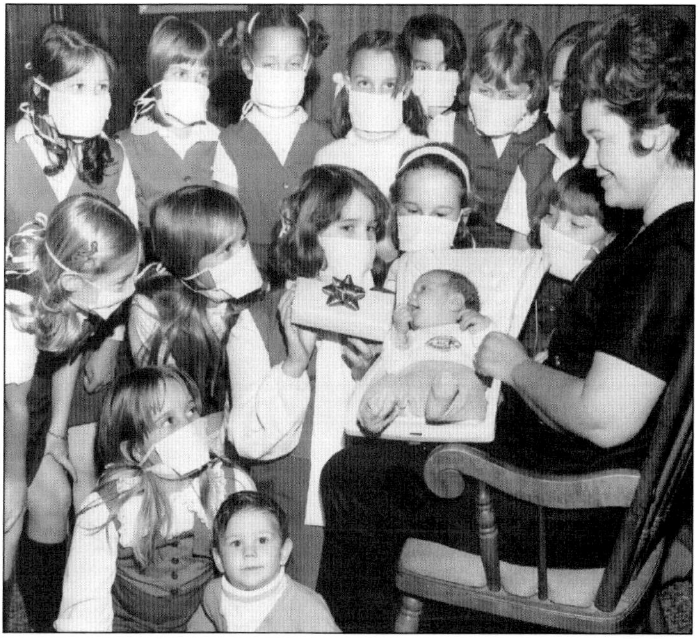

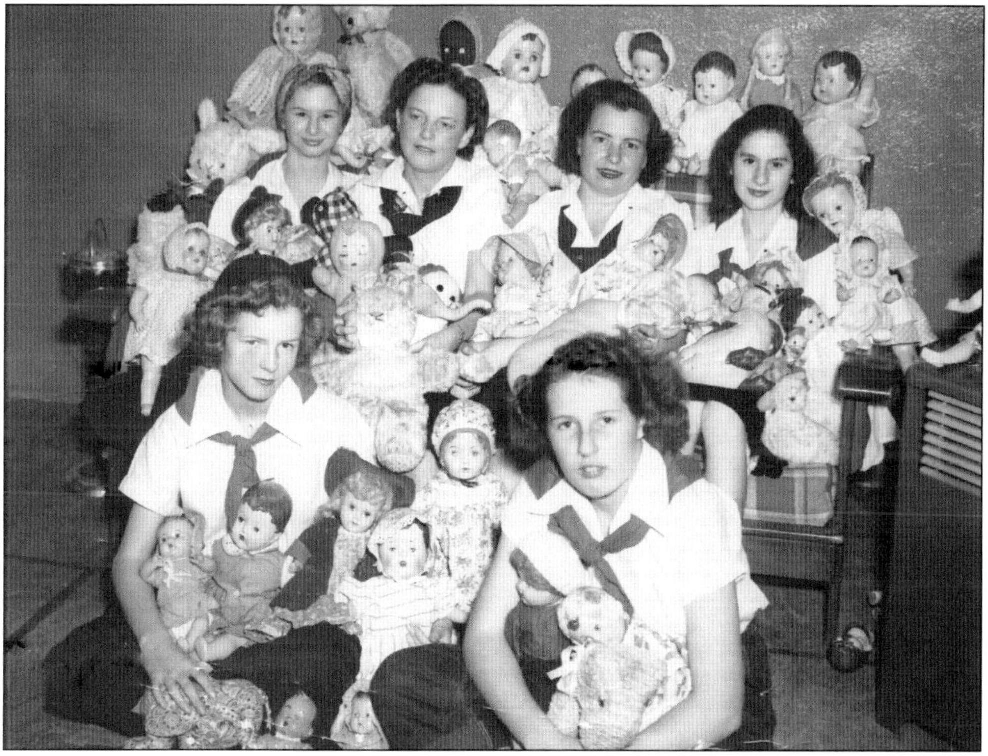

Tanda Camp Fire Girls repaired and dressed 500 dolls for the Denison Lions Club's Goodfellows organization in 1949. The dolls, donated by other Camp Fire Girls, went to little girls who otherwise would not have received one as a Christmas gift. Pictured here from left to right are (first row) Ruth Ann Overbeck and Alice Smith; (second row) Loretta Hales, leaders Marie Beckham and Ruby Coonrod, and Wanda Hales. (DHH.)

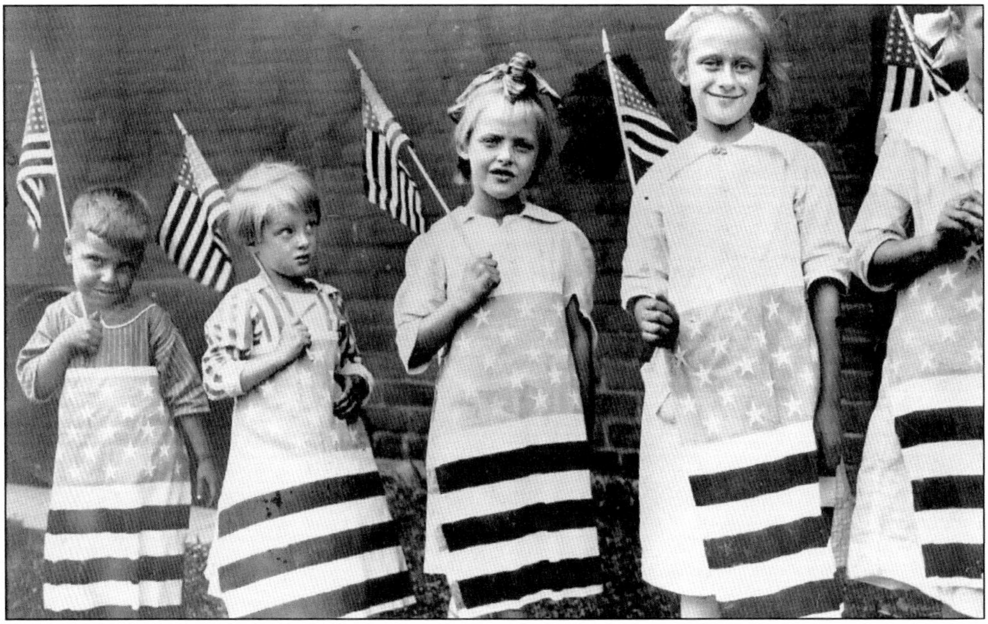

Schoolchildren played an important part in local parades in the early 1900s, just as they do today. In this photograph from an old Denison scrapbook, these siblings (perhaps preparing for a Fourth of July celebration) are dressed to show off their patriotism with flags and matching Stars-and-Stripes aprons. (Anne Clymer Goddard, in MAB.)

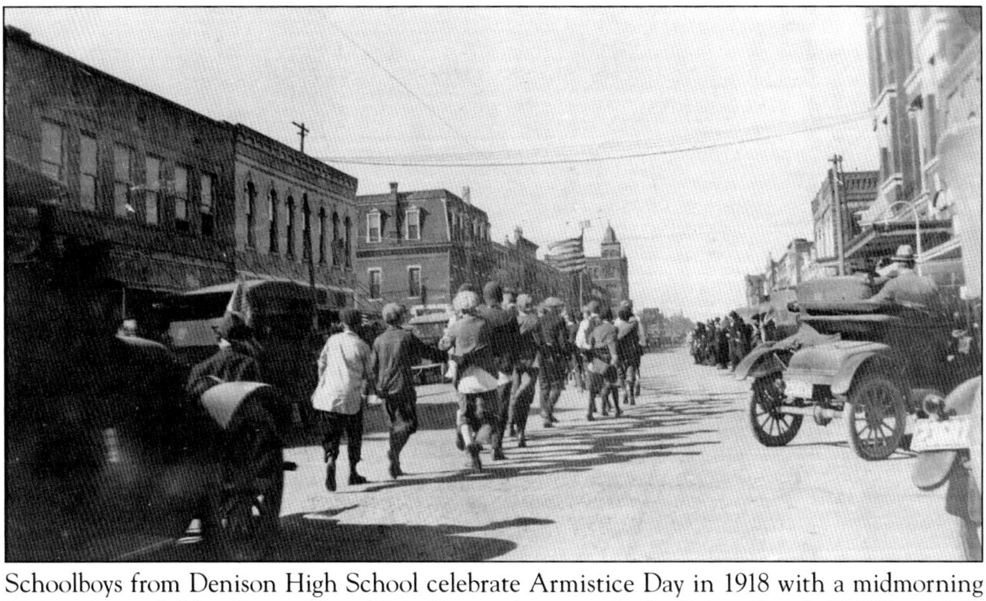

Schoolboys from Denison High School celebrate Armistice Day in 1918 with a midmorning "shirt-tail parade" heading west on Main Street. At center is the Palace Hotel, 400 West Main Street, flag flying, while the first Denison Hotel/Denison Commercial College building can be seen in the distance. At the curb on the right, two men sit in their open-air roadster beneath the sturdy walls of the Leeper/Security Building. (MAB.)

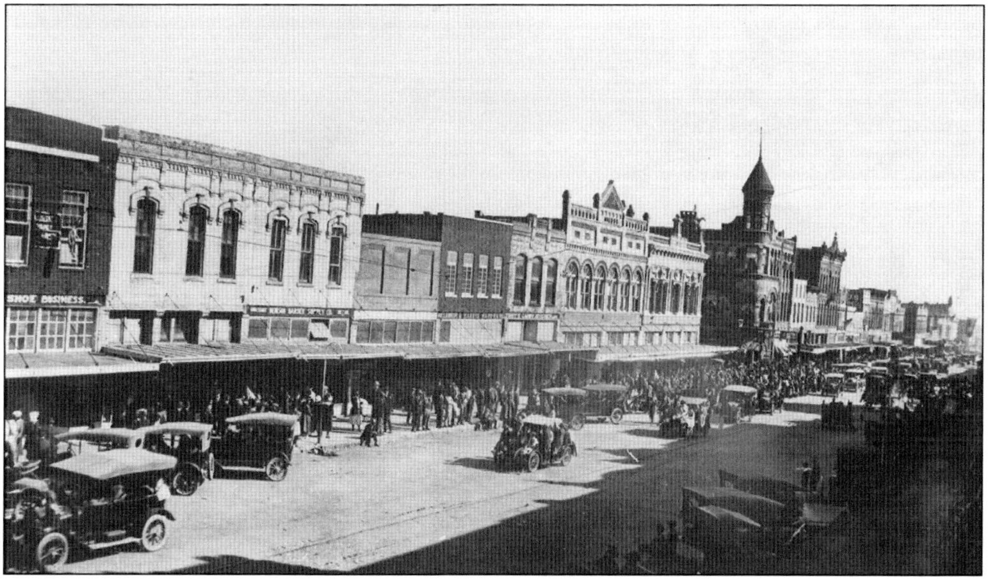

Automobiles and pedestrians throng the 200 and 300 blocks of West Main Street, celebrating the end of World War I. The parade is heading four blocks west to hear speakers and patriotic music on the outdoor stage at the four-year-old Denison High School, built in 1914. Some of the businesses pictured here include Denison Barber Supply, Dollarhide and Harris Hardware, and Tony's Candy Kitchen. This photograph looks east on November 11, 1918. (MAB.)

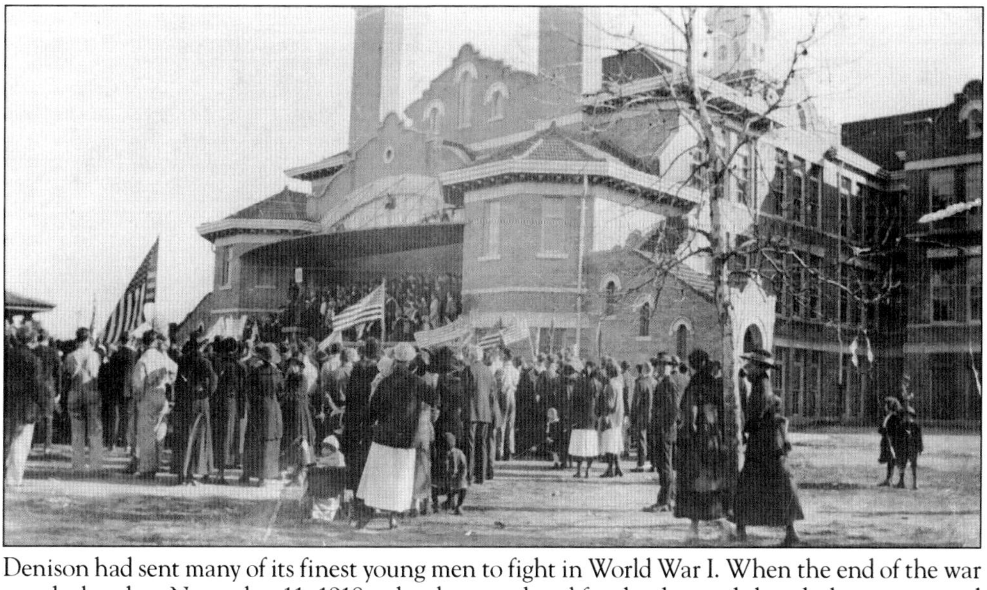

Denison had sent many of its finest young men to fight in World War I. When the end of the war was declared on November 11, 1918, schools were closed for the day, and the whole town turned out to celebrate. The key Armistice Day events took place on the outdoor stage at Denison High School. (MAB.)

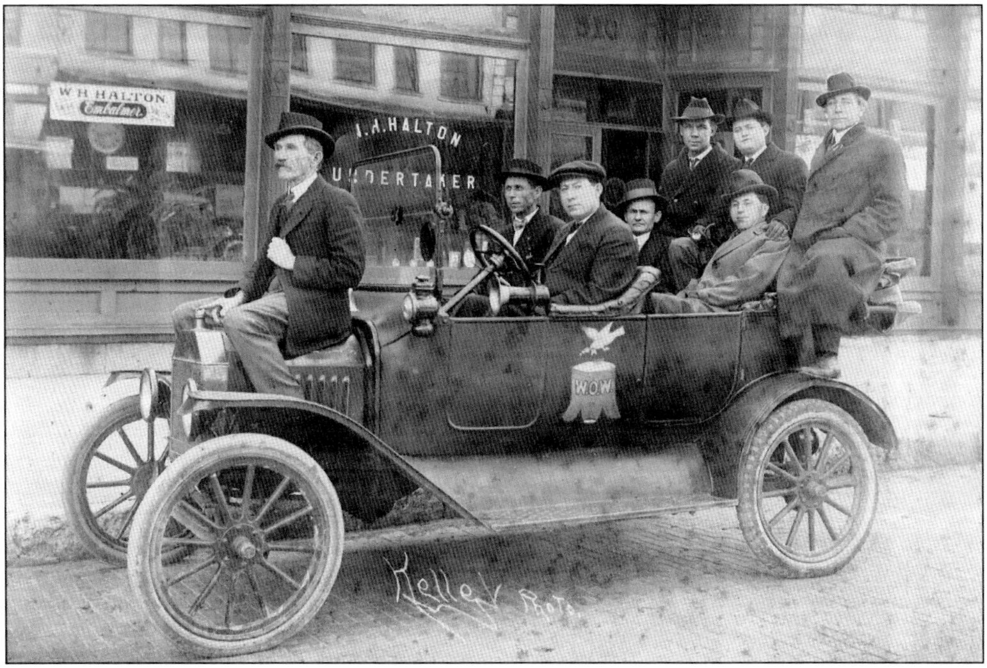

Woodmen of the World was founded in 1890 in Omaha, Nebraska, with the Denison camp organized in 1891. Offering its members aid in times of need, the WOW is noted for the distinctive tree stump–shaped tombstones that it erected nationwide prior to 1930. In this c. 1912 image, the WOW's trademark stump adorns a vehicle carrying local Woodmen. They pause in front of W.H. Halton, Undertaker, at 508–510 West Main Street. (DHH.)

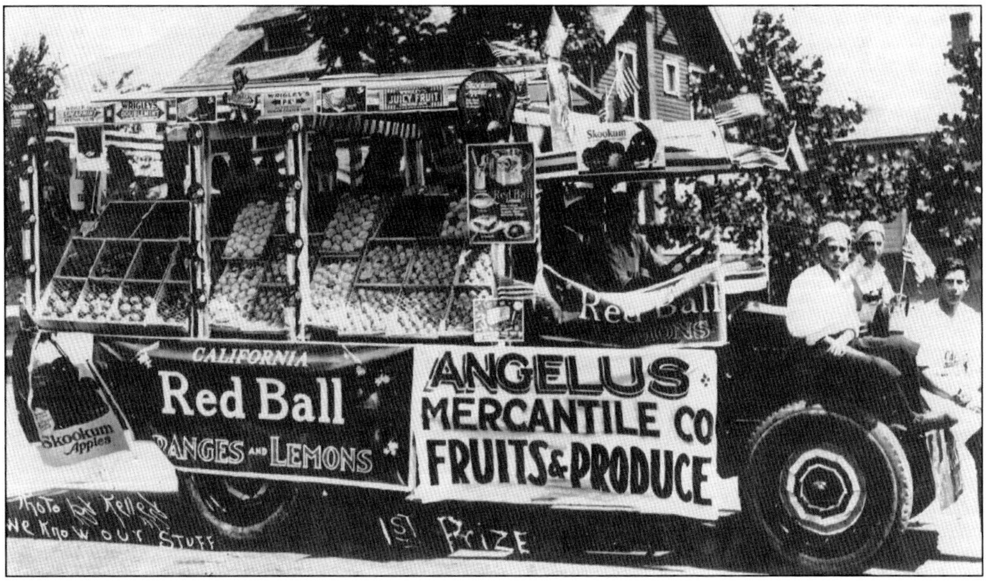

A colorful truckload of Skookum apples and California Red Ball oranges and lemons took first prize in a Labor Day parade. Angelus Mercantile Company mounted the display. Beginning around 1907, the company at 311 East Woodard Street was owned by Charles Bruno and Frank Massie. The photographer, Kelley Studio, took the opportunity to advertise his business with the motto "We Know Our Stuff" scratched at lower left. (MAB.)

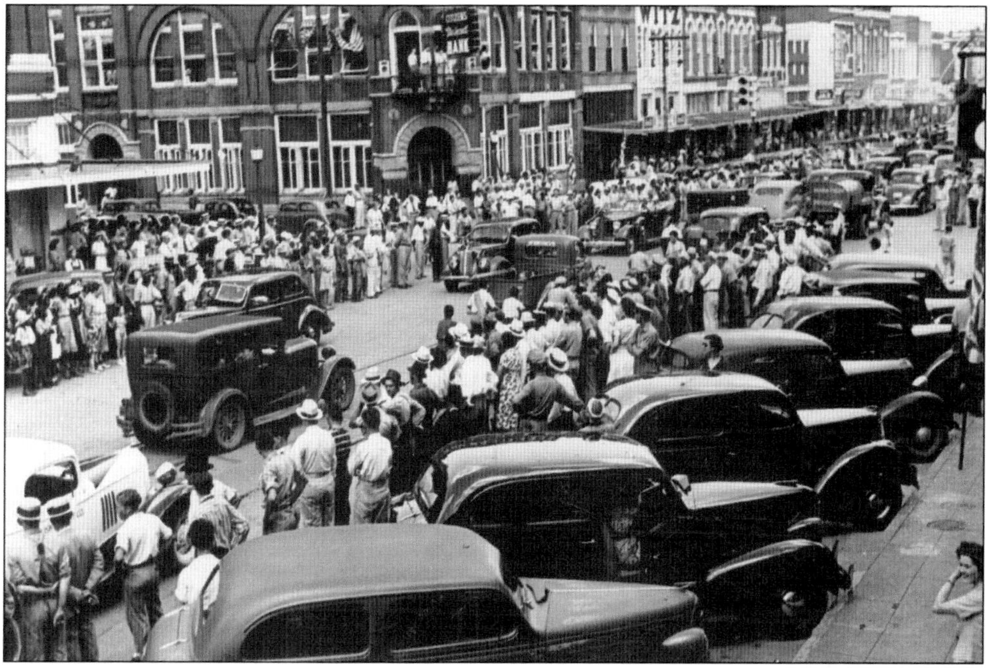

When Denison learned that Congress had made funds available to construct the Denison Dam, citizens came out for an impromptu parade on June 29, 1937. US House majority leader representative Sam Rayburn had fought long and hard for passage of the bill authorizing the project. Cars paraded up and down Main Street, while drivers honked their horns to celebrate the occasion. (DHH.)

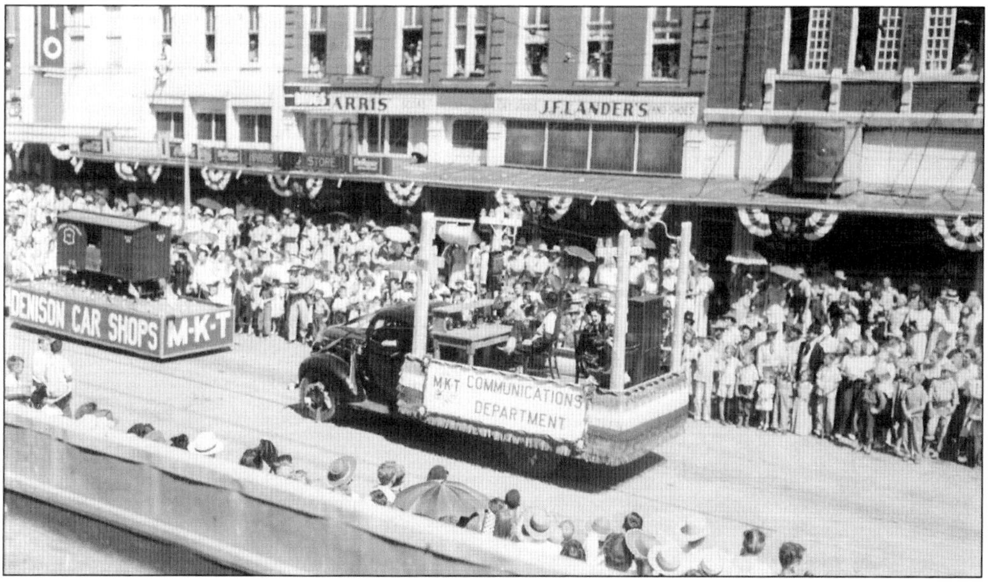

Industries and businesses got into the spirit of Denison's 75th anniversary celebration in September 1947. Traveling west, Katy Car Shops features a miniature car on its float, while the MKT Communications Department combines a piano played by a gleeful female musician with a work desk. The 200 block of West Main Street (north side) was so crowded that many people took to second-story windows to watch the parade. (DHH.)

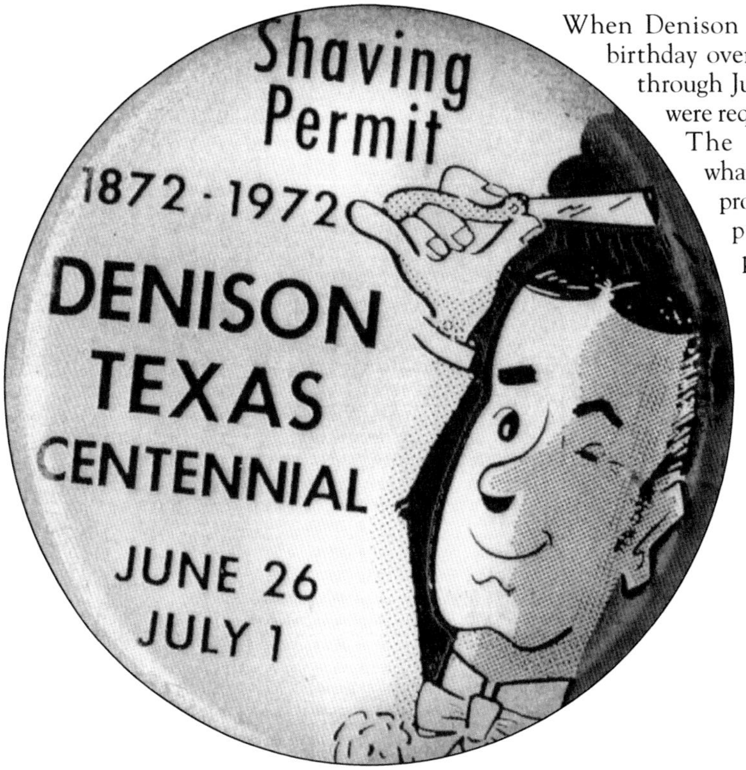

When Denison celebrated its 100th birthday over the week of June 26 through July 1, 1972, gentlemen were required to grow whiskers. The rare man who, for whatever reason, could not produce facial hair could purchase a "shaving permit" for a small fee. It would exempt him from being tossed into the watering trough. However, on occasion, the sheriff was known to ignore a button worn in a man's lapel. (MAB.)

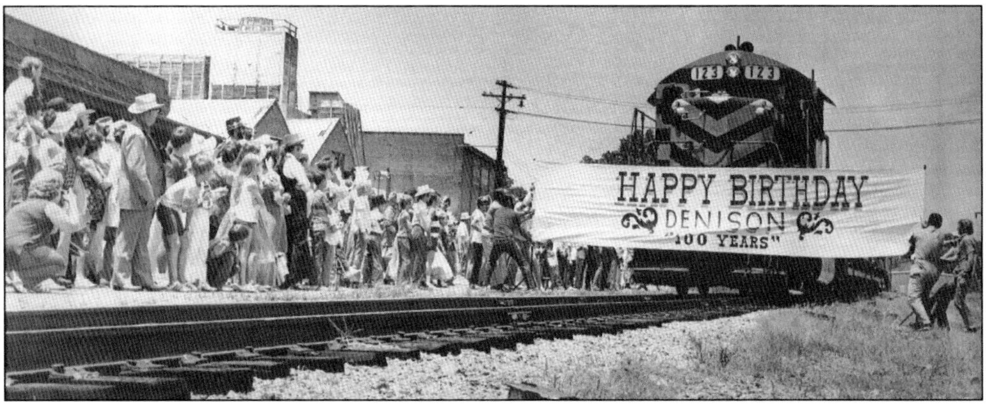

In 1972, Denison celebrated its 100th anniversary. Here, a Katy locomotive breaks through a "Happy Birthday Denison" banner, marking the occasion. Denisonians, dressed in the fashions of the 1870s (when the town was established), line the station platform, waiting to ride the commemorative train. The first MKT train arrived in Denison on Christmas eve in 1872, thus, establishing the town that would later become MKT headquarters. (HD.)

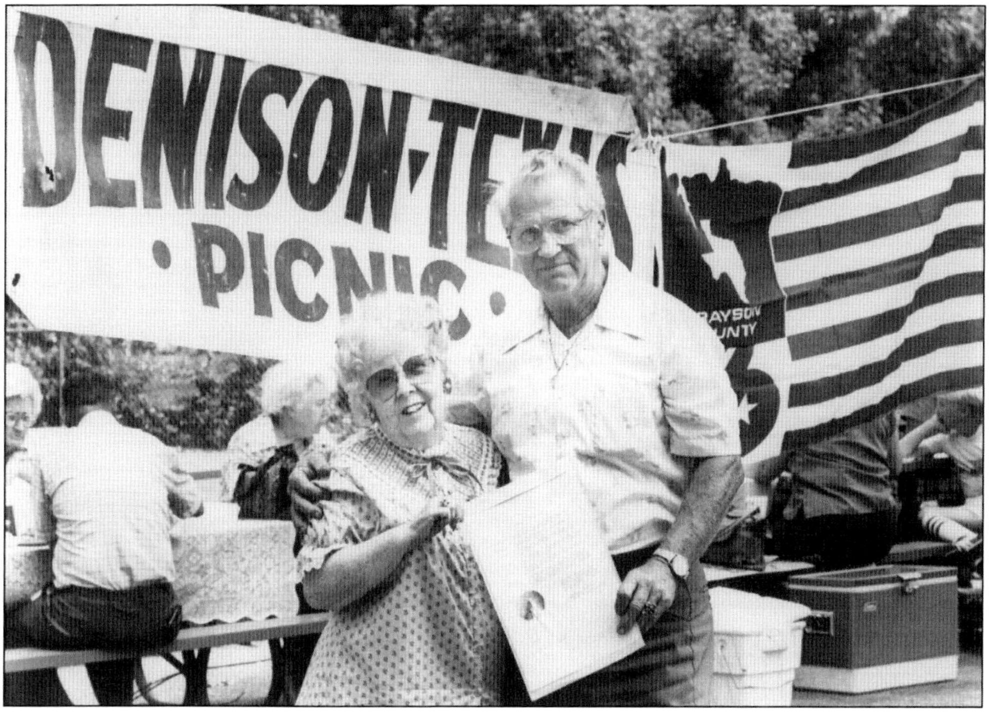

In 1983, Ethel Waddell Thorn and Fred Schweisinger hold a proclamation issued by Denison mayor Ronnie Cole as the annual Denison, Texas, Reunion celebrates its 60th year in Long Beach, California. The reunion was organized in 1923 on the lawn of a Denison native in Santa Monica, California, and former Denisonians met every year until the early 1990s. At one point, the gathering drew more than 300 attendees. (HD.)

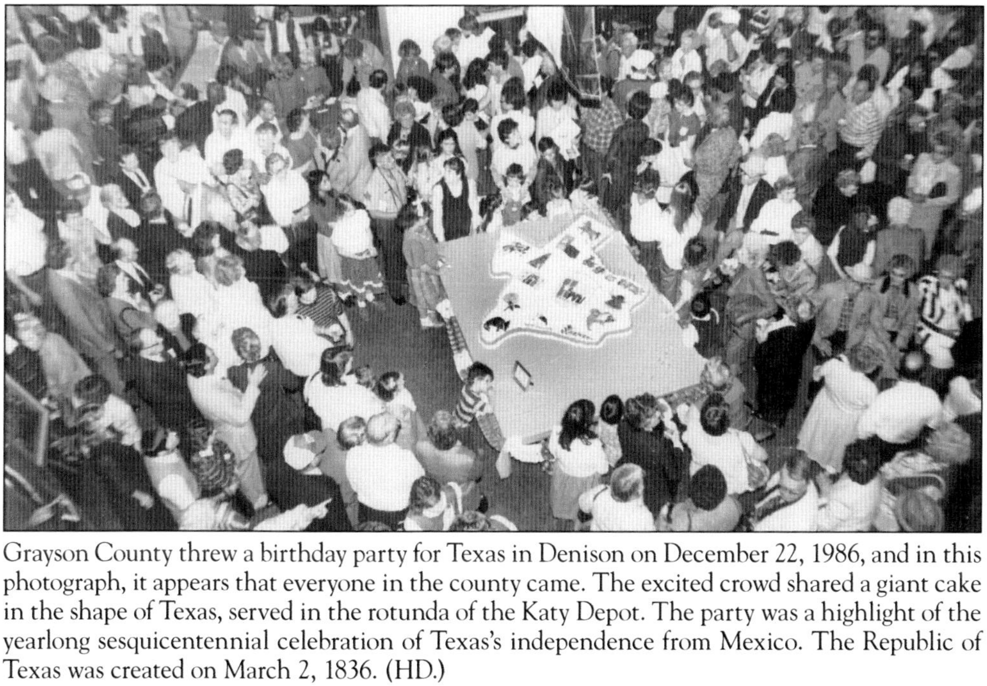

Grayson County threw a birthday party for Texas in Denison on December 22, 1986, and in this photograph, it appears that everyone in the county came. The excited crowd shared a giant cake in the shape of Texas, served in the rotunda of the Katy Depot. The party was a highlight of the yearlong sesquicentennial celebration of Texas's independence from Mexico. The Republic of Texas was created on March 2, 1836. (HD.)

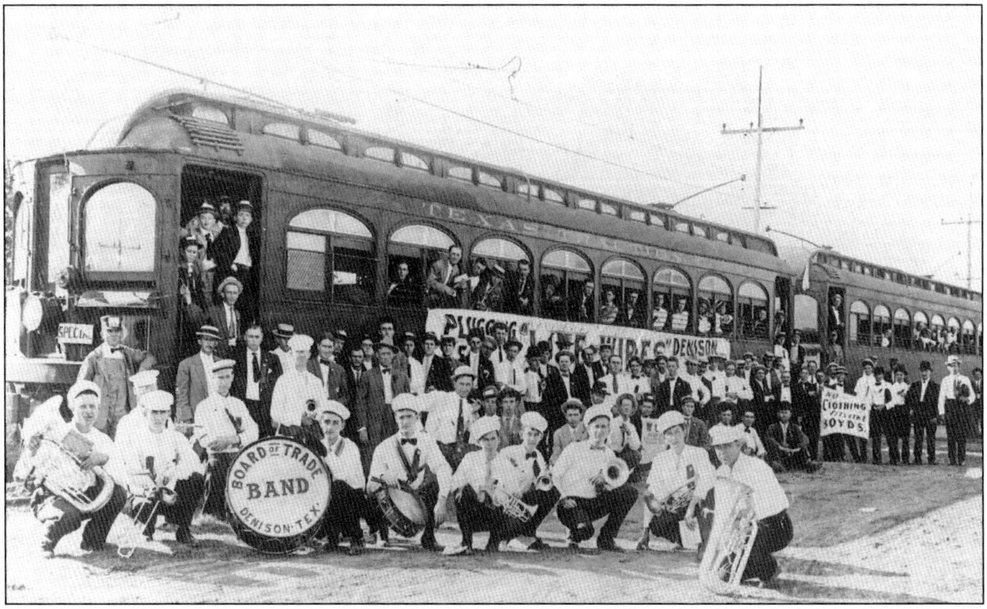

Taking to the rails to advertise Denison are city leaders and the Live Wires, an organization of young businessmen. They fill two special Texas Traction coaches, later known as interurbans. On hand to entertain crowds at each stop is the band for the Denison Board of Trade, which later became the Denison Chamber of Commerce. Boyd's Clothing Store takes the opportunity to advertise: "No Clothing Fits Like Boyd's." (MAB.)

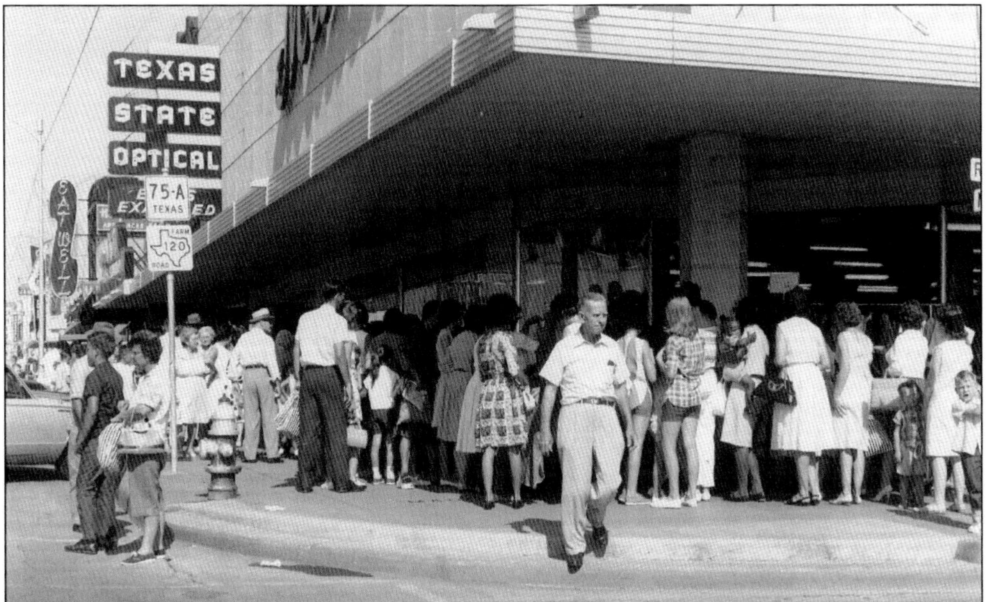

During the 1960s, merchants in downtown Denison moved their merchandise to the sidewalks once a month to entice shoppers to stroll Main Street looking for bargains. Everything from clothes to automobiles could be purchased at large discounts. Madden's Department Store, at 301 West Main Street, recently had been renovated. At this time, Highway 75 and FM 120 still ran up Main Street; later, both would be rerouted. (MAB.)

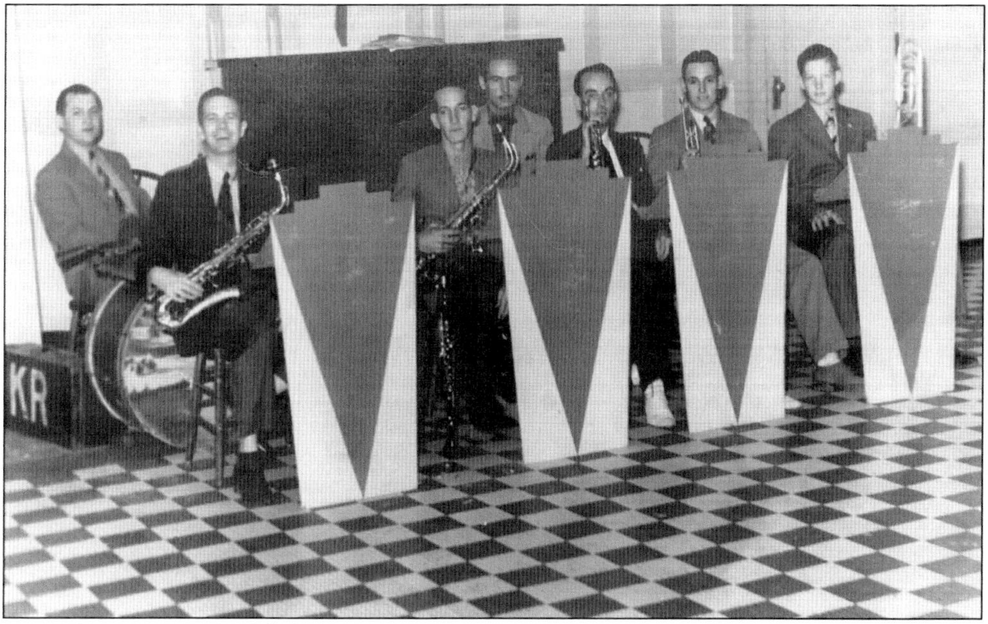

Kenneth Ransom, at back left, formed this band in the 1930s to play for special events in Denison. Seen here at a gig at the Hotel Denison are, from left to right, Ransom on drums, Jimmy Ellison and Dan Williams on saxophone, Kenneth Middleton on piano, ? Blanton and Bob Bomer on trumpet, and Henry Calvert on trombone. (C.J. Ransom, in DHH.)

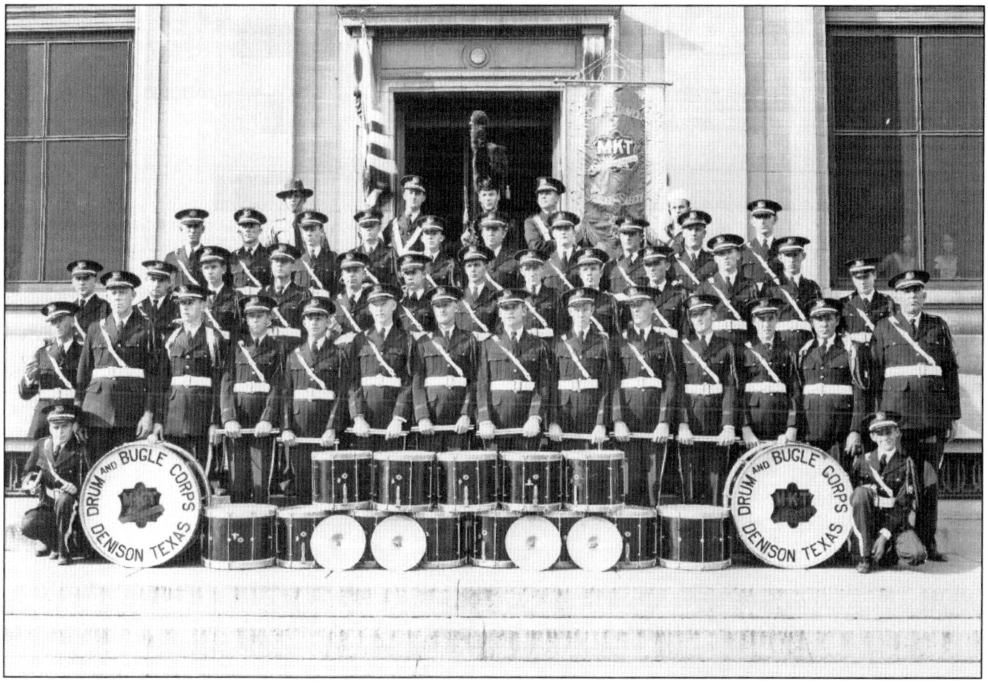

The MKT Railroad had a drum and bugle corps. Here, around 1930, the group poses on the steps at the Denison Post Office with its instruments, ready to perform. The unidentified director stands in the back row, middle. The MKT "Service and Safety" banner hangs to the right of the door near a sailor. A soldier stands at back left. (WPL, in HD.)

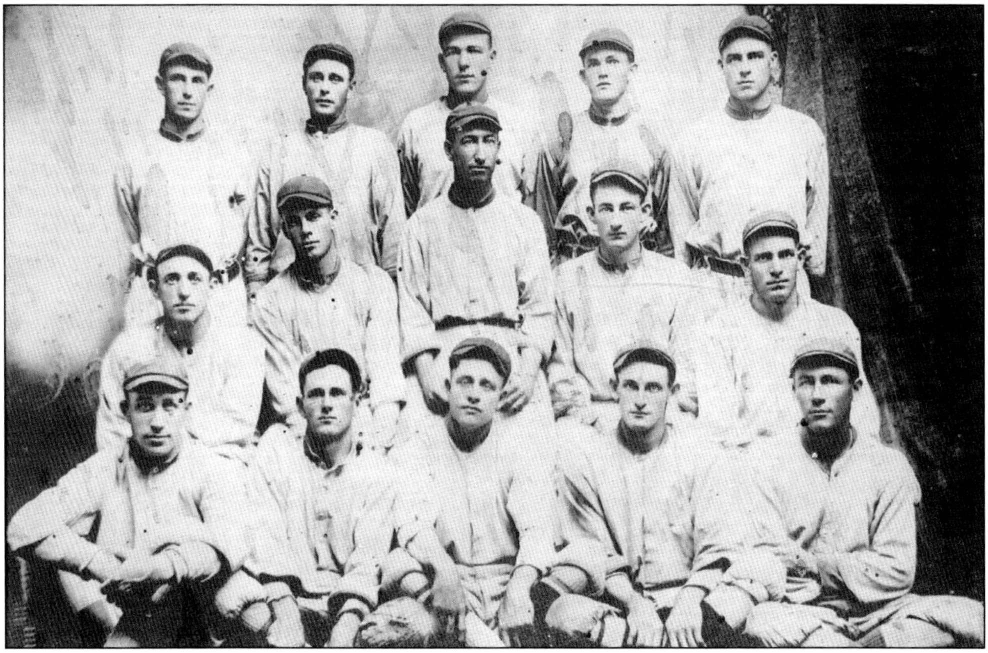

In 1915, the Denison Railroaders won the Western Association league championship. From left to right are (first row) William "Boston" Campbell, Bill Harper, Dick Spear, Bob Covington, and ? Edmiston; (second row) "Jew" Hellman, Ray Query, Aldridge "Babe" Peebles, Ezra Glenn, and Duggan Brooks; (third row) Fred Nicholson, Tex Merritt, Walter Kinney, Rogers Hornsby, and ? Sheffield. Campbell and Peebles established Denison's Rialto Theater. Future baseball hall-of-famer Hornsby went on to play 23 years in the major leagues, most of them with the St. Louis Cardinals. (DHH.)

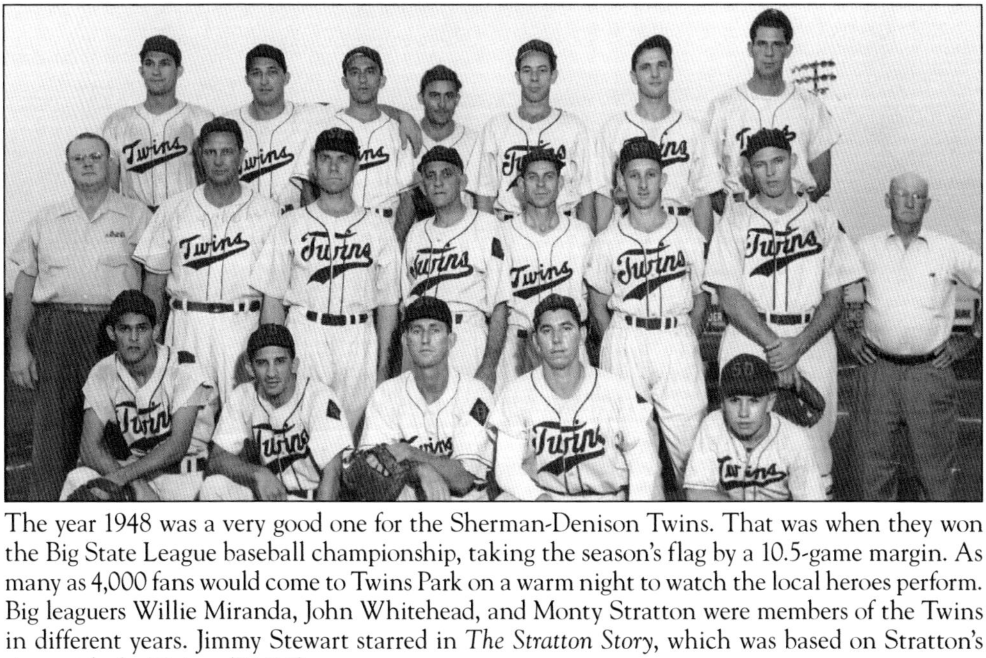

The year 1948 was a very good one for the Sherman-Denison Twins. That was when they won the Big State League baseball championship, taking the season's flag by a 10.5-game margin. As many as 4,000 fans would come to Twins Park on a warm night to watch the local heroes perform. Big leaguers Willie Miranda, John Whitehead, and Monty Stratton were members of the Twins in different years. Jimmy Stewart starred in *The Stratton Story*, which was based on Stratton's time with the Twins. (DHH.)

Eight

PUBLIC SERVANTS

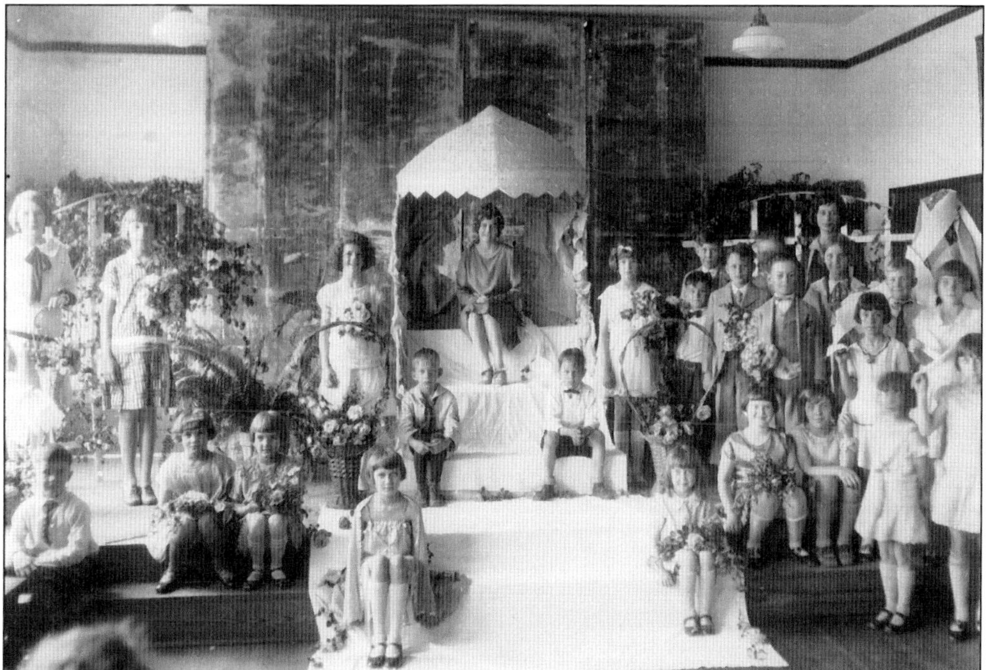

Raynal Elementary School held a pageant in the late 1920s, when Anna Mosse (1876–1959) was principal. This photograph by Kelley Studio shows costumed students at what may have been a May Day event. Teachers at the time were Wilma Carroll, Mildred Parrish, Ethel Cummins, Edith Adamson, Anna Mosse, and Mrs. Alwild Bassinger. (MAB.)

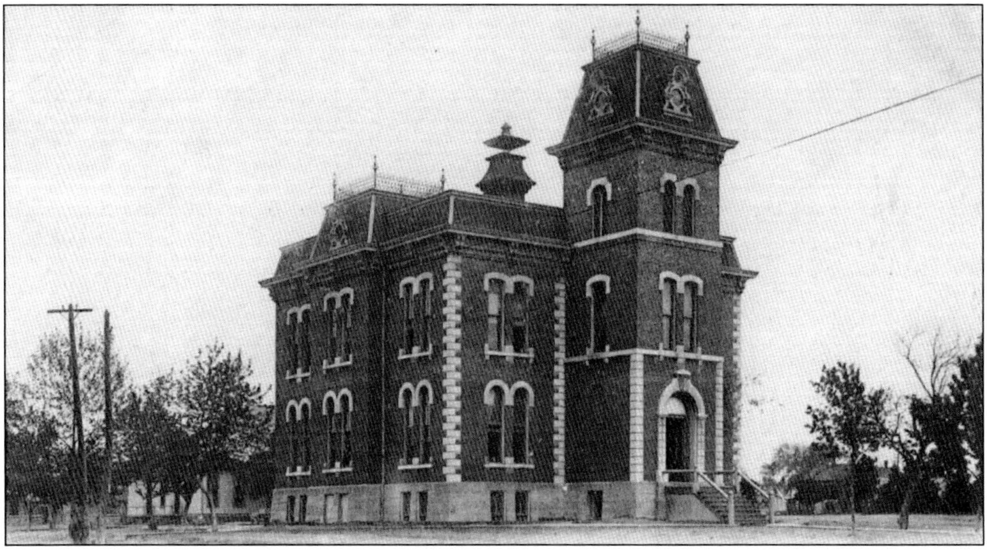

Denison's early leaders believed firmly that an outstanding school would attract settlers to help build their newborn town. Aware of educational trends in the East, they built the first, free, graded public school in Texas. Charles Wheelock of Sherman prepared the plans. Visitors—including US president Ulysses S. Grant—came from far and wide to admire the tall, elegant Educational Institute (also called Union Seminary) completed in 1874. (AWGC.)

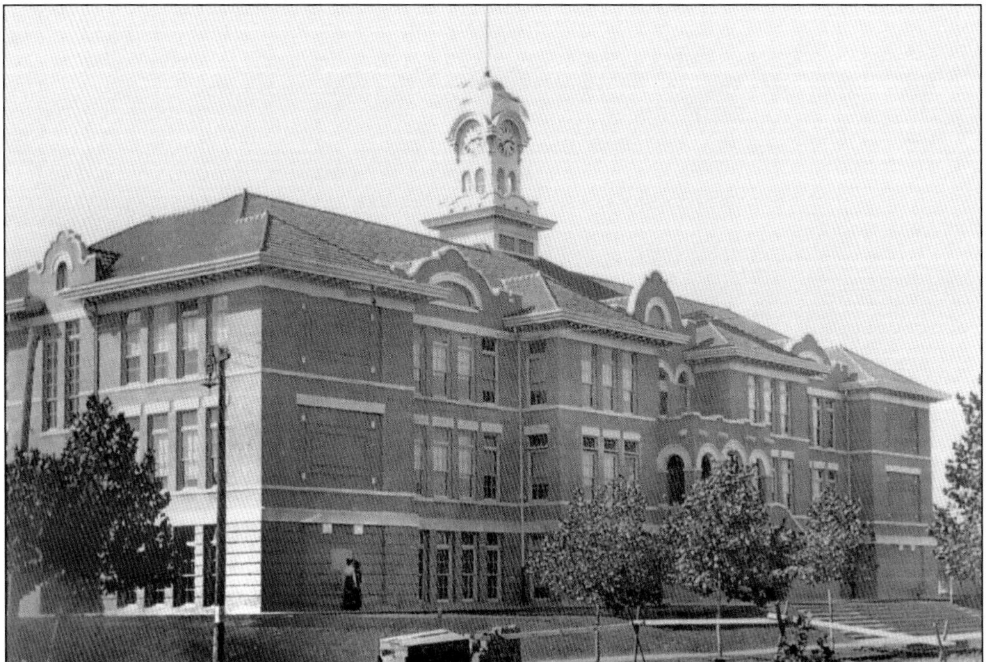

In 1914, Denison replaced its 1874 high school with a larger, more modern facility on the same Main Street site. Arthur O. Watson of Austin, a leading Texas architect, designed the Mission Revival–style structure seen here around 1940. New wings were added in 1927 and 1939. The building became Denison's first junior high school from fall 1954 through May 1986. After heated controversy, it was razed in 2007. (BCT.)

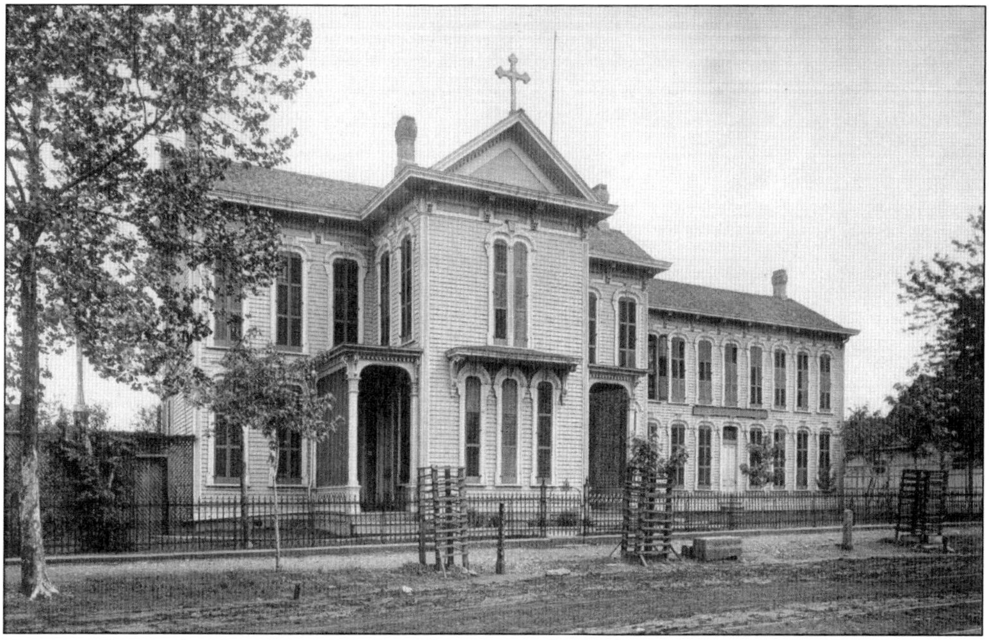

To serve the needs of settlers on the North Texas and Oklahoma frontier, the Roman Catholic Sisters of St. Mary of Namur founded St. Francis Xavier Academy, a girls' school, in 1876. For many years, the academy had both boarding and day students; the boarding department was discontinued in 1939. Boys were admitted in 1924. Initially, the nuns bought banker Edward Perry's two-story home at 300 North Houston Avenue. In 1881, as the student body neared 100 students, the Italianate frame structure shown in the c. 1895 image above was completed. After the move, the former house burned. In 1900, adjoining the frame building, the order completed a striking four-story Gothic Revival brick edifice at the northwest corner of West Sears Street and Rusk Avenue, seen below around 1935. The school closed in 1968; its buildings were razed in 1971. (Above, AWGC; below, MAB.)

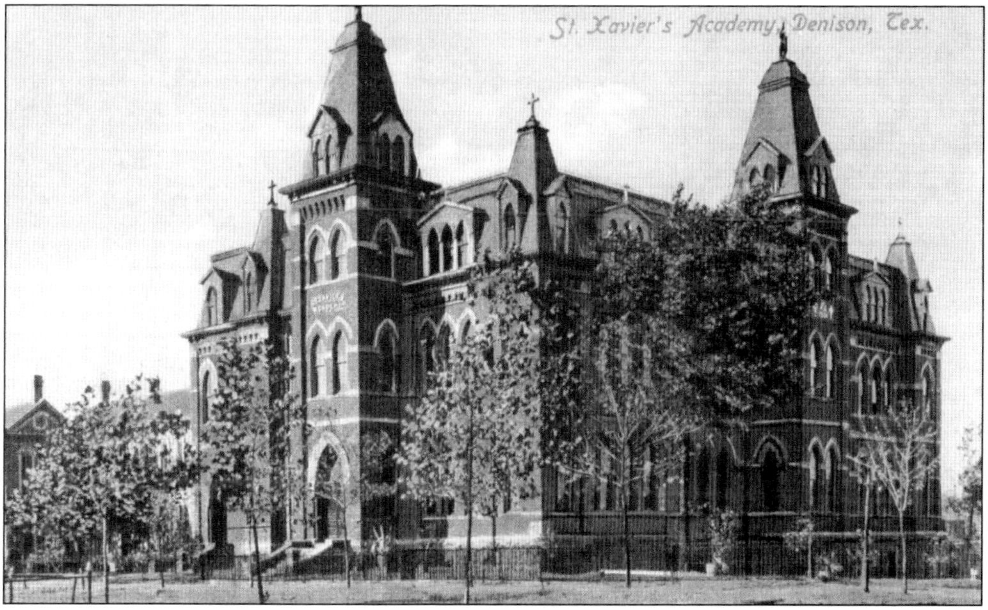

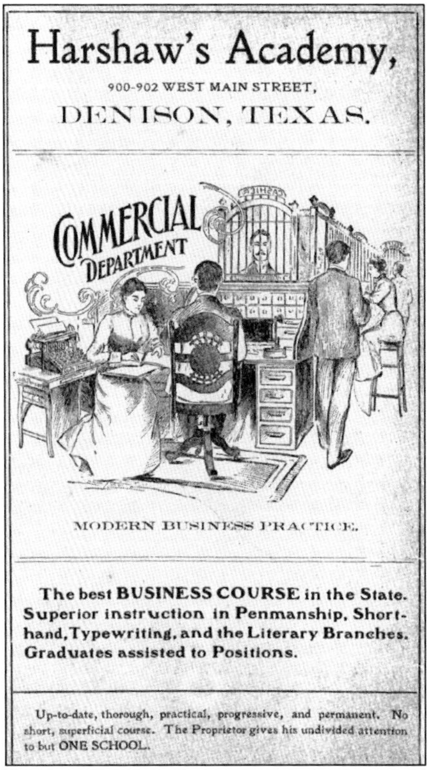
Harshaw's Academy,
900-902 WEST MAIN STREET,
DENISON, TEXAS.

MODERN BUSINESS PRACTICE.

The best **BUSINESS COURSE** in the State. Superior instruction in Penmanship, Shorthand, Typewriting, and the Literary Branches. Graduates assisted to Positions.

Up-to-date, thorough, practical, progressive, and permanent. No short, superficial course. The Proprietor gives his undivided attention to but ONE SCHOOL.

Prof. George L. Harshaw (1854–1908) came to Grayson County from Missouri shortly after the Civil War. By 1885, he was in Denison, operating a private school. Harshaw's Academy began as the English Literary Academy at 1431 West Main Street, where George and his family also lived. Soon, the school was renamed Gate City Literary and Commercial Academy and relocated to 900–902 West Main Street, where it taught students practical business skills until 1907. (MAB.)

Grayson County College (GCC), located at Denison's southwest edge, opened in September 1965 with 1,479 students. Enrollment in fall 2010 was over 5,300. In 2010, the college completed an eight-year, multimillion-dollar expansion, including this new administration building. Students of all ages choose among the college's 79 academic and technical majors. GCC offers an array of online classes and works closely with area businesses, both large and small. (GCC.)

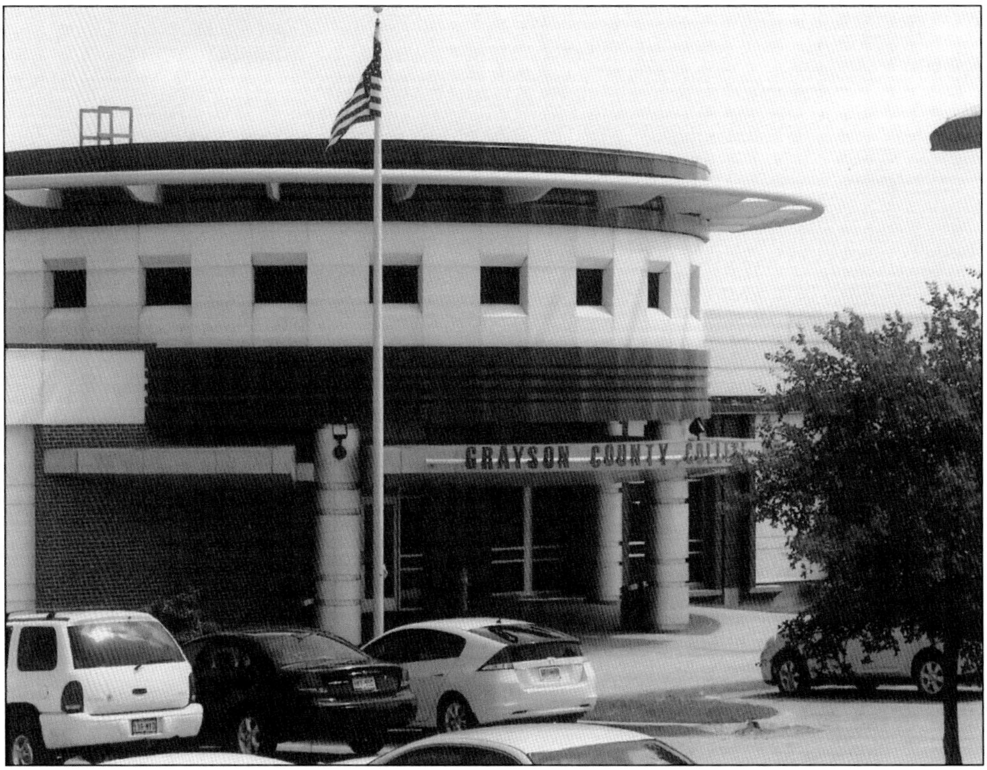

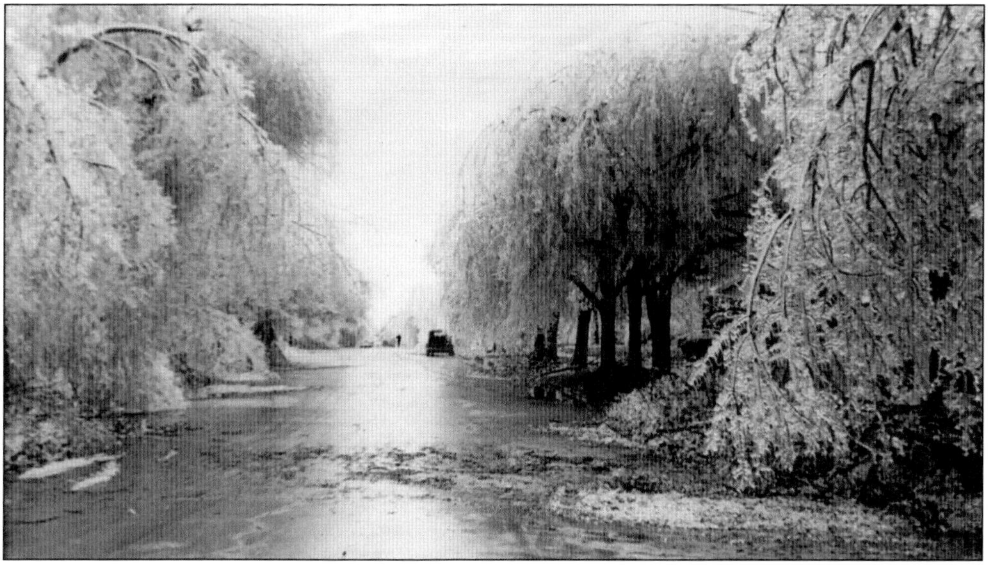

Ice storms have kept Denison people on their toes through the years. This one paralyzed the city on February 26, 1945. In different years (1888, 1919, 1930, 1945, and possibly 1949), temperatures dropped, and freezing rain caused tree limbs to break, electricity to go out, and streets and highways to become dangerously slick. A record low temperature of 16 degrees below zero was recorded in Denison on February 12, 1899. (MAB.)

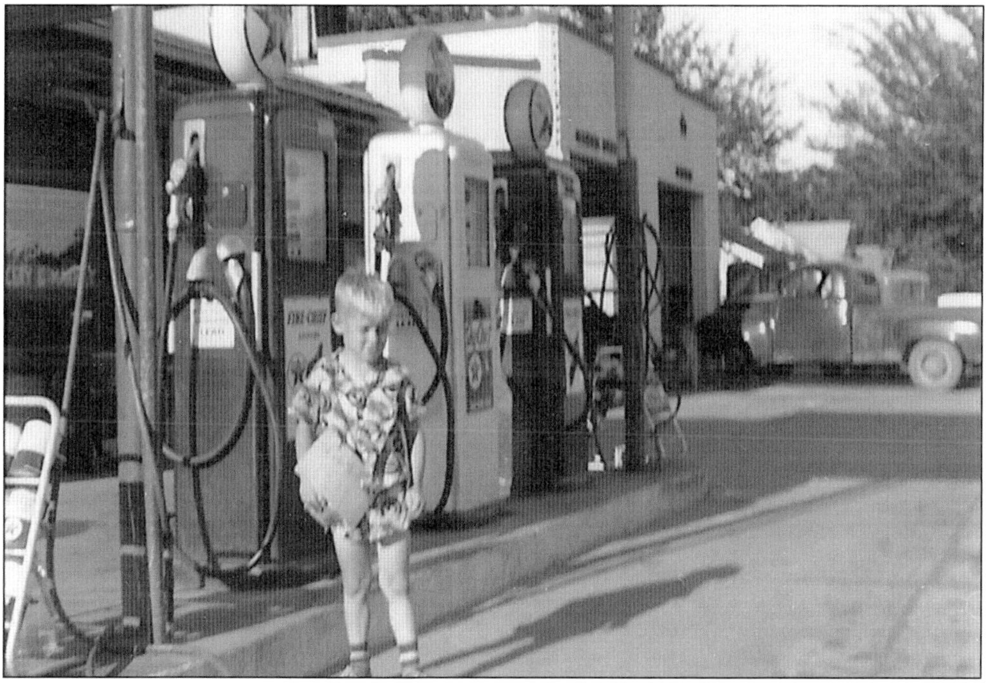

A youngster stands in front of the Texoma Service Station and Fisher Grocery at the intersection of Morton Street and Maurice Avenue. Here, on November 21, 1944, a collision between a butane gas truck and a passenger car killed 13 people and injured 15 more. The service station and several homes in the area were destroyed. That day has been called Denison's Black Tuesday. (Becky Fisher Oubre Rains, in DHH.)

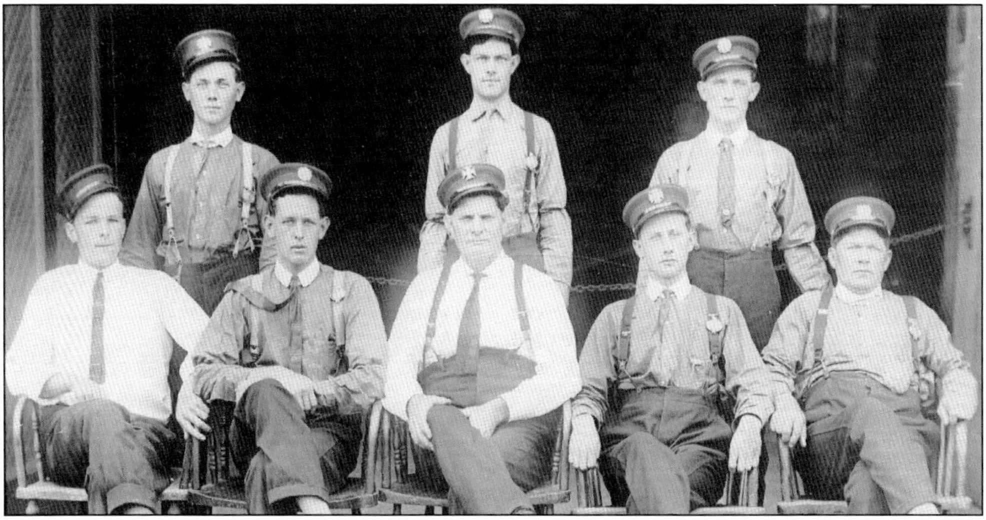

In 1910, Denison had two hose carts and a hook and ladder wagon, all drawn by horses. John Cooper (seated, center) was fire chief; Joe Capelle (standing, left) was fire marshal. The other firemen are unidentified. Cooper died while fire chief. Eight men usually staffed the Central Fire Station. In 1913, the city got its first motorized fire engine, an American LaFrance 750-gallon pumper. A hook and ladder truck was added in 1914. (DHH.)

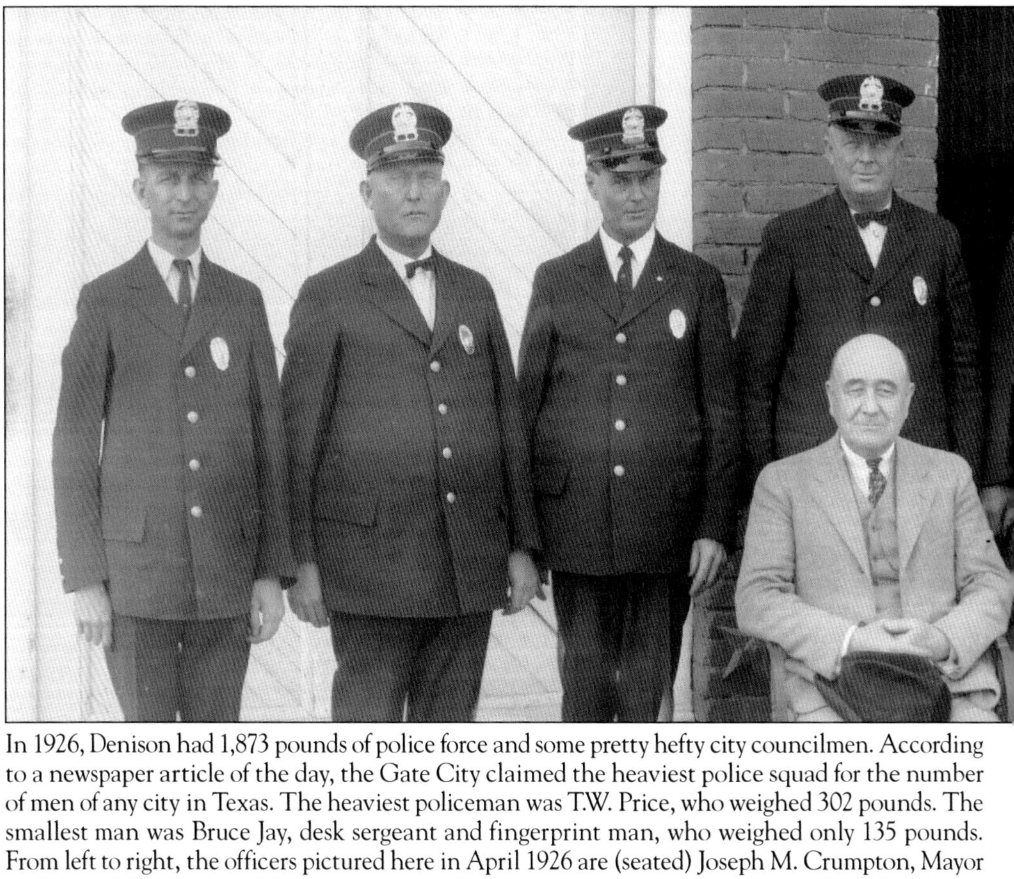

In 1926, Denison had 1,873 pounds of police force and some pretty hefty city councilmen. According to a newspaper article of the day, the Gate City claimed the heaviest police squad for the number of men of any city in Texas. The heaviest policeman was T.W. Price, who weighed 302 pounds. The smallest man was Bruce Jay, desk sergeant and fingerprint man, who weighed only 135 pounds. From left to right, the officers pictured here in April 1926 are (seated) Joseph M. Crumpton, Mayor

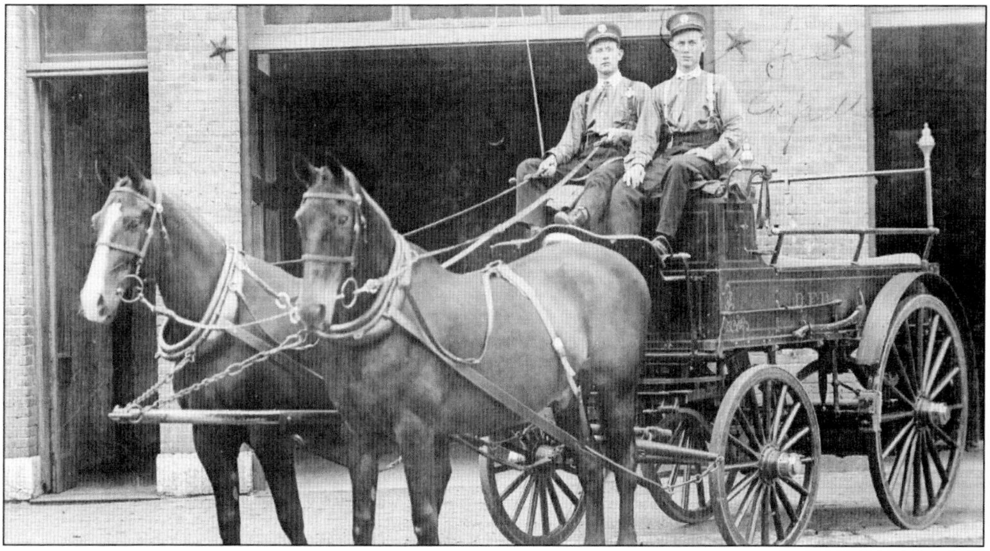

Fire Marshal Joe Capelle (right) and an unidentified fireman show off their prized horse-drawn fire wagon in front of the Central Fire Station at 320 West Chestnut Street. By 1876, fire protection had taken a leap forward, as the hand-drawn cart gave way to a horse-drawn fire wagon. That year a team of horses was purchased. A fire bell, later sold as junk for $4.75, sounded the alarm. (DHH.)

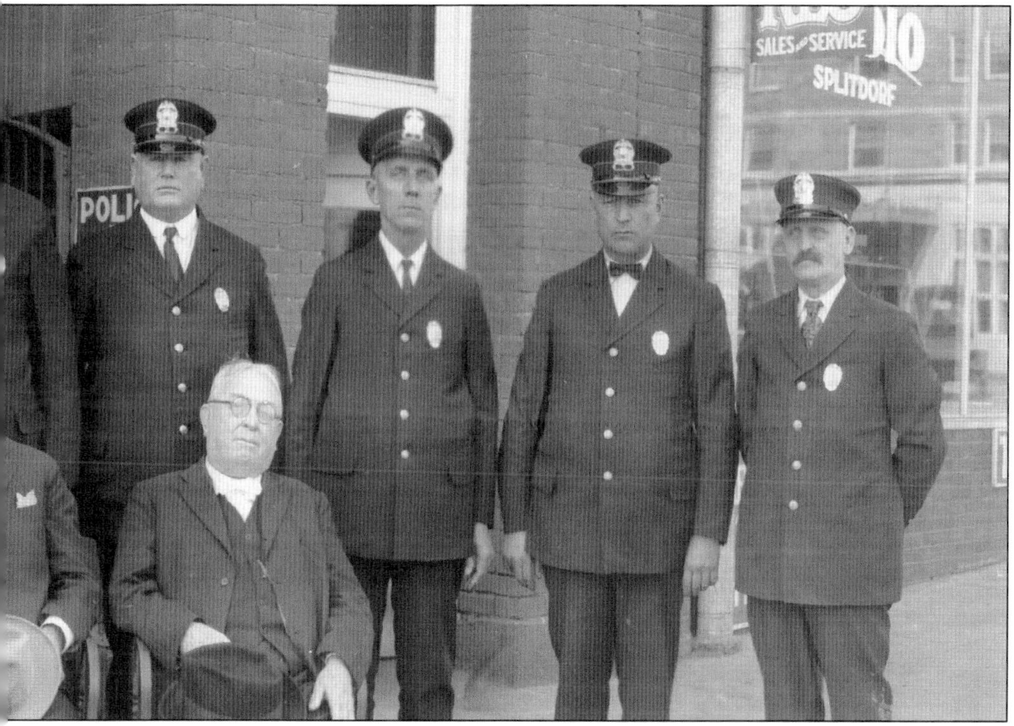

W.S. Hibbard, and Patrick H. Tobin; (standing) Bruce Jay, Walter A. Truett, J.B. Roberts, V.L. Caldwell, Chief ? Nix, Thomas W. Price, J.R. Dishner, G.C. Ballew, and J.G. Tripp. The Denison City Council assigned Crumpton, Hibbard, adn Tobin as police commissioners. Later, in 1926, Mayor Hibbard and Councilman Tobin were reelected to the City Council. (MAB.)

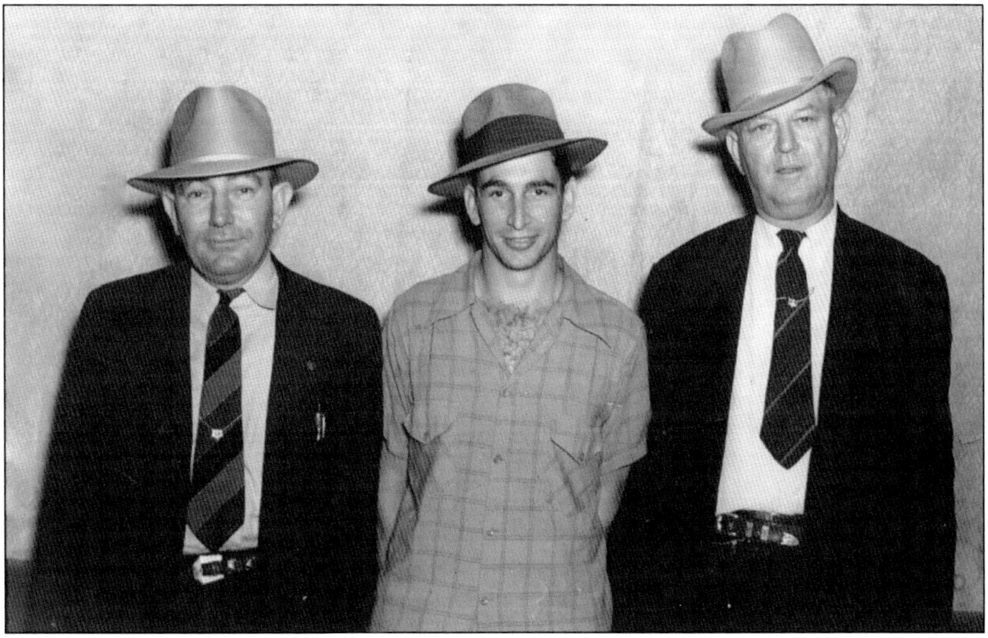

Grayson County deputy Paul Smith, left, and Deputy Virgil Evans, right, seem to have captured their man. Earl Scobey, 24, Denison, was wanted as a payroll bandit. Things could not have been too serious, judging from the smile on Scobey's face. A young man named Earl Scobey was a member of the Denison High School class of 1933, placing this photograph in the late 1930s. (MAB.)

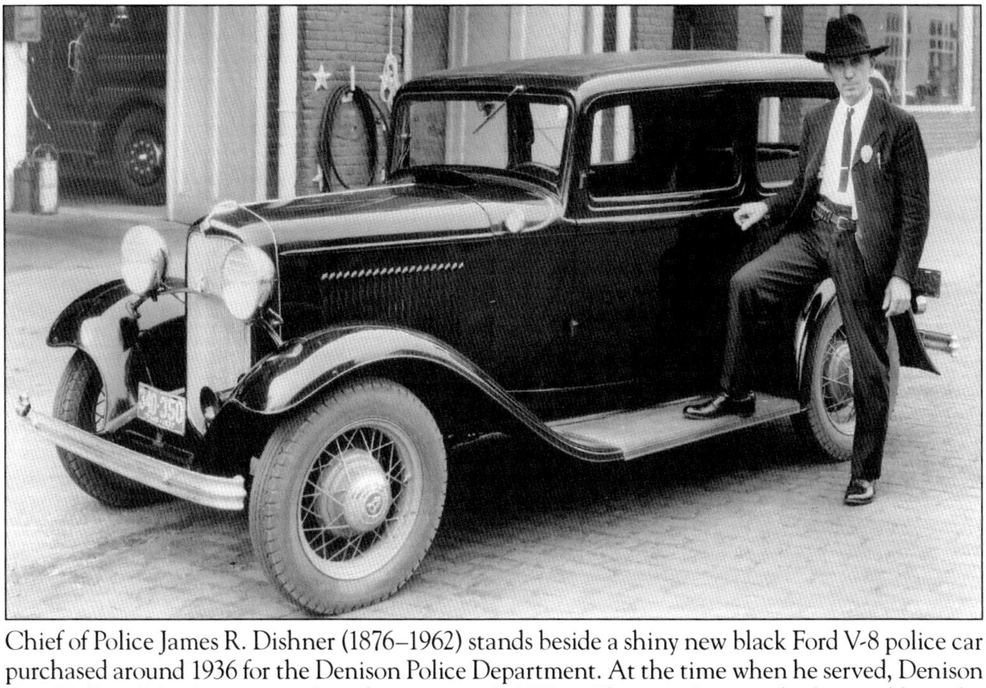

Chief of Police James R. Dishner (1876–1962) stands beside a shiny new black Ford V-8 police car purchased around 1936 for the Denison Police Department. At the time when he served, Denison City Hall and the fire station shared quarters at 320 West Chestnut Street, which is visible in the background. Dishner was identified from a 1939 photograph of the police force; he was the only one wearing a black cowboy hat. (DHH.)

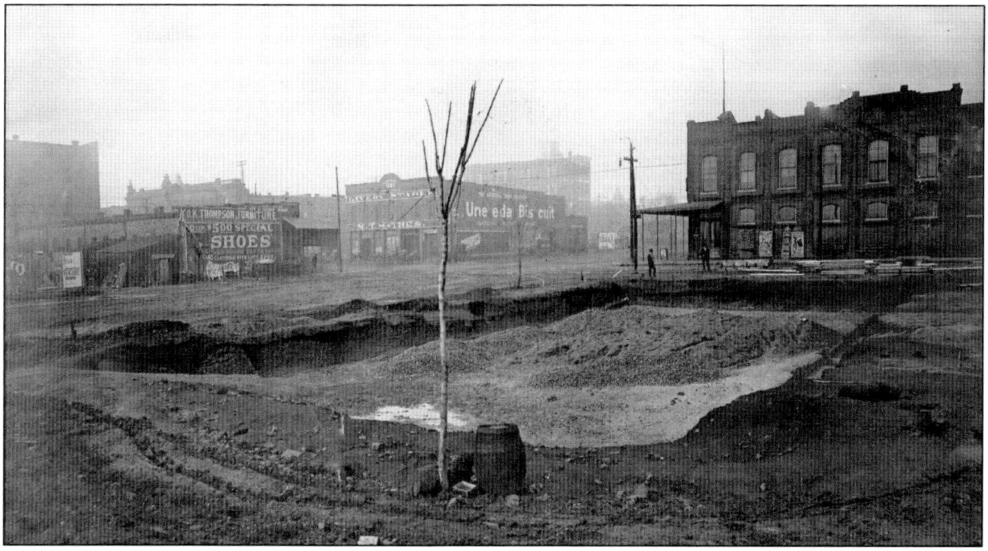

In 1910, workers stabilize walls of the foundation and basement for a new post office (today's Federal Building) at 231 West Woodard Street at the corner of Rusk Avenue. The post office formerly was located in the Munson Block, seen across the avenue. Across Woodard Street, M.T. Mathes Livery Stable advertises Uneeda Biscuits, while D.K. Thompson Furniture advertises Boyd's Clothing Store. (DHH.)

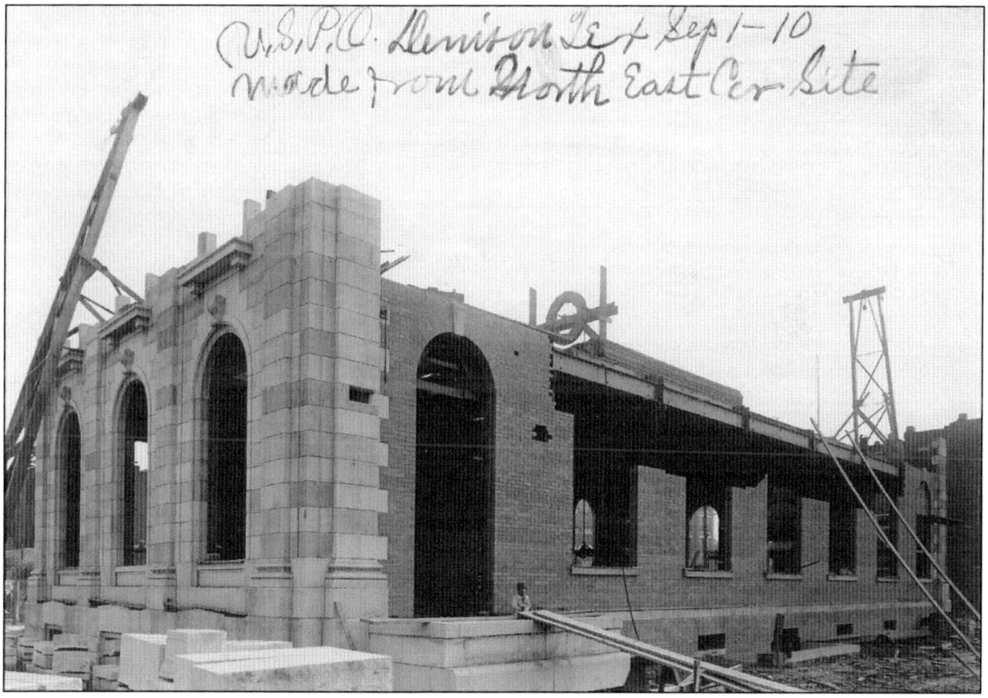

On September 1, 1910, construction of the first floor of the Denison Post Office was well under way. This photograph shows the northeast (alley) corner of the site; giant granite blocks stand ready. Building the giant structure was tedious business and took until 1912. Its design is attributed to James Knox Taylor. Fell and Ainsworth were contractors. Appointed in July 1907, William J. Scott was postmaster during construction. (DHH.)

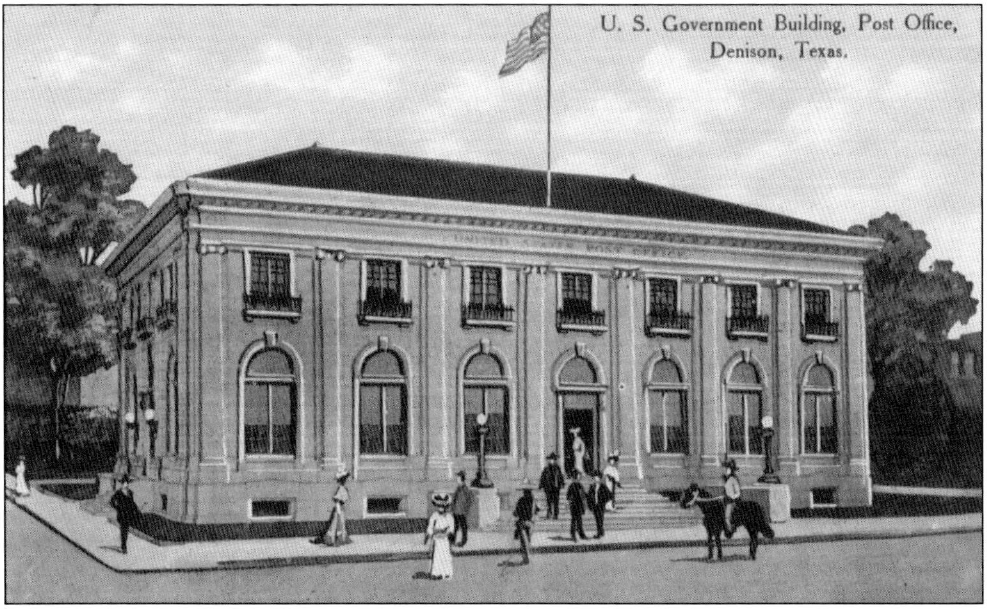

Denison had mail service as early at 1872. Charles W. Nelson was the first postmaster. In 1901, Denison pioneered in offering rural free delivery. When the town was six months old, the post office had a separate entrance for women. The post office shown here (built in 1910 through 1912 and still in use in 2011) cost $125,000. The facility was enlarged in 1964 and 1966. (DHH.)

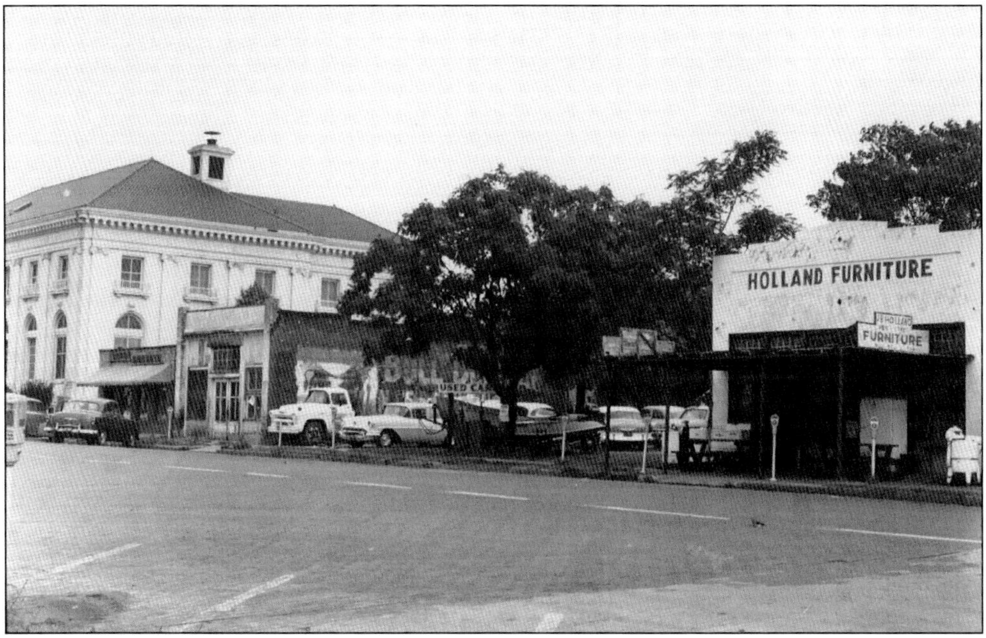

The 200 block of West Woodard Street was a busy block before the Denison Post Office was enlarged in 1964. East of the post office, businesses prospered until they had to close to make way for the Federal Building's expansion. These businesses included Langford Printing (a used-car lot that also sold boats), J.B. Holland New and Used Furniture, Zenthoefer's Poultry and Eggs, and Chris Waltz Plumbing Supplies (upstairs was the meeting hall for the Woodmen of the World). (MAB.)

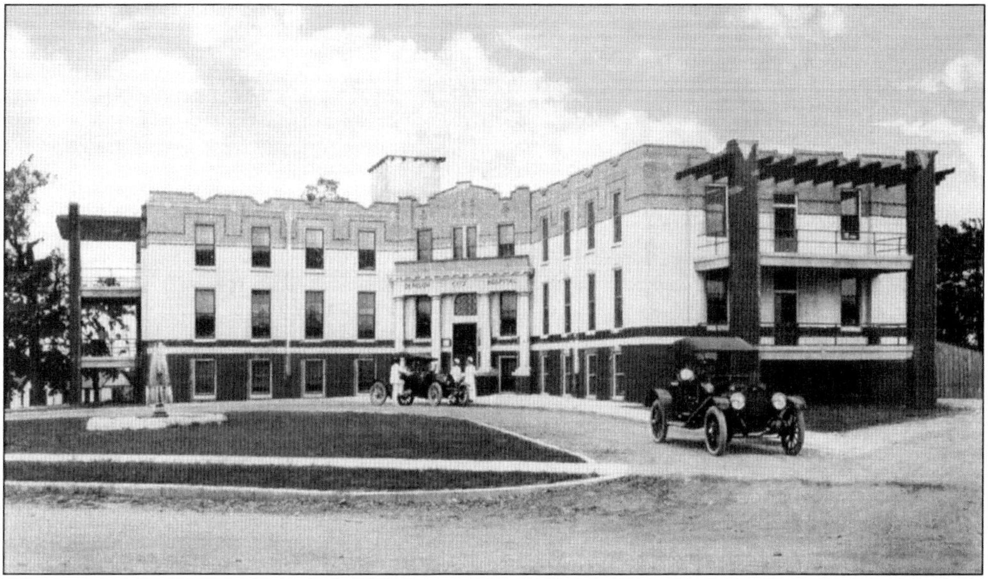

Denison City Hospital was constructed at 411 East Hull Street in 1913 and opened in 1914 under private management. The Sisters of Divine Providence, a Catholic sisterhood, took over operation of the property in 1943, and Madonna Hospital opened its doors on September 1, 1945, as a first-rate medical facility. By the mid-1950s, it had become too small to serve the population, and a larger hospital replaced it. (DHH.)

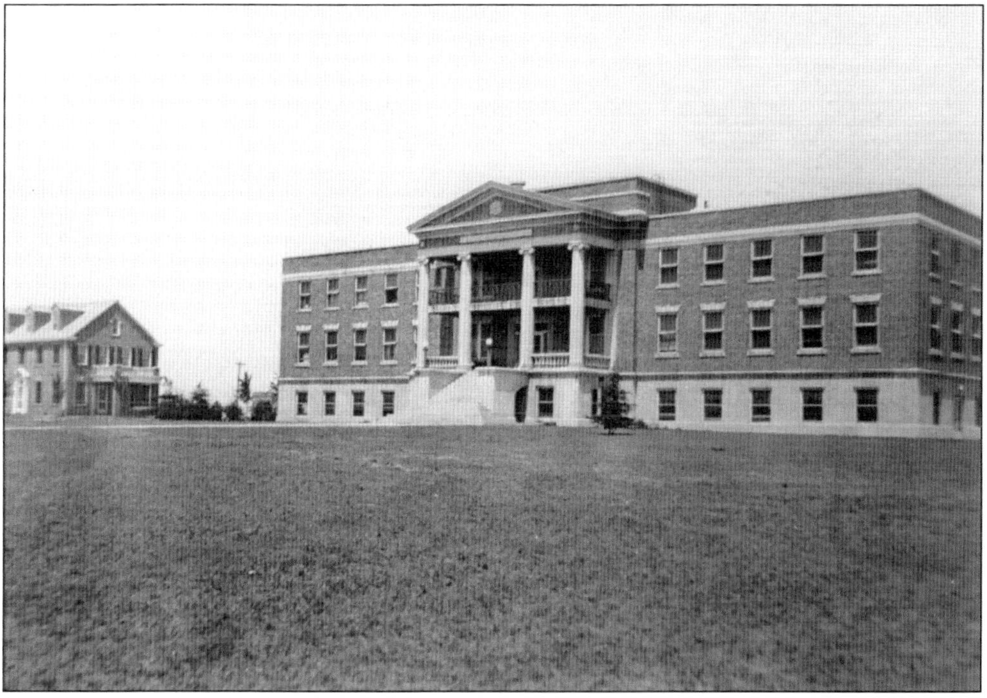

Work began on the MKT Employees Hospital on North Tone Avenue in 1920, and opening day was November 1, 1921. The 65-bed hospital was built on 27 acres deeded to the railroad by the City of Denison. Dr. T.J. Long was division surgeon, and Dr. A.G. Sneed was resident physician. The two-story building to the west was a home for nurses who worked at the hospital. (DHH.)

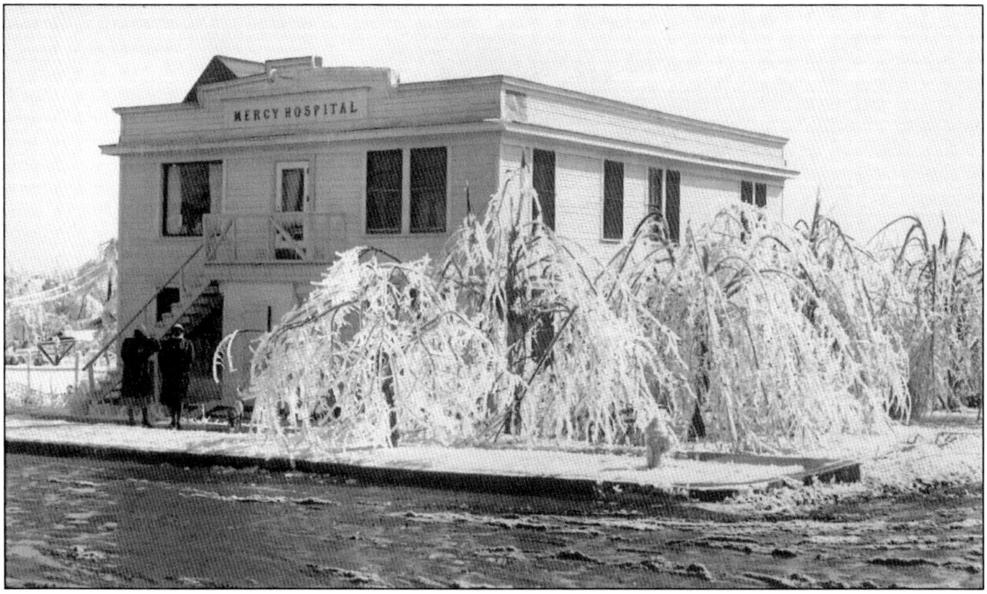

When Mercy Hospital was dedicated on June 21, 1926, several hundred blacks and whites were on hand. The nonprofit Sons and Daughters of Mercy built and operated the hospital, which only accepted African American patients. Dr. Roscoe C. Riddle, M.D., headed the hospital at 1030 West Munson Street; patients came from great distances. The facility closed in the mid-1940s. Dr. Riddle contracted to operate thereafter at the Denison City Hospital. (MAB.)

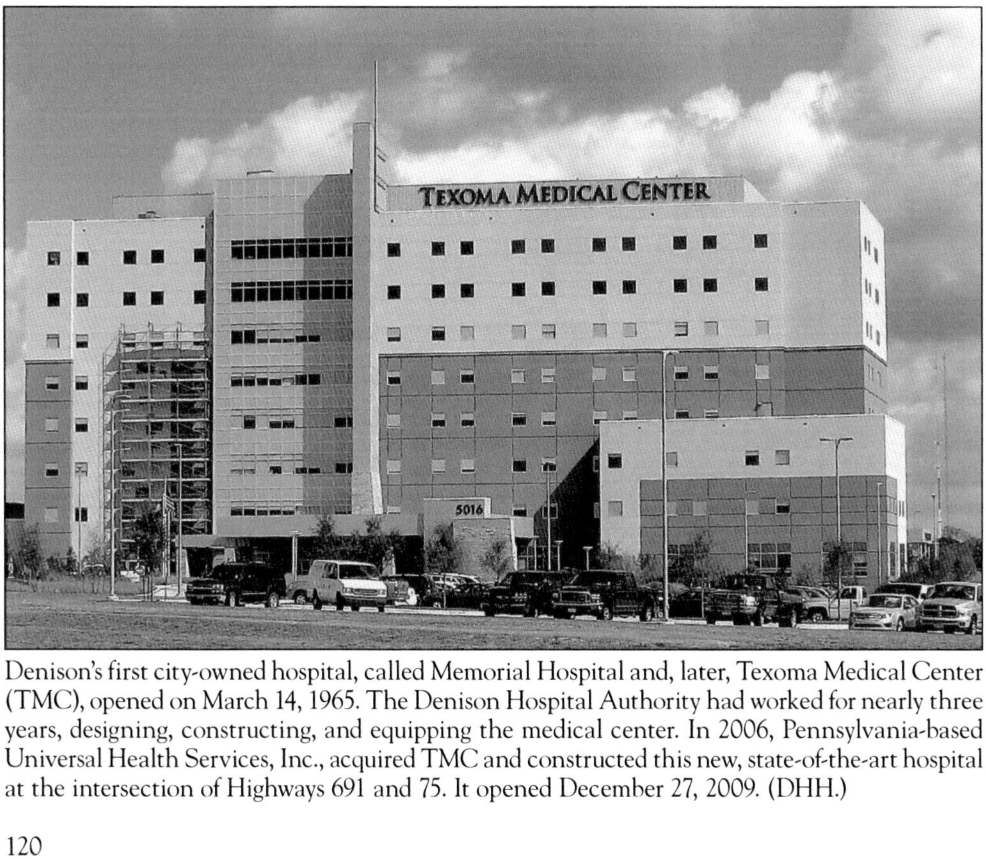

Denison's first city-owned hospital, called Memorial Hospital and, later, Texoma Medical Center (TMC), opened on March 14, 1965. The Denison Hospital Authority had worked for nearly three years, designing, constructing, and equipping the medical center. In 2006, Pennsylvania-based Universal Health Services, Inc., acquired TMC and constructed this new, state-of-the-art hospital at the intersection of Highways 691 and 75. It opened December 27, 2009. (DHH.)

Nine

Hometown Heroes

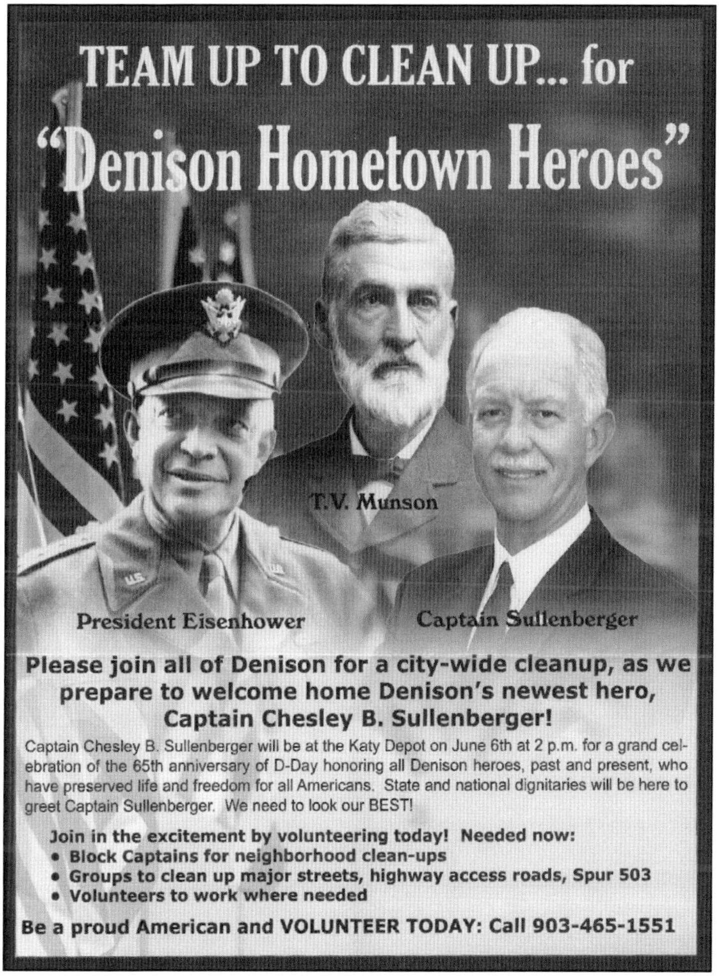

US president Dwight David Eisenhower, Thomas Volney Munson, and Chesley Burnet Sullenberger Jr. are three Denison men who made their mark on history. A D-Day Hometown of Heroes celebration honored them, along with all veterans, on June 2, 2009. Sullenberger, whose historical January 2009 airplane landing in the Hudson River saved the lives of 155 passengers and crew members, was present to greet Texas governor Rick Perry and a large crowd at the Katy Depot. (MAB.)

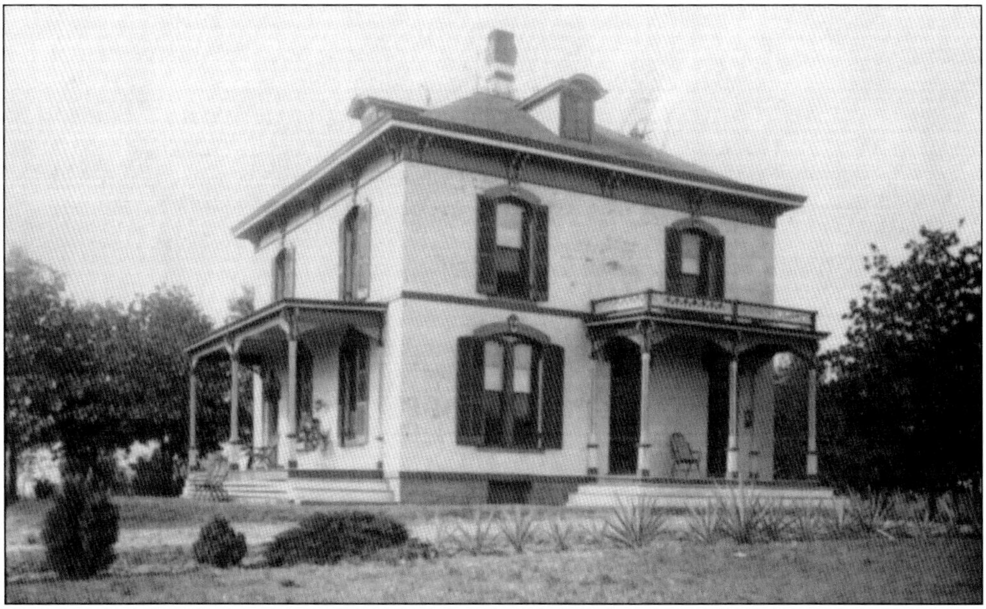

Thomas Volney Munson (1843–1913), an eminent Texas horticulturalist, is best known for his fight against the phylloxera epidemic of the late 19th century. Grafts from his wild grapevines in Denison sent to the Bordeaux vines of France saved the European wine industry. For that service, Munson received the Chevalier du Merite Agricole and the French Legion of Honor. He built this home, Vinita, in 1887 at 530 West Hanna Street. (AWGC.)

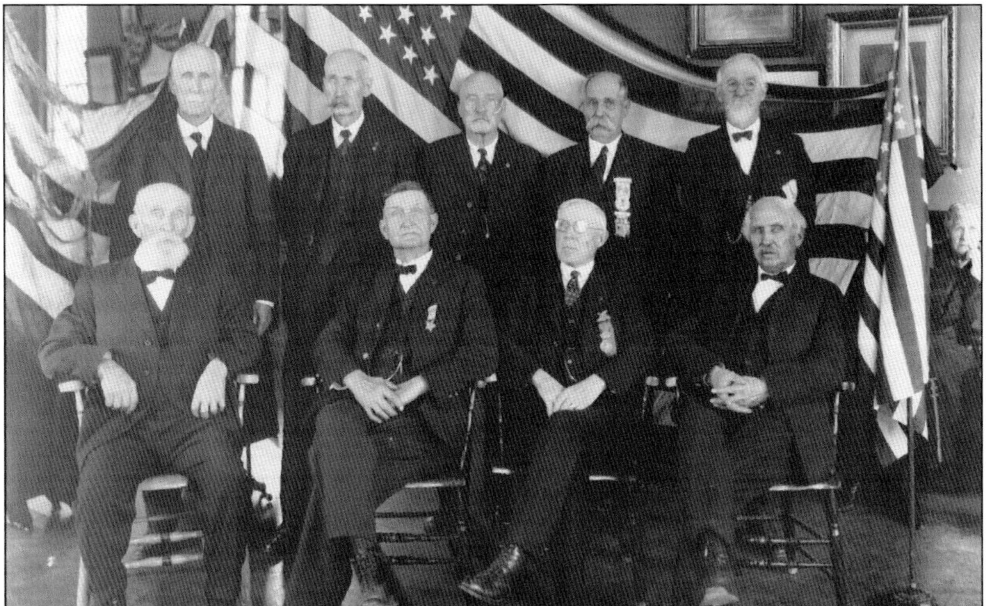

The Grand Army of the Republic (GAR) was a fraternal organization composed of Union army veterans of the Civil War. Many such men followed the Katy Railroad south to Denison. Seen here around 1925 are, from left to right, (first row) Charles Klein Wagner, C.C. Hotchkiss, Simon Ely, and S.E. Wertz; (second row) ? Mickels, unidentified, J.D. Dunn, unidentified, and Charles Eldredge. Note the tattered American flag on the left. (WPL, in MAB.)

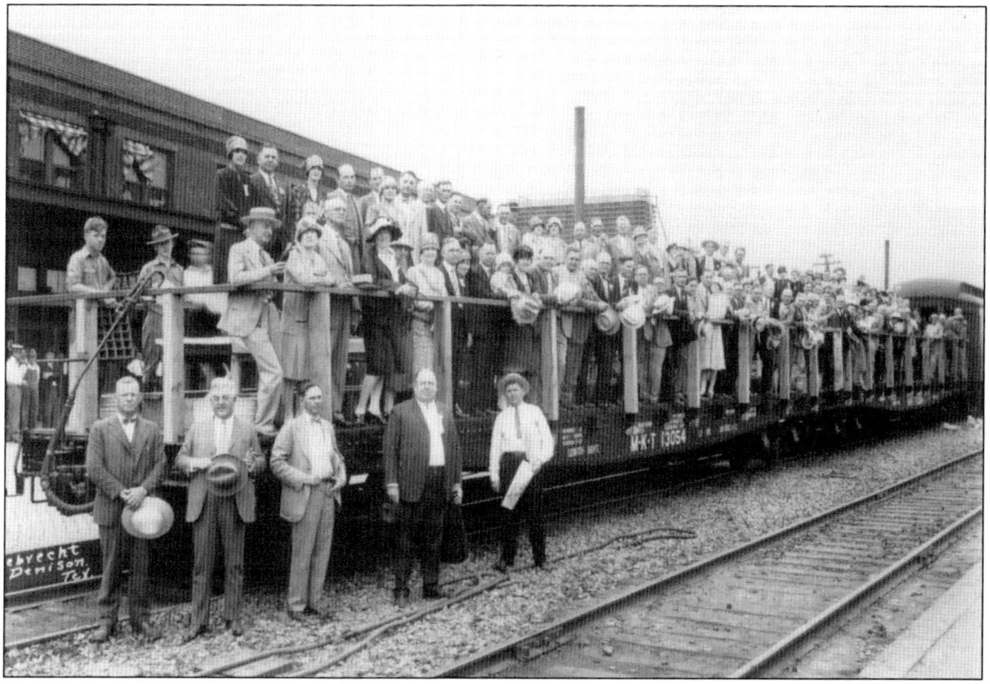

A big celebration was in order when John Nance Garner came to Denison around 1930. Garner, a Texas Democrat, had been in the US House of Representatives since 1902. He would become US speaker of the house in 1931 and serve as vice president under Franklin Roosevelt. A Katy platform car was pulled up next to the station so that arriving dignitaries would see the eager crowd. (MAB.)

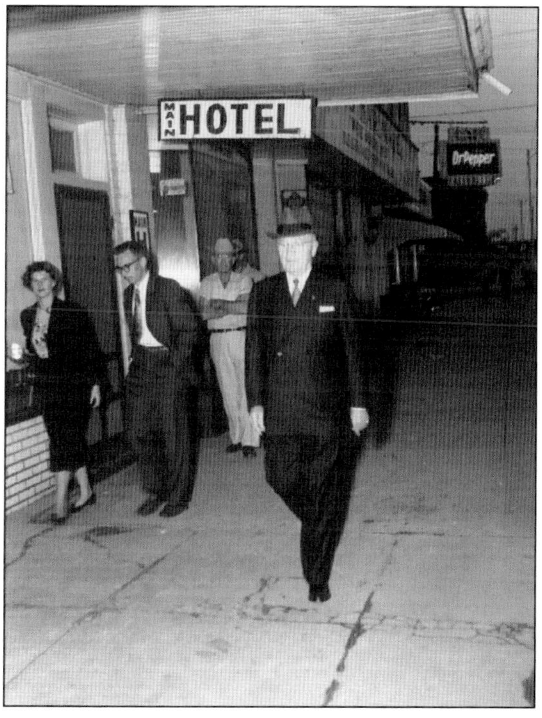

US president Harry S. Truman rode the train to Denison in 1947, got off, and took his morning walk up Main Street before moving on to speak in Sherman. He was joined by *Denison Herald* editor Claud Easterly, who interviewed him as they walked up Main Street. Here Truman is in front of the Main Street Hotel in the 100 block near the Saratoga Café on the corner. (Claud Easterly, in HD.)

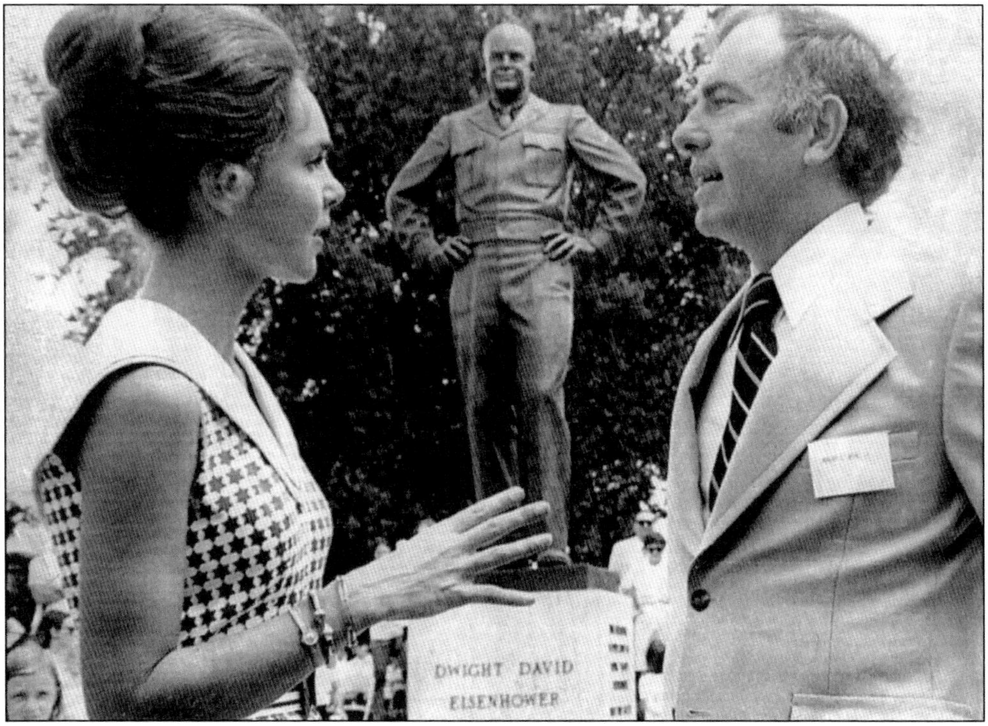

US president Dwight D. Eisenhower was born in Denison in 1890, and the Eisenhower Birthplace has been carefully preserved as a state historic site. The Denison Historical Society, under the leadership of Sidney Johnson, raised funds and commissioned sculptor Robert Dean (right) to erect this eight-foot statue at the birthplace. Julie Nixon Eisenhower, daughter of Pres. Richard Nixon and wife of Eisenhower's grandson David, unveiled the statue on July 9, 1973. (DHH.)

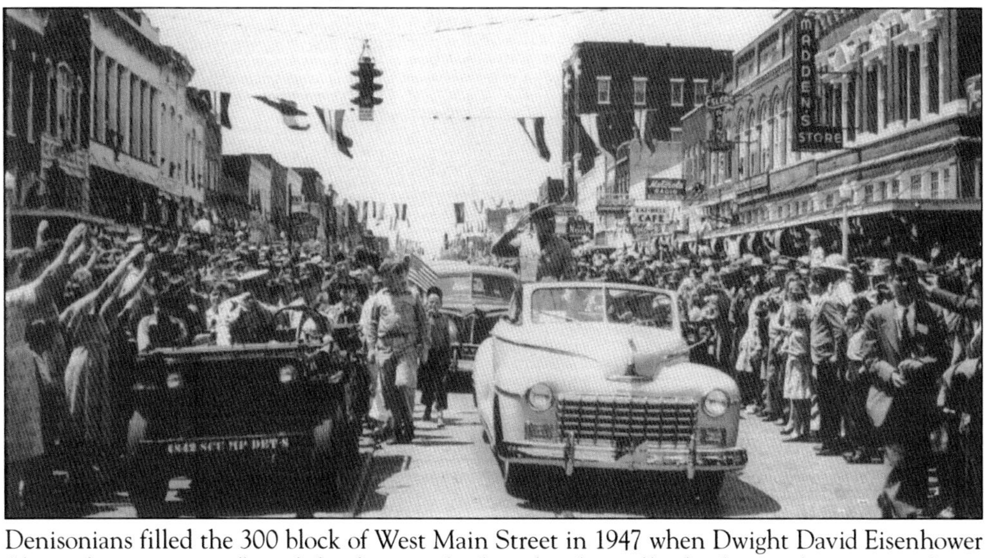

Denisonians filled the 300 block of West Main Street in 1947 when Dwight David Eisenhower (then a five-star general) made his first visit back to the place of his birth since leaving as a three-year-old boy. Some 50,000 people attended the downtown parade and speech in Forest Park. The future president and his entourage then went to his birthplace at 208 East Day Street. There, he lunched with Denison dignitaries. (DHH.)

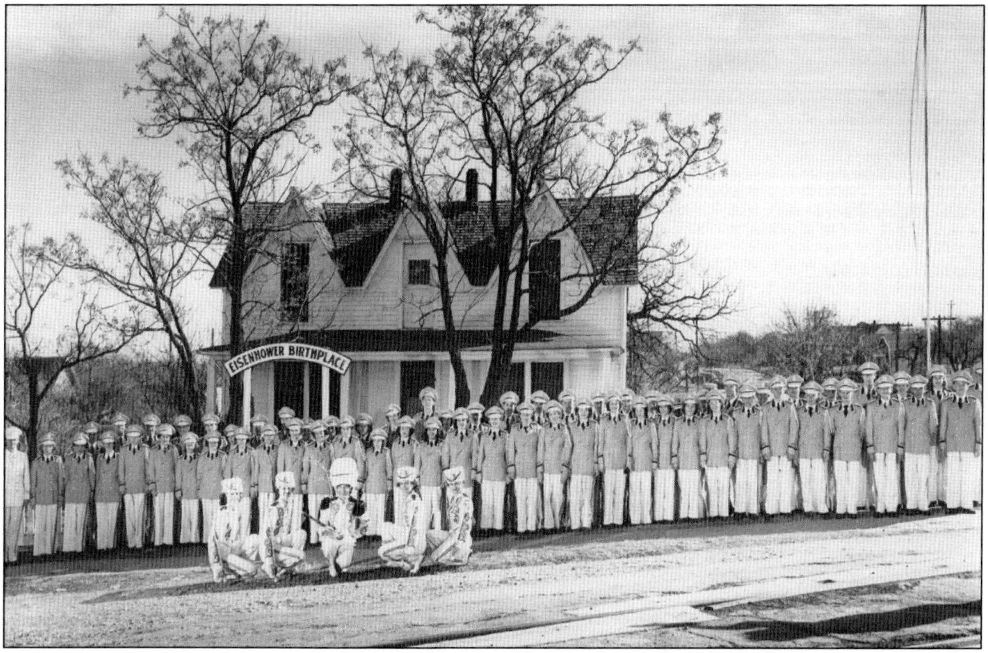

Denison High School's Yellow Jacket Band members pause in front of Pres. Dwight Eisenhower's birthplace in Denison as they prepare for a trip to Washington, DC. The band marched in Eisenhower's inaugural parade in January 1953. With Lavada Crook as drum majorette and Larry Thomas as band director, the musicians wear new uniforms, purchased especially for their history-making trip. (Lavada Crook Linder).

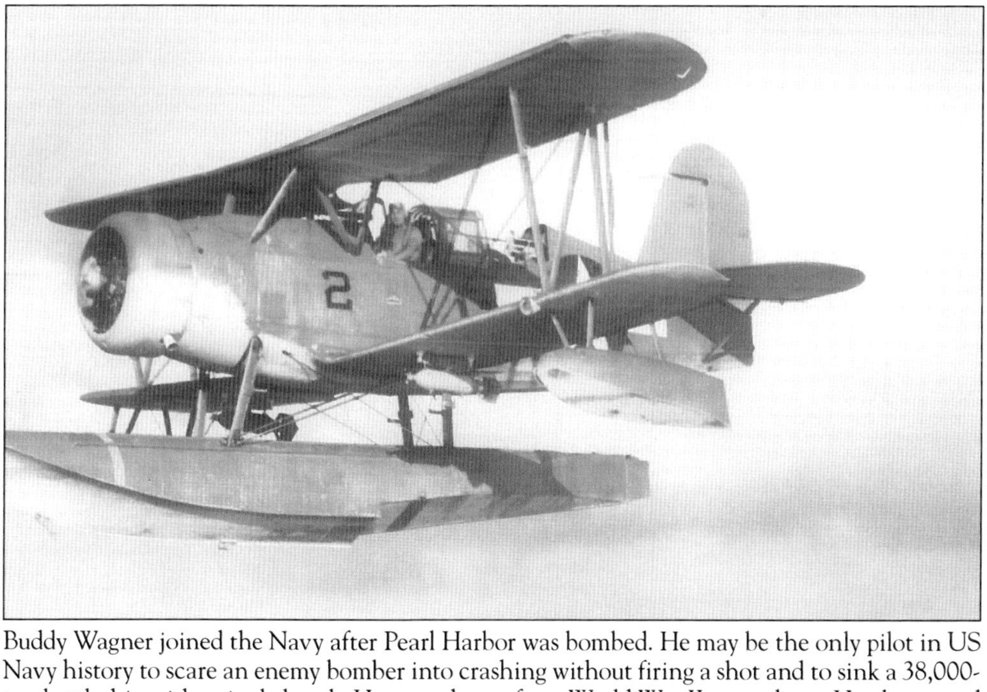

Buddy Wagner joined the Navy after Pearl Harbor was bombed. He may be the only pilot in US Navy history to scare an enemy bomber into crashing without firing a shot and to sink a 38,000-ton battleship with a single bomb. He came home from World War II a true hero. He also served in the Korean Conflict before he passed away on February 9, 2009. (US Navy.)

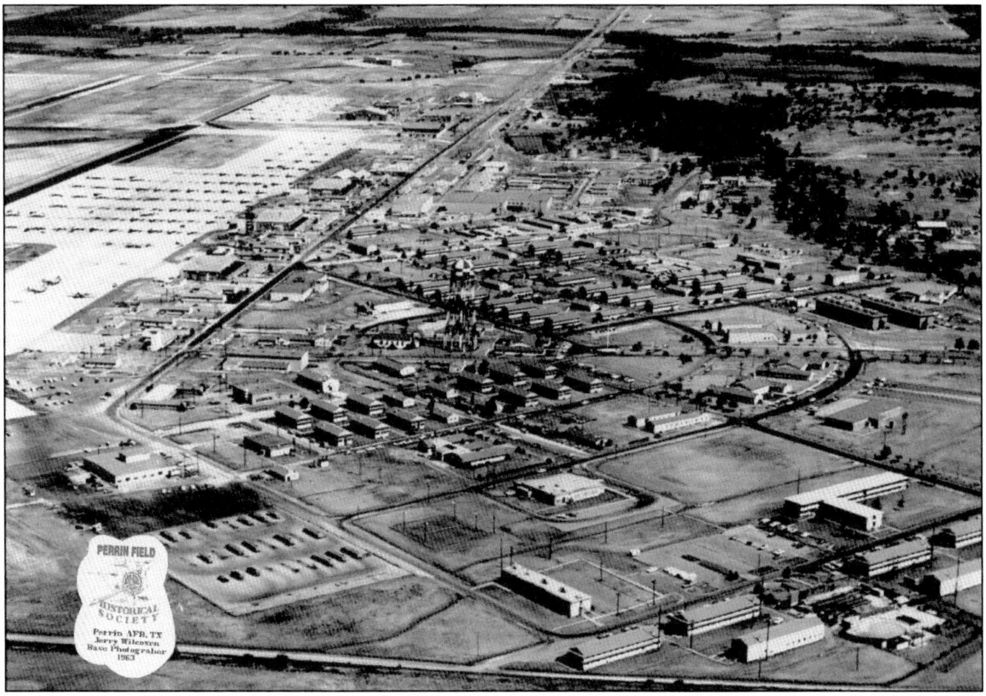

A US Army airfield in Denison saw its first class of pilots in 1942. In 1946, the airfield was deactivated after having trained 10,000 pilots. Reactivated in 1952 to support the Korean War, its name was changed to Perrin Air Force Base, and the first jets arrived. Seen here in 1963, Perrin closed in 1971. The field became North Texas Regional Airport–Perrin Field. (Perrin AFB Museum.)

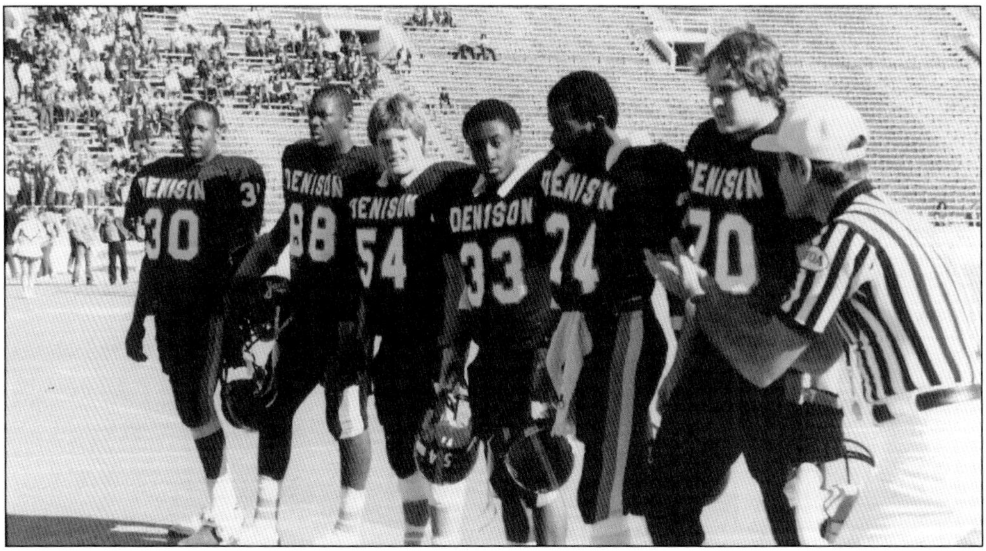

The Denison Yellow Jackets went all the way to the top on December 23, 1984, when they defeated Tom Ball in Baylor University's stadium for the Texas AAAA championship. Two days before Christmas, the town of Denison all but shut down as Yellow Jacket fans made the trip to Waco. From left to right, pictured on the field are Tony Brown, Fred Washington, Scott Skelton, Ray Taylor, Leslie DeHorney, Kevin Krueger, and an unidentified referee. (Dr. Don and Kay Skelton.)

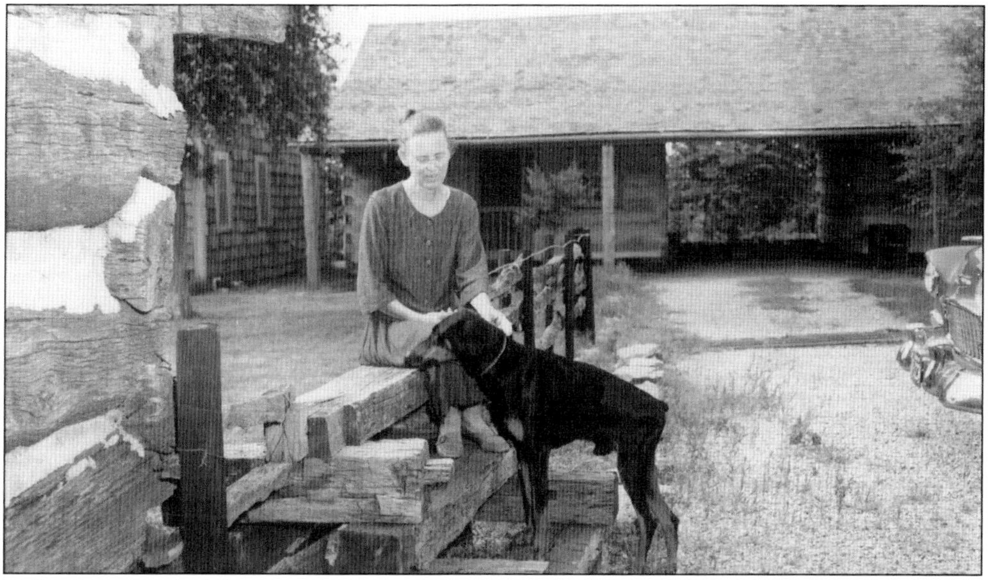

Nellie Chambers built her own domain atop Paw Paw Hill and amid the irises she grew so beautifully. Here she sits with her dog, surrounded by pioneer houses that she collected and preserved. One, perhaps the oldest house in Grayson County, was home to Judge James G. Thompson. On Chambers's death, it and other log structures were moved to Frontier Village, a museum at Loy Park. (John Crawford, in HD.)

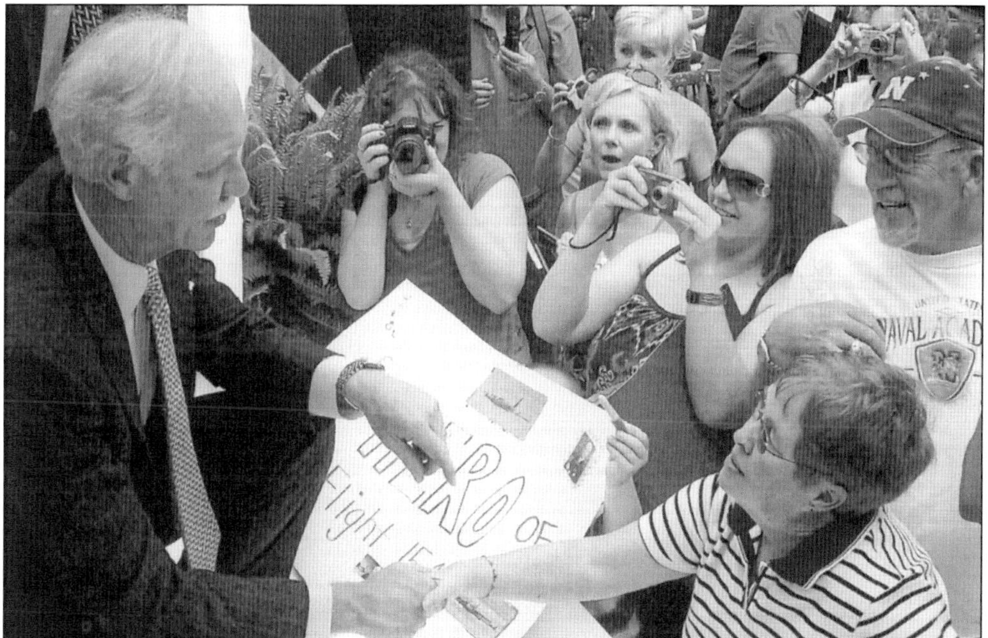

Airline captain Chesley Burnet (Sully) Sullenberger Jr. is a Denison native who saved 155 lives when he landed his crippled jetliner on the Hudson River in January 2009. Local citizens honored him on June 6, 2009, as hundreds attended a parade on Main Street and a program at the Katy Depot. Sullenberger also spoke at Denison High School's graduation and attended the reunion of his DHS class of 1969. (DHH.)

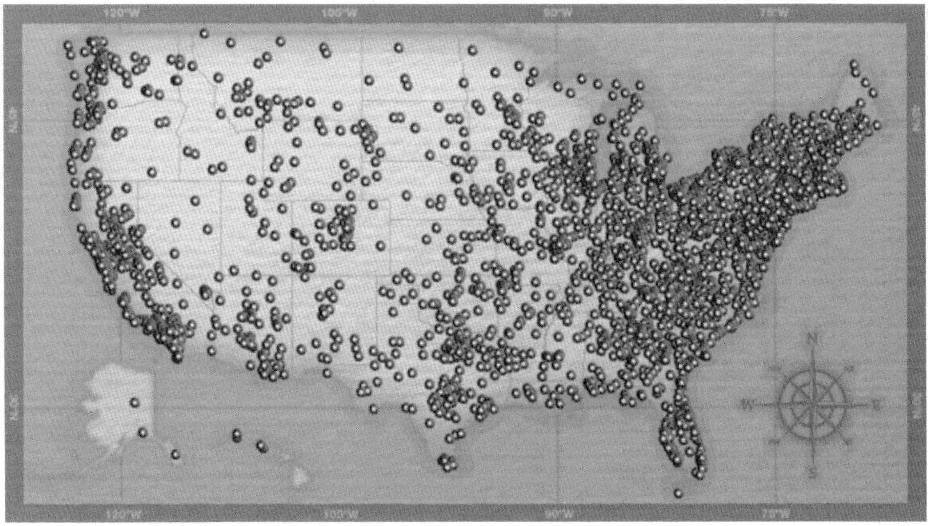